The Politics and Reality of Family Care in Corporate America

THE POLITICS AND REALITY OF FAMILY CARE IN CORPORATE AMERICA

JOHN P. FERNANDEZ

Lexington Books

D.C. Heath and Company · Lexington, Massachusetts · Toronto

Library of Congress Cataloging-in-Publication Data

Fernandez, John P., 1941–
  The politics and reality of family care in corporate America / John P.
Fernandez.
    p.   cm.
  Includes bibliographical references.
  ISBN 0-669-21562-7 (alk. paper)
  1. Employer-supported day care—United States. 2. Day care
centers—United States. 3. Day care centers for the aged—United
States. 4. Work and family—United States. I. Title.
HF5549.5.D39F47 1990
331.25—dc20   89-29170
                                                                  CIP

Copyright © 1990 by Lexington Books

Published simultaneously in Canada
Printed in the United States of America
Casebound International Standard Book Number: 0-669-21562-7
Library of Congress Catalog Card Number: 89-29170

The paper used in this publication meets the minimum requirements of
American National Standard for Information Sciences—Permanence
of Paper for Printed Library Materials, ANSI Z39.48—1984.

Year and number of this printing:

90 91 92 93 94 8 7 6 5 4 3 2 1

This book is dedicated to my mother, Julia E. Fernandez. I wish that she had lived to see the book. I miss her.

Contents

Figures and Tables

Acknowledgments

I would like to express my great appreciation to those companies who have made this book possible, and I would particularly like to express my deep appreciation to several people who helped me immensely.

Lee Pennisi, vice president of research for Dependent Care Management Services, played several crucial roles. She encouraged me to understand the importance of elder care to corporate America. She put me in touch and assisted me in interviewing key people in the aging and child-care network. She did extensive research for all parts of the book and helped edit the manuscript. Finally, she was the friend who went through the ups and downs during the course of writing this book.

Jackie Dubois spent many long hours doing research and editing and typing the manuscript. In addition, she did the graphics and some of the data analysis. She was always there when I needed her.

Eleni Julia Fernandez spent many hours calling key people, collecting and sending materials, and keeping her father organized. Michele Fernandez's assistance with data analysis was greatly appreciated, and she offered a number of crucial suggestions.

Andrea Trank came to this project at a crucial time when I needed a professional who could put some of my sociological jargon into clear, concise English.

Paulette Gerkovich worked many weekends assisting me with numerous tasks and never once complained about the personal time she was giving up.

Doreen Yochum and Mary Ridge were two friends who were extremely supportive during the good times and the bad times. I also thank Jim Pagos for his encouragement.

In addition, I would like to thank Ann Nelson and Liz

Casey for reading the manuscript and assisting me in clarifying my ideas. They have been friends for years and have helped in my other books.

Karen Hill-Scott was her usual supportive self. She directed me to a great deal of valuable research.

Finally, I would like to thank the professionals who were generous with their support and research information. All were generous with their knowledge; such generosity is the hallmark of true professionalism. I am lucky enough to count many of these people among my friends:

Judith Barr, The New York Business Group on Health, New York, New York

Margaret Beale-Spencer, Emory University, Atlanta, Georgia

Mary Brown, Corporate Child Care Consultants, Atlanta, Georgia

Carol Crecy, U.S. Administration on Aging, Washington, D.C.

Michael Creedon, National Council on Aging, Washington, D.C.

Carol Fraser-Fisk, *Aging Network News*, McLean, Virginia

Leslie Gaynes-Ross, *Fortune* magazine, New York, New York

Jean Holland, U.S. Administration on Aging, Washington, D.C.

Dorothy Howe, National Institute of Adult Day Care, Washington, D.C.

Theresa Lambert, National Association of State Units on Aging, Washington, D.C.

Robert Levin, Washington Business Group on Health, Washington, D.C.

Diane Levitt, Head Start, Pasadena, California

Jon Linkous, National Association of Area Agencies, Washington, D.C.

Charlotte Nusberg, International Federation on Aging, New York, New York

Jeff Ostroff, Prime Life Marketing, Plymouth Meeting, Pennsylvania

Suzanne Palestrone, Women's Bureau, U.S. Department of Labor, Washington, D.C.

Dan Quirk, National Association of State Units on Aging, Washington, D.C.

Betsy Richards, Corporate Child Care Consultants, Atlanta, Georgia

Janet Sainer, New York City Department on Aging, New York, New York

Anita Shallit, U.S. Administration on Aging, Washington, D.C.

Ed Sheehy, National Association of Area Agencies, Washington, D.C.

Diane Sherwood, St. Margaret's House, New York, New York

Robyn Stone, U.S. Department of Health and Human Services, Washington, D.C.

Mike Suzuki, U.S. Administration on Aging, Washington, D.C.

Leon Warshaw, New York Business Group on Health, New York, New York

Introduction

T HE evidence is mounting that the United States is losing its position of world economic superiority. As a result, American corporations are looking for innovative ways to increase their efficiency and productivity so that they can once again improve their global position. Some corporations are realizing that one issue they must address if they are to remain viable in a competitive global environment is their employees' need for assistance in family care.

The American family and the American workforce have both undergone tremendous changes in the last twenty years, as women have entered the workforce in great numbers. During the nineteenth and twentieth centuries, as industry and commerce replaced agriculture, the roles of women and men became narrowly defined. People were increasingly segregated by gender: men were clearly recognized as breadwinners and women as homemakers.

But the traditional distinctions between gender roles at home and at work have since blurred, especially in the past twenty years. Traditional gender lines have been erased as more and more women work outside the home. As a result, child care—traditionally a woman's concern—has become a matter of general concern.

But the American child-care system—to the extent that there is one—is presently riddled with problems. Day care is limited in supply, it is difficult to afford, and it is often of distressingly poor quality. Waiting lists at quality facilities can be so long that some parents apply for a spot months before their child is even born.

The Corporate Response

With a few exceptions, most businesses have not kept up with the changes in the American workforce and the American family during the past twenty years. Most business executives have an intellectual understanding of such issues and the problems they cause some employees, but they have not yet taken the step of assisting their employees. So far, most of the solutions that corporate America has tried have amounted to little more than Band-Aids. Most of the proposals are piecemeal and lack sufficient funding, like the congressional bills for child care that have any chance of passing.

Basic human nature can explain some of this reluctance to change—it is often difficult for people to accept change and the new behaviors and accompanying problems that change brings. Businesses are also saddled with another obstacle—their bureaucratic structure, based on years of established practices, which often slows down the process of change even further.

But perhaps the main reason for corporate reluctance to change is that traditionally, businesses have avoided family-care issues, drawing a distinct line between workplace and family matters. Family care is still considered primarily a "women's issue" and therefore peripheral to corporate success.

The Bottom Line

The fact is that corporate America should respond to these demographic changes. Even as corporate executives and others argue against addressing family-care issues in a systematic and serious manner, the United States loses billions of dollars each year in productivity. Corporate America must now grasp the fact that family care is a corporate competitive issue, not a "women's issue." Assisting employees with family care is in fact a bottom-line productivity issue.

The lack of adequate affordable care for children of all ages adversely affects employees in corporate America. Employees' family-care problems can have a negative effect on their stress levels, can cause stress-related health problems, can lead to absenteeism, unproductive time at work, and internal work conflicts, and ultimately, can drive away productive workers. Benign neglect or halfhearted approaches to family care will eventually show up on the corporate balance sheet—as a loss.

A review of demographic changes in the American workforce demonstrates just how important women have already become, and will continue to be, to American economic survival. The labor pool as a whole is expected to shrink over the next decades, and labor shortages have already begun. The competition for a shrinking pool of talent is projected to increase as the "baby-bust" generation enters the labor market. Companies that implement progressive family-care policies and programs will have a tremendous competitive advantage over those that do not. Corporate America would reap billions of dollars in productive time, in lower health-care costs, and in retention of good employees.

Corporate Excuses

Many corporate executives raise arguments against offering assistance to their caregiving employees. One argument is that information about family care is unavailable. An April 1988 report by the U.S. Department of Labor, for example, noted that "among the clear deterrents to employer involvement with child care are the lack of information, awareness and technical assistance as well as the lack of documented evidence that such involvement could improve productivity."[1] This book itself provides employers with the information and technical assistance they say they need.

Another argument that employers raise against offering assistance is cost. Most employers believe family-care assistance would increase their expenses. But this is true only in the short run and only for a few of the many family-care solutions. Even the costs of those solutions that have high price tags, such as day-care centers, are actually lower than the costs of failing to take action.

Most of the other reasons employers offer for their failure

to act are more aptly termed "excuses." This book seeks to dispel the notion that these excuses are viable. One such excuse is the threat of liability. However, several corporate executives who ventured into the world of child care have suggested that corporations have greater liabilities with products and services than they do by getting involved in child care. They argue that by developing a quality program based on known risk-management concepts corporations can limit their liabilities.

A second excuse is equity—an unwillingness to appear to be favoring employees with families over other employees. But business complaints that family-care practices are discriminatory are not substantiated by the facts. Most employees recognize that one worker's stress can affect the entire work environment; other employees must often pick up the slack when a working caregiver is forced to come in late, leave early, call in sick, or quit because of family-care problems.

The Role of Government

A majority of Americans—63 percent—believe the federal government should develop policies to make child care more affordable and available for working parents. This view is shared even by the 59 percent of Americans who are not currently raising children, which indicates that even those who are not parents understand the importance of child care to society.

Expanding the availability of quality, affordable child care might ease the drain on government budgets caused by programs for the poor, as well as increase the federal, state, and local revenues through the taxes these employees will pay into government coffers rather than drain them. Children who receive quality child care will have a better chance of becoming assets to society rather than liabilities, saving the country billions of dollars due to less crime, less need for drug programs, and less need for protection from delinquent children.

The issue of affordable day care has captured the attention of some of our politicians. Governor Thomas Kean of New Jersey stated in June 1988 that there were only 105,000 slots in child-care centers in New Jersey, but that there were "three times that number of children with working mothers." According to Edward Ziegler, "We are at about the same place with child care as we were when we started universal education."

In the 1988 presidential campaign, both candidates placed child care high on their agendas, promising a variety of care initiatives in their platforms. President George Bush now has a responsibility to keep his promise to American children. He has said, "This nation's children represent our future—and our responsibility. Good health care and nutrition, sound education, and access to safe child care should be a concern for all of us."

President Bush is supporting tax credits to help low-income families with child care. Prominent Democrats are supporting a plan to subsidize day-care centers that serve families with low and moderate incomes. These are steps in the right direction, but more money and other direct measures must be taken to stave off a further crisis.

I am convinced that all three of society's major components—family, government, and business—must work together to generate and implement solutions. If these three groups do not act in concert, family-care problems will continue to cost American society billions of dollars.

The Present Book

This book provides a wealth of hard data and realistic solutions that corporate executives, government officials, family-care providers, social agencies, and educators can use to help position their organizations as leaders in family-care assistance, giving the United States a competitive edge necessary in the new global marketplace. The three surveys I have conducted in the past five years on child care show that a significant majority of employees believe that corporations should actively assist employees with family care.

Four years ago, in my first book on these issues—*Child Care and Corporate Productivity: Resolving Family and Work Conflicts*—I concentrated on one family-care issue alone: child care. My research for the present book inspired me to pursue the problems of dependent care generally and their impact on corporate productivity. This book focuses specifically on both child care and on elder care, with brief reference to adult-dependent care.

The first four chapters of this book deal with child-care problems and their solutions. The following two chapters analyze elder-care problems and their solutions. Chapter 8 discusses and analyzes the problems of dual dependency. Chapter 9 deals with the politics and reality of corporate family care, and chapter 10 presents a comprehensive plan for family care.

SURVEY METHODS

The primary research for this book is based on a survey of thirty companies conducted during 1987 and 1988. The companies are diverse, in fields such as telecommunications, finance, and real estate.

The number of employees within each company ranges from fifty to more than fifteen thousand. The employee participation rate ranged from 35 percent to 71 percent. The total number of participants was over 26,000.

Occupational workers made up 58 percent of the survey participants. Women constituted 54 percent of the participants; they represented 63 percent of the occupational workers and 43 percent of the managerial employees. People of color (American Indians, Asians, blacks, and Hispanics) made up only 11 percent of the participants. My 1989 study involved 3,300 corporate participants. This survey differed from the 1987/1988 survey by focusing much more detail on adult dependent care issues.

FAMILY CHARACTERISTICS

Table 1–1 shows the percentage of employees in each marital/parenthood category. More than twice as many women (13 percent) as men (5 percent) are single parents. Many more men are married with children eighteen and under (55 percent) than women (35 percent).

Table 1–1
FAMILY STATUS OF SURVEY PARTICIPANTS
(Percent)

	Women	*Men*
	(N = 14,064)	(N = 12,140)
Single, No Children	24	13
Single, Children 18 and Under	13	5
Married, No Children	12	8
Married, Children 18 and Under	35	55
Married, Grown Children	12	16
Unmarried Couple, No Children	2	1
Unmarried Couple, Children under 18	1	.5

RESEARCH INSTRUMENT

The data were collected through a self-administered, mailed questionnaire that contained both multiple-choice questions and open-ended questions that allowed participants to elaborate and develop their answers. Both quantitative statistical data and qualitative individual comments were solicited to achieve a better understanding of employee feelings, beliefs, and attitudes. On all the questionnaires, improper responses (such as replying to questions that one should have skipped or giving more than one response to a question that required only one) were eliminated.

I developed the questionnaire using information from several sources: from the companies, from groups of company employees who listed issues they believed their employers needed to face in the next five years, and from extensive open-ended interviews with working people. Areas covered in the questionnaire were "You and Your Career," "Performance Appraisal," "Training and Development," "Employment Security," "Your Health," "Pluralism," "Questions About Women," "Questions About People of Color," "Questions About White Men," "Family/Work Issues," "Child Care/Elder Care and Work/Family Problems," "Supervisory Relationships," "Work

Group Relationships," "Perceptions of Top Management,"
"Your Company's Management," "Participation and Decision
Making," "Your Social/Cultural/Civic Activities in Your Com-
munity," "Demographic Information," and "Reaction to the
Survey."

Although the questionnaire covered twenty areas, this book
focuses only on the responses from "You and Your Career,"
"Performance Appraisal," "Training and Development," "Your
Health," "Questions About Women," and "Family/Work Issues."
Some readers may question the relevance of some of these
factors to family care, but as we shall see, all are related to
family-care issues.

Summary Of Key Findings

Some of the overall findings I discovered are:

- Almost double the percentage of men said they have no
  child-care problems as compared with women.
- Many married women are, in reality, single mothers when it
  comes to caring for children.
- Over the past four years, some men have become more
  involved in the care of children.
- Children's ages have a significant impact on child-care
  problems: the younger the child, the more the problems.
- Child-care problems significantly contribute to the loss of
  productive time due to employees missing work, coming in
  late, leaving early, and dealing with family issues during
  work hours.
- Many employees experience stress at home or on the job
  because of child-care problems. The younger the child, the
  more the stress.
- There is clear evidence that stress resulting from family-
  care problems leads to health problems such as back pain,
  headaches, and insomnia. These stress-related health problems lead to such consequences as work absence, lower productivity and the loss of employees.
- Supervisors who are supportive of employees' child-care

problems help reduce stress, missed days of work, and other unproductive time.

- Many employees base their career decisions—such as quitting and turning down transfers or promotions—on their family-care problems.
- Child-care arrangements and flexible work hours influence many employees' views about when and if they will return to work after the birth of a child.
- While only about 10 percent of the employees currently have elder- and adult-dependent responsibilities, 25 percent of them expect to have such responsibilities in the next five years.
- Most caregivers to the elderly and to adult dependents are responsible for more than one of the following tasks: providing financial assistance, completing various forms, coordinating medical activities, providing transportation, and providing home and personal care.
- Elder-care responsibilities in and of themselves are not problems. They become problems as the elderly become less financially viable and more physically impaired.
- Employees who have difficulty caring for these groups have significantly more stress, stress-related health problems, and unproductive time at work than those who do not.
- Employees in the sandwich generation experience more stress, stress-related health problems, and unproductive time than those who are not in the sandwich generation.
- For both child-care and elder-care problems, the most frequently favored solutions are quality, affordable day-care centers, flexible work options that do not decrease income, and financial assistance.

1

The Changing American Workforce

A MERICAN adult life centers on work and family. But increasingly, conflicts are emerging between these two aspects of life, resulting in stress and stress-related health problems for people both at home and at work. Perhaps the single greatest reason for this is the increasing number of women in the workforce.

Although women have always worked, in the past two hundred years industrialism helped stratify society along class and gender lines, creating the "traditional" family. In the traditional family, most middle- and upper-class women remained at home as caregivers, while men assumed the role of provider outside the home. In the last twenty years, however, the need for talented labor has begun to erase these gender lines at work and at home, causing "role chaos" and stress.

Most modern mothers work outside of the home because of economic necessity; approximately two-thirds of women in the workforce are single, widowed, or divorced, or have husbands who earn less than $15,000. Quite simply, women work because they have to—to support themselves and their families. Female workforce participation has slowed the decline in the standard of living for two-parent families with children.

Because of the increased participation of women in the workforce, 26 million American children need some type of supervision every day. This demand is expected to double in the 1990s. Understandably, this situation creates a great deal of stress for working parents. A 1989 survey of 278 mayors and city managers cited not crime or drugs as their major concern, but child care.

Where do these children go while their parents are at work? In 1986, 9 million of them spent the day in some type of child care, but it was often of distressingly poor quality. Today, as many as 11 million school-age children come home to an empty house.

In my 1989 study of 3,300 employees, I found that about one-quarter of the children look after themselves. Overall, the most commonly used forms of child care that allow employees to remain at work in my study are:

	Percent
Child Looks After Him- or Herself	23
Day-Care Center	19
Family Day Care	15
Care by an Adult Member of the Household	14
Care by Other Relatives	12
Care by an Older Brother or Sister	6
Before-and-After-School Program	6
Other Arrangements	6
Someone Comes to the Child's Home	1

Compounding the stress between home and work, increasing numbers of employees are also becoming responsible for the care of the elderly and adult dependents. Over the next few decades, the elderly population will increase dramatically as the baby-boom generation grows older. Some experts speculate that by the middle of the twenty-first century, more employees will be caring for an elderly relative or friend than for their young children. In addition, increasing numbers of employees will become part of a "sandwich generation": they will simultaneously have responsibility for their children, for their elderly relatives or friends, and for their work.

Vignettes

The problems, concerns, stresses, and strains of employees who participated in surveys I conducted in 1988 and 1989 are representative of those that a growing number of working American families face as a result of changing demographics.

Karen W. is a white, married, lower-level manager in her mid-thirties with two teenage children (thirteen and fourteen). She and her husband both work full-time, but Karen has primary responsibility for caring for the children. Their annual household income is $74,000.

Although Karen's children usually look after themselves, caring for them when they are sick is a big problem because Karen's hours are very long and, at times, inflexible. "When my children are sick, I have to depend on a neighbor to help me with picking them up from school," she said. Doctor appointments and home emergencies use up much of her vacation time.

Worrying about her children and planning her schedule around their care also limit Karen's ability to travel on the job.

Karen summarized her dilemma this way:

My children are young teens. Idle hours after school and during summer vacations give them prime time to get into big trouble! There's no one at home to guide them in their decisions or to discipline them when needed. I feel that this is a major cause for teenage delinquency. I have basically good children, but like any normal kids, if they can get away with it (whatever *it* may be), they will, and this leads to major problems. The stress for me is knowing that no one is at home to take care of these problems.

Karen said her male supervisor does not understand her family/work conflicts and is unsupportive of her needs.

These conflicts create substantial stress both at home and on the job. Karen indicated that as a result of her stress, she had been tiring quickly in the previous six months, had difficulty falling asleep, and had frequent headaches.

Karen listed summer and vacation-care programs as the employer-assistance options that would be most useful to her. Before-and-after-school programs, a compressed work week, and flexible hours would also relieve some of her child-care problems.

Taking care of an elderly parent can be more stressful and difficult than finding care for young children, Rita C. pointed out. A white single occupational worker in her late thirties, Rita has no children, but she does have primary responsibility for caring for an adult dependent—her mother. "It's about time you included the elderly" [in the survey], she wrote.

In the previous year, Rita arrived late at work or left early several times because of work/family conflicts. She makes care-related phone calls during work hours. She uses vacation days to care for her mother's needs and has missed several days due to her own health problems. She said that caring for her mother is difficult because of the financial drain, the numerous doctor appointments, and her mother's frequent illnesses.

As a result of this caregiving, Rita has been bothered by a variety of stress-related health problems such as back pain, overeating, smoking too much, and having difficulty getting up in the morning. She thinks her company should play a more active role in employee health care and strongly supports greater company assistance with family/work conflicts.

Matt S., a white, lower-level manager in his late thirties, earns $41,000 annually. His wife works part-time, and they have no children. Matt is responsible for his two elderly parents. Because his parents' health is poor, he and his wife take care of their cooking, cleaning, and shopping needs, as well as their medical needs and transportation. Matt said the dual roles of dependent caregiving and working present problems, including finding and affording quality adult day care. These factors create stress for him both at home and on the job. Nevertheless, he admitted, since his wife works part-time, he is relieved of many elder-care responsibilities. As a result, he has no stress-related health problems that he knows of.

Matt would like to see his company provide an off-site adult day-care center in conjunction with other local companies. Some form of financial assistance and more flexible work hours would also be helpful.

Veronica D. is a thirty-five-year-old black middle-level manager. Her household consists of a husband who works full-time and two children, aged four and thirteen. Her family's annual household income is $65,000.

Veronica's position in middle management demands a great amount of her time and energy and requires her to work overtime. Veronica said this situation has caused a great deal of stress at home and at work: "Sometimes if I'm in the middle of a report, a meeting, or whatever . . . I have to make sure I get to the day care. If I'm not there, it's a dollar a minute late fee." Veronica pays $95 per week for her four-year-old's care. She complains that very few programs exist for her thirteen-year-old and that not enough attention is paid to the care of school-age children.

Veronica's problems and responsibilities do not end with finding care while she is at work. After work, she must rush home, cook dinner, wash the dishes, and so on. Balancing these two roles with little assistance from her husband "makes life impossible sometimes. I'm always tired, I'm always stressed out." But she reported no stress-related health problems besides feeling fidgety and occasionally overeating.

Veronica admitted that she has seriously considered leaving her company for one with better child-care asistance. She, too, feels that her company should play a more active role in helping employees with dependent-care needs and would like to see an on- or near-site day-care facility or employee discounts at local day-care centers as well as before-and-after-school programs.

Jeanette M. is a member of the sandwich generation. A pregnant Asian occupational worker, she already cares for her elderly mother and is beginning to experience the effects of work-related stress in anticipation of her role as caregiver to both her baby and her mother: "I have restless sleep, headaches, and aches all over my body. It isn't the pregnancy—it's my worrying about who is going to take care of my baby, and if I will be able to be a good mother and a good worker at the same time." She believes that . . .

The baby needs to be with the mother at least one year before being taken care of by strangers who could be trusted and love the baby. It would be good for the employees if the company provided day care by the office (better if at the same location as the office) so that employees can be with the children during lunchtime. If there's an emergency, if a child is sick, the employee could be with the child in minutes and bring him or her to the emergency center.

Jeanette said that caring for her dependent mother has already impaired her effectiveness at work. She anticipates having more difficulties in the years to come, since her mother will require more attention and financial support. Jeanette would like her company to implement a program with "volunteers to run errands for elderly and/or disabled people." More flexible hours would also be helpful.

Steven F. is another sandwich-generation employee. He is a thirty-six-year-old white occupational worker with a three-year-old daughter, a wife who works full-time, and a dependent mother-in-law who suffers from osteoporosis. Steven and his wife earn $47,000 per year.

His mother-in-law requires assistance in all areas including: financial, medical, transportation, home care, and personal care. Steven's responsibilities to her and his rigid work schedule hamper his ability to properly care for his daughter. He has been unable to find affordable, quality child care; his daughter is currently in a family-care home that Steven said is of poor quality. Other problems include finding care for the girl when she is sick and finding a child-care facility with hours that correspond to his and his wife's work schedules.

> I think that the father's role in raising the child is unrecognized at the company. The possibility of time off should be considered. I think that the company should realize that we're all just people, and as such, we have things that we have to do outside the company. They should be flexible enough to work with us.

Steven feels that a day-care facility near work would be the best solution for his child-care needs. An adult day-care facility would help alleviate his concern over his elderly mother-in-law. In addition, he made a persuasive argument for the compressed work week and working-at-home options that were also requested by many other employees: "I think that a compressed work week—ten hours a day, four days a week—would be more easily dealt with. It would allow me to take care of personal business without having to miss work or take vacation time." Steven is sandwiched between his responsibilities of caring for the young and old while working. He has seriously considered quitting his job either to stay home with his child or to work for a company with better dependent-care assistance.

Clara G. is a twenty-eight-year-old Hispanic lower-level manager. She is the single mother of a nine-year-old son. Her annual income is $32,000. Clara's job requires her to work extensive overtime for eight to ten straight days each month to meet financial book closings:

> I have only one week a month after book closing when I don't feel the stress of the job. If it weren't for my mother, who takes care of my kid, I'd probably have to quit this job. My mother's wonderful; I've had perfect attendance for the past year because she's always there when my child gets sick or I need her. I get so stressed out for most of the month that I overeat and smoke too much. I feel lousy, but I don't know how else to deal with the stress.

Clara believes the company should offer financial assistance, such as a flexible-spending account, so that she can pay her mother more money. She feels that before-and-after-school programs would also be useful "to keep my son off the streets."

Jim D. is a forty-two-year-old middle-level white who has four children, aged seven, nine, twelve, and thirteen. His wife has never worked, but he earns $65,000 annually.

Jim wrote, "My wife and I decided that I would work and she would take care of the kids." As a result of this arrangement, he did not report any stress at home or on the job because of conflicting work and family responsibilities. He also claimed he has no stress-related health problems.

Because of his own family arrangement, Jim feels that the company should not assist employees with their child-care needs: "The company should stay out of the family business. Its job is to make money. My job is to work, and my wife's job is to take care of the kids." One wonders what Jim's position would be if his financial situation did not allow for his wife to remain at home—a luxury that few families can afford anymore.

Even employees who do not have any child-care or elder-care responsibilities worry about the impact these impending responsibilities may have upon their family and work lives in the future. They see the difficulties that working parents and caregivers are now struggling with in the workplace.

Lisa K. is a single black occupational worker in her early thirties. She earns $27,000 annually after ten years of employment. Although she has no children and no elder-care responsibilities, she expects to have both within the next several years and is concerned about the effect they will have on her career: "It's difficult to have enough time for work, caring for others and yourself."

Lisa lives with her parents and expects to be responsible for their home care in the near future: "If my parents were to get sick, I'd take over all activities of running the home." Already she has turned down a transfer to a different city to avoid a potential conflict. Even without current family-care problems, Lisa's rejection of her transfer was a lost opportunity, not only for her but for her company, which was unable to move her into a position that would have maximized corporate efficiency and growth.

She anticipates at least some problems finding and affording quality care for her parents, and she feels strongly that her company should actively assist her with both child care and elder care. She would like to see her company offer adult-dependent care as well as payroll deductions or tax-exempt savings plans for family care.

Lisa believes that "on-site day care would be a great benefit, but not at the expense of other benefits we have already obtained." Regarding her future child-care needs, she said, "I feel people should have up to one year off for a child, without losing their jobs—not necessarily the same position, but some position of equivalent value."

These vignettes demonstrate the wide variety of family situations and problems that today's employees face. It is easy to see that these problems make employees less effective on the job and, in turn, adversely affect corporate productivity. Unfortunately, very little is being done to assist employees and thus to improve the competitiveness of the corporations that employ them.

Working Women

Over the last four decades, women have come to constitute an increasingly large percentage of entrants into the workforce: in 1960 they represented 33 percent of the workforce; in 1980 they represented 43 percent. This trend will continue for the rest of this century—by 2000, women will represent at least 47 percent of the workforce. An estimated two out of every three people who will fill the 21 million new jobs between now and the twenty-first century will be women.

These statistics are very important, but they do not tell the whole story. The greatest changes in the female labor force have occurred among women of childbearing age. Ellen Galinsky, a noted child-care expert, estimates that fully 80 percent of working women are of childbearing age. She projects that 90 percent of these women will become pregnant at some time during their careers. But having young children no longer means leaving the workforce. In 1986, 63 percent of mothers with children under eighteen were employed, compared with 9 percent in 1940. The most dramatic increase in the labor force in recent years has been in the percentage of working mothers with children under one year of age—from 31 percent in 1976 to 51 percent in 1986.

The percentage of working women will continue to increase as women—especially college-educated women—postpone childbearing until later years. Mary Brown, president of Corporate Child Care Consultants in Atlanta, notes, "Increasingly, women are postponing both marriage and childbearing into their late twenties and early to mid-thirties because they are committed to a lifelong work career outside the home. Each year these women postpone having children, their value to their company increases. Thus, it is incumbent upon their companies to make certain that they are providing the family-care assistance which will assure their quick return to their job."[1]

Women now receive more undergraduate degrees than men. In 1985 they received 51 percent of all undergraduate degrees, compared with only 42 percent in 1970. Clearly, as American society becomes more technologically driven, more jobs will require highly educated employees. As the percentage of women pursuing undergraduate and advanced education continues to increase, American society will have to develop new programs and policies to keep these valuable employees in the workforce.

The Changing Family Structure

What effects have the increasing number of working women had on the American family? One of the most striking effects has been the assault on the pervasive idea that the typical family is the "traditional" family, in which the husband works full-time and the wife stays home to care for the children. Fifty years ago, 70 percent of American families were "traditional" in this sense. At that time, corporate policies and procedures were in harmony with the structure and circumstances of many people's family lives. But today, fewer than 10 percent of all American households fit this description. Yet I have found in seminars I have conducted on race and gender issues that a significant number of the participating men, between 35 percent and 45 percent, believe that the traditional family is still the norm. (For women, the figures are between 10 percent and 30 percent.)

Over the past twenty years, the number of dual-career families and single heads of households has grown enormously, changing the profile of the American family. Two-income couples made up only 28 percent of all married couples in the United States in 1960; but in 1985, they made up 49 percent. This rapid growth in two-income couples is projected to rise to 57 percent by the year 2000.

At the same time, since 1971, the number of families headed by women with no husband has increased by 67 percent. Almost 20 percent of all working women are now single parents. In 1986, as many as 61 percent of all black children born were born to single mothers, as were 28 percent of Mexican-American children, 58 percent of Puerto Rican children, and 16 percent of white children. Today, more than one-quarter of all American children live in single-parent homes, while half of all black children do.

As a result of the escalating divorce rate and the growing number of births out of wedlock (5 percent of all births in 1960, but 23 percent in 1986), experts estimate that nearly half the children born in the 1980s will live with a single parent before they reach adulthood. Sixty percent of all single working mothers with children under fourteen earned less than $15,000 annually, and only 15 percent made more than $25,000. More than one-quarter of children born in the 1980s will live in extreme poverty—that is, in families with an annual household income of less than $15,000.[2]

Since the cost of quality child care can range from $3,000 to $12,000 per year per child, it is beyond the reach of many single heads of households and even of some two-income families. In addition to its cost and quality, its availability is also a problem. The availability of child care often determines the amount of time women are able to work. Figures vary slightly from study to study, but about one in seven employed women with preschoolers say they would work more hours if additional or better child care were available. Among non-working mothers in families with household incomes of less than $15,000, more than one in three say they would seek work if reasonably priced child care were available. Among single, divorced, widowed, and separated mothers who are not in the labor force, more than two out of five would seek work.[3]

Attracting these people into the workforce is essential if American businesses are to offset the labor pool shortages that will occur as the baby-bust generation enters the labor market. In fact, the labor shortages have already begun. The labor force is growing by just over 1 percent a year, compared with the 2.2 percent annual increase between 1970 and 1985. The eighteen-to-twenty-four-year age-group is projected to decrease by 20 percent in the next decade.

Aging in America

Recently, a great deal of attention has been focused on the importance of child care for working parents. Only in the past several years, however, has American society become more aware of the connections between working women, dual-career families, and the aging population. Increasingly, women working outside the home are assigned not double but triple duty: they must be wage earners, care for children, *and* care for the elderly. Contrary to popular belief, present-day families do not generally abandon the elderly to nursing homes. In fact, they prefer family care of the elderly, which is the most critical factor in preventing or delaying nursing-home placement.

Some recent demographic data underscore the increasing importance of elder care.[4]

- The median age of the U.S. population is projected to rise from the current thirty-two to thirty-six by the year 2000 and to forty-two by 2040.
- In 1900, only 4 percent of Americans were sixty-five or older. By 1986, 12 percent were at least sixty-five years old, and by the year 2020, 25 percent will be sixty-five or older.
- The elderly population itself is growing older. In 1986, 41 percent of the elderly population was seventy-five or older. But by 2000, half the elderly population is projected to be seventy-five or older.
- The eighty-five-and-over population is growing especially

quickly. By the middle of the next century, this population is expected to be seven times larger than it was in 1980.

How will these changing demographics affect corporate employees? In upcoming years, "baby-boomers" will grow older; at the same time, the small size of today's families means that fewer children will be available to care for their "boomer"-generation parents as they age. This, in turn, means that more corporate employees will be responsible for caring for an elder. Finally, Americans are living longer, but more and more of the aged are chronically ill or unable to carry out routine activities without assistance.

Today, only about 10 percent of all corporate employees, regardless of age, have primary responsibility for the care of an elderly person. (About one out of five employees over fifty say they have such responsibilities.) But in the future those numbers are sure to increase dramatically. The 10 percent statistic I am using is not the only accepted figure; other studies show proportionally higher numbers.

Research by Michael Creedon of the National Council on Aging found that among employees age forty, the percentages ranged between 25 percent and 30 percent.[5] Clearly, corporations with an above-average proportion of female employees and with a high workforce median age are more likely than others to be affected by the elder-care responsibilities of their workers.

The number of employees in the United States who are primarily responsible for caring for an elderly person cannot be precisely calculated, but there is little question that their numbers are growing daily. In 1989, I found that as many as 35 percent of employees over forty said they will have primary responsibility for an adult dependent in the next five years. With this growth, the corporate workforce is increasingly composed of employees who have increased levels of stress because they are responsible for both children and elderly. Presently, the sandwich generation represents about 1 percent to 3 percent of the workforce; but as Dr. Creedon points out, as increasing numbers of baby-boomers enter their forties and fifties, up to 25 percent will be sandwiched between the needs of their children and the needs of their parents.[6]

If the employees who have primary elder-care and/or child-care responsibilities are added together, they constitute a majority of employees. Their burdens may negatively affect their job performance. (Approximately 10 percent of the workforce aged eighteen to sixty-four is responsible for the care of an impaired adult. Added to those with elder care and child care, about seven out of ten employees face some family-care responsibilities.)

There will be enormous changes in the demographics of U.S. employees during the next decade. Corporations will be faced with an increasing number of employees who will be responsible for the care of family dependents—not only children, but aging parents as well. In fact, many employees will be responsible for the care of both. As we will see in the following chapters, if corporate America does not assist its employees, the caregiving responsibilities will affect corporate competitiveness.

2

Child Care and
Corporate Productivity

DESPITE the unprecedented focus on child care in the
1988 U.S. presidential election, despite the current debate over child-care legislation in Congress, and despite some
well-publicized corporate efforts, helping employees with
child-care problems still is not a priority for a large segment
of corporate America. Most corporations' approaches are so
weak or limited that their commitment to assisting their employees seems halfhearted. This lack of corporate initiative
comes at a time when the American family is undergoing a
major metamorphosis. Both single and married mothers are
entering the workforce at increasing rates. These workers
need care for their children, and when none is available,
some have no choice but to leave their children unsupervised.
A federal task force recently estimated that 11 million children are "latchkey children." The American family is crying
out for help, and all elements of our society must respond if
the United States is to remain competitive in the new global
economy.

Child care has traditionally been regarded not as a business
concern but as a women's issue and therefore not worthy of
serious economic attention. One white female occupational
worker in my studies stated, "I was told when I took this job
to decide if I was going to be a worker or a mother, and that
I had better not try to do both on company time." A white
male occupational employee added, "All personal problems
cannot be turned off for work and then back on in a family
setting."

This chapter begins to explain why child care is a bottom-line competitive issue.

Key Research on Corporate Child Care

Before I analyze the data from my own studies, let's review some of the recent studies that demonstrate the pronounced effect that employees' child-care problems have on corporate productivity.

In her 1988 study on dual-career couples, Dr. Gayle Kimball found that supervisors most frequently cited tardiness (83 percent), absenteeism (78 percent), scheduling (66 percent), and poor on-the-job performance (62 percent) as effects of inadequate child-care services. In addition, 16 percent of parents reported that they had considered quitting their jobs because of child-care difficulties.[1]

Arthur C. Emlen, in reviewing studies he has done over the years, noted that employees with children eighteen and under miss more work than employees with no children, "except for men employees whose children are cared for at home." In dual-income families, he found that women miss 50 percent more days per year than men, primarily because women are much more likely to be the primary caregivers.[2]

Kathryn Senn Perry found in 1988 that 46 percent of employees with children under twelve had missed at least one day of work in the previous year because of child care. Forty percent said their spouses had missed work because of child care. Forty-two percent said they had been late or left early because of child-care problems.[3]

In a recent study conducted by child-care experts Ellen Galinsky and Diane Hughes, 44 percent of the men and 76 percent of the women with children under six missed work in the previous three months for a family-related reason. The researchers estimated that the organizations they studied paid over $4 million in salary and benefits to employees who were absent because of child-care problems.[4]

It is important for companies to recognize the crucial relationship between the child-care needs of the workforce, existing corporate policies, and the level of community child-care services. For example, in 1979, Intermedics had to increase its workforce by recruiting women. The company analyzed the child care available in Freeport, Texas. Seeing a lack of services, Intermedics built and opened a high-quality day-care facility for 260 children; it costs employees $15 a week for full-time care. The center filled immediately. The company was rewarded with a 60 percent decrease in job turnover in the first two years of the center's operation. During the first year, reduced absenteeism saved fifteen thousand work hours. The combined savings for Intermedics totaled more than $2 million in the first two years of operation.

Experimental research has demonstrated that employers benefit from providing child-care assistance in decreased absenteeism, lowered turnover, enhanced recruitment, and improved productivity. In a 1984 study Ann G. Dawson and associates found that of seventeen companies that sponsored child-care centers, 53 percent of the companies reported a turnover rate of zero for those who used the center.[5]

These studies are part of a growing body of evidence that a lack of child care negatively affects corporate productivity and that providing child care improves productivity. The survey results presented in this book complement, support, and expand upon the conclusions of these studies.

My Research

In my 1988 study, I asked employees with children eighteen and under, "With regard to your child-care needs, how much of a problem is each of the following for you?" Table 2–1 shows the questions and employee responses by marital and gender status. (Notice that overall, the differences in the responses of men and women are significant.)

Overall, the most frequently cited problem was *finding care for a sick child* (40 percent). (*Note:* The percentages I am discussing here apply only to those employees who described these situations as a "big problem" or "somewhat of a problem." They do not include those who said these situations are

Table 2–1

IMPACT OF MARITAL STATUS ON CHILD-CARE PROBLEMS

Respondents were asked: "With regard to your child-care needs, how much of a problem is each of the following for you?" (N=Percent who say "a big problem" or "somewhat of a problem.")

Child-Care Problem	Single Women	Single Men	Married Women	Married Men	Unmarried Women	Unmarried Men	Total Women	Total Men	Total
Finding care for a sick child that fits into your schedule.	57	45	53	26	58	48	55	27	40
Going to school conference or program during working hours.	47	44	45	31	56	35	46	32	39
Handling child(ren)'s dentist/doctor appointments.	47	38	42	22	58	29	44	24	34
Handling dual roles as a parent and an employee.	44	37	40	18	42	17	41	19	30
Traveling on overnight trips.	46	45	37	21	41	34	39	21	30
Handling the sudden loss of child care, i.e., provider quits, gets sick, vacations, etc.	37	30	40	21	47	29	39	21	30

Handling child care during school vacations, holidays, or snow emergencies.	40	34	39	20	48	43	40	20	29
Affording child care.	43	35	36	22	46	36	37	22	29
Finding a child-care provider to work evenings and/or nights when working over-time.	42	35	37	20	43	40	37	21	29
Finding good-quality child care for your child(ren).	33	26	35	18	42	41	35	19	27
Transporting child(ren) between child-care arrangement and home.	23	17	21	10	28	29	21	11	16
Telephoning your child(ren) during working hours.	21	17	19	10	27	17	20	11	15

"a small problem" or "no problem at all.") Some of the employees commented about their difficulties.

> I have two children, ages three and four, with asthma, which is unpredictable as to when or how many times the attacks will occur. (black female occupational worker)

> I believe we need a sick plan similar to the state government and railroad instead of lying each time and saying 'I'm sick,' when in actuality my children are sick. (Hispanic male occupational worker)

> My children are very young. If one is sick, I have to take a day of vacation because the day care doesn't allow parents to bring a child in if sick or if he or she has a fever. (white female lower-level manager)

Going to school conferences or programs during working hours was the second most frequently cited problem (39 percent).

> My job is so demanding that I can't find time for my kid's school activities. I feel like they're growing up without me. (white male middle-level manager)

> Our job doesn't give us flexibility to attend our children's school conferences and programs, but management has that flexibility. This leaves a bad taste in occupational employees' mouths. (Hispanic female occupational worker)

The third most frequently cited problem was *handling children's doctor and dentist appointments* (34 percent). "Who ever sees doctors and dentists working after 5:00 or Saturdays?" asked a black male middle-level manager who said that getting his children (aged eight and ten) to doctor and dentist appointments presented major problems.

As table 2–1 shows, 27 to 30 percent of the survey respondents had child-care problems in seven other areas. Some typical comments show the variety of other problems employees face:

> My major problems are as follows: my start time is too early—my child has unsupervised time at home—and in summer vacation, all the facilities offering programs are in the downtown

area. Also, the programs' start time is after I get to work, and they end before I get home. They are usually for only half a day. Day-care centers don't take children after age eleven, but eleven is too young to be home alone. (black female lower-level manager)

Although I have always found solutions to balance work/family demands, my greatest concern in this area now is finding proper care/supervision for my child while I attend night functions for the company or when I have to travel. I have little time to develop support systems in this area, such as friends and neighbors. (white female lower-level manager)

You put in your request not to be scheduled for nights, and they schedule you for night shifts. You have to find people to keep your baby after the day-care hours. This is very difficult. (black female occupational worker)

I pay $612 a month for day care. That's almost half my net income! I have no idea how a single parent survives. (white male occupational worker)

My children are currently in day care. I'm rushed every day because quality day care in my area doesn't open early enough for my needs, or it doesn't deliver or pick up at my elementary school. (black female lower-level manager)

THE MAIN CATEGORIES OF CHILD-CARE PROBLEMS

Over the six years that I have been conducting my research, there has been little change in the overall concerns of employees about child care. Their most common problems can be grouped into three main categories. The first is their *lack of time to deal with the very unpredictable nature of child care,* such as a child falling sick or the sudden loss of a child-care provider. Even the more predictable events, such as school conferences and dentist and doctor appointments, require time that many modern employees can't find because of their demanding work schedules.

The second major problem category is the *availability of quality care*—care not only for infants, toddlers, and preschoolers, but also for school-age children, including before-

and-after-school care, vacation care, and summer care. Finding care for a sick child also falls into this category.

The third problem category is *affording quality child care.* In 1989, for children of all ages, I found that about 40 percent of employees pay nothing for child care, 22 percent pay $2,600 to $5,200 per year, and 8 percent pay over $5,200 per year. A *Fortune* magazine study uncovered similar findings. Marian Wright-Edelman, president of the Children's Defense Fund, has also noted that on average, employees pay $3,000 to enroll just one child in full-time child care.

But the age of the child affects how much parents pay for child care. Only 17 percent of the employees with children five and under pay nothing for child care. By contrast, 25 percent of employees with children two and under and 36 percent with children three to five pay $4,000 or more per year.

Child-care costs are higher for younger children. Infant and toddler care is more costly than care for preschoolers, and care for school-age children is generally the least expensive. But in general, employees with younger children are those just beginning their careers, and they make less money than older employees. These facts make it understandable that financing quality child care is a major concern for many younger employees.

In the hierarchy of child-care costs, center-based care is usually more expensive than family-based care. In one major metropolitan area I found that the average cost for day care is $85 per week and for family care, $76 per week. Care for summer and regular vacations varies greatly in this metropolitan area, from $12.50 to $150 per week. The most expensive form of care is the in-home caregiver or "nanny" who is unrelated to the child. Regional differences also come into play; child-care costs are highest in the Northeast and the Far West and lowest in the South.

For most working families, child care is the fourth largest item on the budget after food, housing, and taxes. In July 1989, the Census Bureau reported that, as a whole, families with working mothers spend $14 billion per year on care for children under fifteen. Women who earn less than poverty-level wages pay disproportionately more of their total income (22 percent) than the nonpoor (6 percent) for child care. As one Hispanic female lower-level manager said,

> Affordable, flexible child care is not always easy to find. There are waiting lists at preschools, and the hours are not always compatible with company start and end times. Child care is getting so expensive that a large part of our weekly income is going toward this expense. The tax credit is so low that it is hardly a credit at all.

In general, child-care problems are greatly influenced by the age of children, but sick-child care is the biggest problem for *all* women with children under thirteen years of age. For employees with children five and under, the sudden loss of a care provider, affording child care, and finding evening and overtime care are the second most frequently cited problems. For those with children six to thirteen, the second most frequently cited problems are handling child care during vacations, holidays, or snow emergencies, going to school conferences or programs during working hours, and handling doctor and dentist appointments. For women with children over thirteen, the problems most frequently cited include handling dual roles, handling doctor and dentist visits, and going to school conferences.

For men with children under five, finding sick-child care and finding quality care are the most frequently cited problems. For men with children six to thirteen, attending school conferences and finding care for a sick child are the most frequently cited problems. For men with children over thirteen, the most frequently cited problems are going to school conferences and programs, doctor and dentist appointments, handling dual careers, and traveling overnight.

In sum, many employees with child-care needs face time, availability, and affordability problems. (The areas of least concern for both women and men are telephoning children during working hours and transporting children between child-care arrangements and home.)

MEN ARE INCREASINGLY INVOLVED
IN CHILD CARE

The largest difference between my 1984 study and my 1988 study is in the number of men affected by child-care dilemmas. In 1988, a significantly higher percentage of men had at least some child-care problems than in 1984. "As a male, I am shouldering more and more of this burden traditionally held by women," wrote a white lower-management father. "I have a child that I either have to take or pick up from a day-care service. I also take my child to regular doctor and dentist appointments. I have also stayed home with my child when she was sick."

Even married men whose wives do not work are increasingly involved in caring for children. A white male occupational worker wrote,

> Dealing with the need to be at work and meet the needs of sick children or of my wife (who does not work outside the home) when she gets sick or worn out from dealing with sick children is very difficult. Especially when you have been up all night with an illness, and you call in to take time off, and your boss acts indignant and sarcastic about the 'real' need for time off, and demonstrates a pure lack of care or concern for the needs expressed.

The percentage of women with child-care problems did not change much between 1984 and 1988. In 1984, twenty-one percent of the women said affording child care was at least somewhat of a problem; in 1988, 37 percent of the women said so. Additionally, 45 percent of the women said finding care for a sick child was somewhat of a problem in 1984; 55 percent of the women concurred in 1988.

But while only 2 percent more women in 1988 (41 percent) than in 1984 (39 percent) said handling dual careers was at least somewhat of a problem, the percentage of men who responded in this manner increased from 3 percent to 19 percent—more than a sixfold increase. In 1984, at least twice as many women as men had problems in eleven of twelve areas. But in 1988, the percentage of women was twice that of men in only one problem area—difficulty in handling the dual roles of employee and parent.

Some participants' comments support the conclusion that more men are becoming active participants in child care.

> The only reason child care is no problem at this time is because my husband is willing to work midnight to 8:00 A.M. while the kids are little. (white female occupational worker)

> I'm beginning to organize things as much as possible. Without my husband's willingness to help, I'm sure I'd have an attendance problem. (white female occupational worker)

> My child (the youngest) was premature and required care in the home. My husband stayed home with her due to the exorbitant costs of maintaining a full-time nurse. (white female lower-level manager)

These statistics and comments suggest that more and more employees—especially men—are finding it difficult to balance work and family responsibilities.

The fact that more men are sharing the burden of child care, especially as their wives become more career-oriented and their families become more dependent on two incomes, has not come about primarily because men are more enlightened. It is due in large part to women "putting their foot down" and pointing out to their husbands and partners that caring for children is a lifelong commitment. In the focus groups I conduct and from the audiences I speak to, I often hear women insisting that their husbands play a more significant role in the rearing of children and in taking care of the home.

> I had to remind my husband that his job did not stop when I got pregnant. He is okay now. (black female occupational worker)

> My husband was very reluctant to help me care for our three children or to do anything in the house until seven months ago. Then I got promoted, and I now make more money than he does. My job is very demanding, and I decided to put my foot down. He is helping a little more now, but I had to threaten him with divorce. (white female middle-level manager)

I have attempted numerous tactics, both subtle and not so subtle, to get my husband to help with our little girl. He does a
little now and then, but I won't give up. He feels like his
friends will laugh at him if they knew he helped me with our
child. (Asian female lower-level manager)

One reason men are sharing child-care burdens may be that
the gap in pay for women and men has begun to close—at
least in the corporations I have studied. Ironically, an increasing number of women are making more money than their
husbands. As women's economic power increases, they are
becoming less tolerant of husbands and partners who are unwilling to carry their share of the load. And as couples' incomes increase, households are less able to suffer the loss of
what was once viewed as a "secondary income." In addition,
the success of women in corporate America places increasing
demands on their time. Work is no longer a nine-to-five job
but a seven-to-seven job. Women's time, energy, and inclina-
tion to be "Supermoms" are becoming limited.

Social researchers once thought that the final years of this
century would usher in an age of leisure. But pollster Louis
Harris says the average American work week, including commuting time, increased from just under forty-one hours in
1973 to nearly forty-seven hours in 1988—about the same
length as the work week of the 1940s. Subtracting sleep,
meals, and personal care, time available for leisure fell from
twenty-six hours to less than seventeen hours—a 37 percent
drop. Money was the biggest reason for the shift. The dis-
couraging news reported by Harris was that a need for two
incomes, longer commuting time to today's jobs, and a general economic change toward lower-paying service jobs were
adversely affecting leisure time.

There are many other reasons why more men have child-
care problems today than in 1984. For one thing, men are
more aware of the issue. As child care becomes more publi-
cized as a "legitimate" corporate issue, people feel more comfortable admitting that they have child-care problems and can
view men as successful caregivers without sacrificing the "ma-
cho" image.

Also, many older top corporate executives who have children are beginning to have firsthand knowledge of the problems their employees experience. I have heard and seen top executives discuss the child-care problems that their children—especially their daughters—are experiencing while trying to balance family and careers. One vice president of personnel of a Fortune 50 company told me that his daughter had to leave her job at another Fortune 50 company because of her problems finding quality, affordable child care for her toddler and her infant. After this incident, he began to believe that corporate America should take a more active role in assisting employees with child care. He recognized how much it had cost his daughter's company to lose an employee in whom they had invested five years and thousands of dollars of formal and informal training.

This growing awareness at the top and throughout the upper hierarchy of corporations has prompted a slow change in some corporate cultures, making it acceptable to talk about and admit to child-care problems. But in most companies those problems are still considered personal matters rather than corporate concerns.

WOMEN STILL DO THE MOST CARING FOR CHILDREN

While an increasing number of men are becoming more actively involved in the care of their children, my recent studies show (see table 2–1) that married women in many homes continue to perform a majority of household and child-care tasks.

> Children are not a priority of this company or this society. For the next six months, I wish every father was required to attend every doctor visit, school conference, arrange for care or stay home with the children. Until males (who are this country's leaders) recognize children as a priority, there will be no changes. (white female occupational worker)

Table 2–1 reveals some startling differences between women and men of the same marital status. Single parents and unmarried couples respond similarly on more questions than do married women and men, and the differences are much smaller. For married couples, in only four of the twelve problems is the difference between men and women 14 percent or less. But among singles, on nine out of the twelve questions the difference is only 7 percent or less. For unmarried couples, on eight of twelve questions, the difference is 10 percent or less.

Single mothers and married women respond similarly to most of the questions. This similarity suggests that many married women behave like single mothers when it comes to caring for children.

Married men seem to be the least burdened with the problem of caregiving. This may be attributed to the number of male employees who maintain "traditional" values or to males' lack of involvement in child-care issues. One white male lower-level management employee stated, "I don't take care of my family situations at work. Everything is all right because my wife has made a commitment to raising our children and not getting paid to work for a corporation." By contrast, single and unmarried men with children respond more like women in most areas.

The role of men in child care varies according to age of the children. For children aged two and under, there is generally a smaller gap between women's and men's responses than in the age group of three to five. It seems that men enjoy "playing daddy" early on. After a period of time, however, the play turns to work and the fun of "playing daddy" wears thin. As the child becomes increasingly independent and curious, men often relinquish the caregiver role.

After children enter school, aged six to thirteen, the gap between the responses of women and men narrows. The gap decreases dramatically between women and men with children over thirteen. These facts seem to indicate that men are slightly more likely to assist with infants and toddlers than with preschoolers aged three to five. As children grow older, go to school, and become less time-consuming, men again begin to play a more active role as daddy.

From these responses, an index was formed to measure the

Table 2–2

THE RELATIONSHIP BETWEEN THE NUMBER OF
CHILD-CARE PROBLEMS AND THE AGE OF CHILDREN

(N = percent)

Age of Children	*None* Women	Men	*1 to 4* Women	Men	*5 to 8* Women	Men	*9 to 12* Women	Men
2 and Under	11	31	23	32	37	24	28	14
3 to 5	6	31	26	32	36	23	32	14
6 to 13	17	36	32	35	29	18	23	12
Older than 13	49	65	37	27	10	6	6	3
Total	24	45	31	32	25	13	20	10

overall degree of employee problems (see table 2–2). Viewed from this angle, only 24 percent of women but 45 percent of men believe they have no significant child-care problems. Conversely, 45 percent of the women and 23 percent of the men have significant problems in at least five of the twelve problem areas.

Using table 2–2, one can see that the age of the child greatly affects women's child-care problems. For example, 65 percent of the women with children two and under, said they have child-care problems in at least five of the twelve areas, but only 16 percent of women with children over thirteen said this. (The figures for men are 38 percent, and 9 percent, respectively.)

Responses also varied according to employees' level in the corporate hierarchy. Unexpectedly, upper-level female managers (55 percent) were most likely to say that they have problems in at least five of the twelve areas, compared with only 39 percent to 45 percent of the women at other levels. One reasonable explanation for this difference is that women at higher corporate levels are in jobs that are extremely demanding in terms of responsibility, time, and travel.

Men in occupational positions (28 percent) were the most likely to say that they have at least five or more child-care problems. (The figures for the other levels are 13 percent to 23 percent.) The fact that occupational women (with the exception noted) and men have more overall problems than employees at higher levels can be attributed to their lower salaries, the inflexibility of their work schedules for both normal and overtime hours, and their lack of power to make decisions and prioritize work and family responsibilities.

A white male occupational worker stated, "Managers have such freedom. Craft should be able to stay home with a sick child without it going against our record. This is shameful harassment." Added a Hispanic male occupational worker, "I'm afraid to take much time off for family-related problems, for fear that it could affect my job situation/status."

RACE AND GENDER

Statistics related to race and gender in the 1988 study are similar to those in the 1984 survey. Black women and Hispanic women were the women most likely to say that they have no child-care problems, while American Indian women and white women were least likely to say this. For men, American Indians were the least likely to say they have no child-care problems; white men were again most likely to respond in this manner, followed by blacks, Asians, and Hispanic men.

The findings on black and Hispanic women may appear surprising, considering that they are most likely to be single heads of households and in low-paying occupational jobs. But on closer analysis it makes sense because black women indicated in both my 1984 and my current studies that they have *always* faced difficult life issues such as dealing with racism and trying to keep the family structure together, so they are better prepared to handle work/family conflicts. In fact, black women were least likely to respond that they have much stress on the job.

In addition, both Hispanic and black women said that they receive support from family members, whether from an immediate nuclear-family member or from an extended-family member. Black and Hispanic women were least likely to say that finding quality child care is much of a problem. White women and American Indian women were most likely to say this.

For the same reasons, it is not surprising that black and

Hispanic women also have the fewest problems with the sudden loss of child-care providers. Finally, despite their lower positions in the corporate hierarchy, black and Hispanic women do not find it any more difficult than white women to afford child care because child care, for many people of color, is handled by family members.

> I'm very glad to have done this survey. A lot of people aren't as fortunate as I am. My mother-in-law doesn't work, and she's the person who takes care of my child while my husband and I are at work. When he's old enough to go to a child-care center, fine. If he gets sick or anything, I'll stay home with him, but if it isn't that bad, he can go over to his grandparents'. (black female occupational worker)

> My mother keeps my child. Therefore, I don't worry about her and that helped me to return to work sooner. (black female lower-level manager)

> The grandparents kept my first child. If I didn't have them, I don't know what I would have done. (Hispanic female occupational worker)

Finally, black women claim that black men are accustomed to women being employed and therefore have a much more egalitarian attitude than other men. This claim is supported by my research: black men are significantly less likely than other men to hold sexist stereotypes (see chapter 9). One black male middle-level manager presented a typical nonsexist view: "Day-care issues are very important issues for our company. Both spouses have responsibility for the child care, which a company needs to recognize." In contrast, a white female lower-level manager stated, "Working mothers are generally required to take care of sick children, doctor appointments, and problems at school or after school, while male parents are rarely required to take this responsibility."

Vignettes

Mary C. is a married American Indian occupational worker in her mid-thirties. She and her husband have four children and a combined annual income of $33,000. She gets very little help from her husband and as a result has missed work, arrived late and left early, each more than six times in the previous year.

> Because my job has certain due dates, I have to be at work on certain days. Being a working mother of four, I use my vacation for my children's sicknesses, doctor appointments, school appointments, and so on. There have been times when I've taken work home to meet due dates. One time when my son had just come home from the hospital after being in the intensive care unit, I was advised to stay home with him for a week. When I requested personal time instead of vacation, my supervisor didn't want to charge my time in this manner. His attitude toward me changed when I explained that I couldn't use a week's vacation in April still having to go until December, especially after having just had one son in the hospital.

Because of the wide range of her children's ages and because one child is epileptic, Mary has a variety of child-care problems.

> The most stressful times *on the job* are summer vacation, school holidays, and after school. Being a transferee, I don't feel I have a good support system should I require a great deal of help during these times. My school children are twelve, ten, and eight—somewhat too old for baby-sitting, but too young to be entrusted on their own. Yet we have no before-and-after-school-care programs. My three-year-old son is in day care.

When her children are ill or have to be somewhere at a certain time, stress results.

> There are times when your children are running a fever, and you pray their fevers will go down so you can go to work. You either want them to be sick enough to know they need to be home or well enough to go to school—nothing in the middle.

All these concerns create a great deal of stress for her, both at home and on the job. She said that in the previous six months she has been fidgety, has had frequent headaches and backaches, and has had difficulty waking up in the morning.

Linda R. is a first-level-management Hispanic employee in her mid-twenties. Her household consists of a husband who is employed full-time and a two-year-old child in a day-care center. They plan to have another child in the near future. Their annual household income is $52,000.

Linda's experiences are roughly commensurate with those of other dual-career couples. She enjoys her work but admitted to having difficulty in managing her work/family responsibilities. Finding care for a sick child, handling child care during day-care closures, handling overtime requirements, and affording quality child care are, for her, "big problems."

Although she is a manager, she has little control over her scheduling and consequently incurs a great deal of stress when she must take an unexpected day off or work overtime. She wrote, "Needs of the business dictate, yet outside child-care is not run on this principle. Also, child-care costs are tremendous, making child-care expenses a big part of a family's budget." She must pay a dollar for every minute she is late in picking up her child, and this happens a few times each week. Her child-care costs are over $400 per month. "Whenever I work overtime, dinner schedules and so on are pushed so far back, I feel as if I never left the job. To prevent working overtime, I take work home to do after I meet my family responsibilities. This leads to an overworked and stressed individual. This then affects my family interaction." To avoid additional pressures on herself and her family, she has seriously considered turning down any offer of promotion, and she is seriously considering moving to another company that does provide child-care assistance.

When asked to select the *one* most useful out of thirteen different child-care solutions, she selected a company day-care center that is reasonably priced and whose hours correspond to her own. In all, Linda chose twelve solutions that would be helpful. (See chapter 5 for child-care solutions.)

Mark V. is a white occupational worker in his late twenties. His gross family income is $33,000. Although his wife only works part-time and is primarily responsible for the care of their three children (aged two, six, and seven), Mark still has problems balancing his family and work roles. In the previous year, he missed work, was late, or left early several times each, always to take care of family matters. He also made numerous personal calls during work hours. "Being a working parent, there have been times when phone calls must be made during work hours concerning school, child care or medical problems," he wrote.

Traveling overnight, attending school conferences, and handling children's doctor and dentist appointments all pose significant problems for Mark. He has trouble finding care for his children when they are sick or during emergencies and his wife has to work. He says that his supervisor is not supportive of his family needs.

> I'm involved in many activities with my kids, but sometimes management acts as though there should be only this job. Conflicts come up when you're made to stay late when other plans have been made. They don't force me to stay, but from their tone you wonder if you'd be cutting your own throat if you don't.

Mark thinks his company should play a more active role in assisting employees with family and work conflicts and child-care needs. He would like to see an on- or near-site day-care center, flexible hours, and "programs for school-age children."

Single Parents

As other studies have shown, increasing numbers of employees are single heads of households with children under eighteen. The Women's Bureau of the U.S. Labor Department reported that in 1985, 21 percent of all households with children under eighteen years of age were headed by single mothers and 2 percent by single fathers. The numbers reflect a significant increase since 1960, when only 9 percent of households with children under eighteen were headed by single parents.

Who are these single parents? They include people from every race and both genders, but the vast majority are women and a high percentage are women of color. They are a quickly growing minority, yet little support is offered to them. The average annual income of a working single mother is about $10,000, and high-quality child care costs about $3,000 per year. Children living with single parents now constitute 24 percent of the entire child population—up from 20 percent in 1980.

For the single parent, the problem of "role overload"—combining full-time employment and family—is especially severe.

> Being a single parent of two, conflicts arise, child care is very expensive, and day cares don't take sick children. It's hard to balance family and work sometimes. Employers need to be sensitive to this. (white female occupational worker)
>
> I'm a single mother. Many things, like school conferences, must be dealt with on company time. A single mother has so few options—she needs some flexibility with work hours. (Hispanic female occupational worker)

Although husbands or male partners in dual-career families may not participate fully in child-rearing and other household duties, they do take some of the pressure off women by contributing income and by performing traditional male tasks. But the single mother generally has very little, if any assistance in these areas. This accounts for the fact that slightly higher percentages of single mothers than married women indicated that they have certain child-care problems.

Single fathers' responses to most questions are quite similar to those of single mothers. The difference between them could arise because men generally make more money than women and consequently experience fewer problems. Nevertheless, compared with married men with children eighteen and under, single fathers are significantly more likely to experience various child-care problems.

One of the major stressors for parents, regardless of marital status, is the financial strain that child care places on the family budget. For single mothers, this is an especially serious problem because women are normally in lower-paying jobs. In 1989, I found that 49 percent of single women, compared with 22 percent of single men, spend about 30 percent of their income on child care.

Cynthia V. is a black occupational worker, aged thirty-one. She is a single mother, has a child one and a half years old, and has an annual household income of $17,000. She pays $95 a week for child care.

She reported that although she is generally satisfied with her job, her scheduling gives her a great deal of difficulty. She has no control over her hours and must frequently travel overnight. Compounding this problem is her company's excessive concern about tardiness:

> I wish that our hours were more flexible. Could the company give us a grace period of five minutes in the morning? What I mean is this: Why couldn't they wait until 7:05 before officially saying that we're late? I have to be at my desk at 7:00, but sometimes I'm late by one minute because of traffic and my child's day care doesn't open until 6:30. Sometimes they're late opening the day-care center, and I still get docked.

Not surprisingly, Cynthia admitted to feeling stress at work and has considered leaving the company to work for one with better child-care benefits. She feels stress at home as well, noting, "Sometimes I go home thinking about work that needs to be done or things that I didn't have time to do. I become frustrated when things aren't done right, and sometimes I take it out at home."

She would like to see her company assist employees with their dependent-care needs, and specifically she would like payroll deductions for child-care expenses and an on- or near-site day-care facility. Cynthia would also like to see her company actively help employees with dependent elderly parents. She is concerned about her fifty-nine-year-old mother, who is currently under a doctor's care: "It would be difficult financially, emotionally, and physically to try to take care of my mother." Cynthia would like to see more flex-time options and expanding community-based home-care services in order to help her future responsibilities for caring for her mother.

Caring for Children with Limitations

The "normal" stresses of parenting and working full-time are compounded when a child is handicapped, whether in an emotional, a physical, or a mental capacity. Approximately 10 percent of the employees I studied have children eighteen or under with special needs resulting from physical, emotional, and/or learning limitations. (In my 1989 study, about 15 percent of the employees were responsible for dependent adults—eighteen to sixty-four—who have some form of limitation.)

Such children require more parental attention, but child-care arrangements tend to be less available for them. Families of these children therefore often experience a serious imbalance in work and family life. For example, 67 percent of the employees who have children with special needs, compared with 46 percent of those who do not, say they have stress at home to "a great extent" or to "some extent." As one might expect, the employees who have children with special needs have a "very difficult" or "difficult" time finding appropriate care and are much more likely to have considered staying home with their children than those who are having only "slight difficulty" or "no difficulty at all."

In 1984, the Center for Social Policy and Practice in the Workplace at the Columbia University School of Social Work began a study to develop services for families struggling to maintain their work roles while caring for a disabled child. The project sought specifically to identify families with very young children, on the assumption that early intervention would be most effective.

The study was conducted using union members who had recently drawn maternity benefits for themselves or hospitalization benefits for a child. Eight percent reported that they had a handicapped child under the age of two and a half. From the report:

> Disabilities included chronic illness (hearing, vision or speaking problems) and other physical problems. These families scored high on a measure of work interference, i.e. dealing with family matters during working hours, missing work, arriving late and leaving early. . . .[6]
>
> As Susan G., a black, occupational, single mother with two young children, one of whom has a severe learning disability, explained: "I try not to bring my personal problems to work. I do have a handicapped child and to meet her needs there are times I have to change my normal schedule. When the problem arises, my supervisor refers me to EAP (Employee Assistance Program). The company seems to feel that by making an exception in my schedule another employee would complain. I feel each case needs an individual examination, and my situation is different from everyone's in my group. I don't want special treatment, but I'm a single parent with a handicapped child and I have to work."

Like the great majority of workers who are attempting to balance work and home responsibilities, this worker doesn't want special treatment. What she would like is to be able to perform her position responsibly without compromising her family's needs. Flex-time, she feels, has helped her perform both functions: "Since the inception of flex hours, the schedule works out when you need to change hours because of appointments."

Child-Care Problems and Their Impact on Productivity

Employees' responses differed depending on the ages of their children, their marital status, their demographic background, and the health of their children, but one commonality is obvious from their comments and data: most female employees and a solid majority of male employees have child-care problems. They cannot leave these problems at the corporate door, as many corporate executives would like to believe they can. The problems, instead, are translated into lost productivity, increased health-care costs, and potentially, a loss of good employees to another company or from the workforce altogether.

Some employees recognize that their child-care problems negatively affect their effectiveness as workers. Marsha Love, Ellen Galinsky, and Diane Hughes have found that almost equal percentages of women (43 percent) and men (42 percent) believed that their work and family responsibilities interfered with each other a great deal. A much higher percentage of women with children under six (68 percent) reported this type of interference.[7] This compares with 51 percent of the

Table 2–3

WHO SAYS CHILD-CARE PROBLEMS IMPAIR THEIR WORK EFFECTIVENESS?

(N = Percent who say at least to some extent)

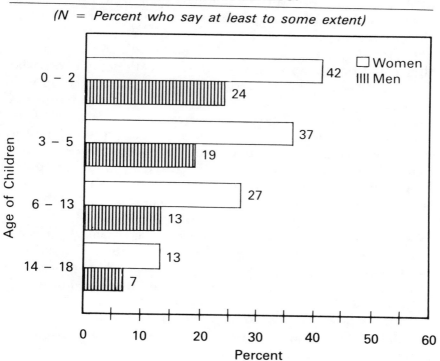

men with children under six. And Kathryn Senn Perry found
that 53 percent of the participants wasted time or made mis-
takes, or their quality of work suffered, because they were
worried about their children.[8]

Table 2–3 shows employee responses to the question, "To
what extent do you believe your child-care problems impair
your effectiveness as an employee of your company?" Overall,
one out of five employees in 1988 with children eighteen and
under said that child-care problems impair their effectiveness
as employees to a "great extent" or to "some extent." More
than twice as many women (27 percent) said this as men (12
percent). In 1989, 54 percent of the women and 25 percent
of the men responded in this manner. (That sample had a
much higher percentage of occupational employees with more
child-care problems generally.)

Notice the significant effect the age of the children had on
the employee responses. The younger the children, the more
likely the employees were to feel that their child-care responsibilities impair their job performance. In addition, the more
the employees missed work (came in late, left early), the more
likely they were to believe they are not as effective at work as
they could be. For example, 45 percent of the employees who
have never been late compared with 70 percent of those who
were late more than six times because of work/family conflicts
said they were not performing their jobs as effectively as
possible. It is clear from focus groups and from employee
responses that the major reason that more employees do not
believe that their effectiveness is impaired by child-care problems is that they try to make up the lost work time by working overtime and by bringing work home.

> As a management employee, I don't feel comfortable perform-
> ing personal business at times at work, but I also feel commit-
> ted to making up the time. (white female lower-level manager)
>
> I feel that I make up any work time spent on personal matters
> by adjusting hours, including unreported overtime. I try to
> keep my hours flexible. (black female occupational worker)
>
> I think it also balances out, since I often have worked through
> my lunch to meet commitments, as well as overtime and

weekends—this is without additional compensation. (black female middle-level manager)

Employees often work through vacation days and holidays to get work done (I'm doing this survey on Thanksgiving Day) or try to keep up with a growing work load. And because of continuing work demands, chances are that they will not have the opportunity to take the time off at another time—what a joke. (white male middle-level manager)

The fact is that a growing number of employees believe their company gets more than its fair share out of them, because the time they spend at the company encroaches on their family and personal time.

Family needs (children or not) shouldn't be considered a work problem, as often as family intrudes on work—work more often intrudes on family. (White male occupational worker)

Now ask me how many times work has delayed me going home, prevented early leave, canceled my vacation or personal plans, or worked during personal time. I cannot believe you asked one question and not the other. As a matter of fact, I find it insulting. [This man said that he had missed work three times, been late for work six times, left early three times, and dealt with personal calls numerous times in the past year.] I spend well over forty-five hours per week without work-related affairs. The family-related matters that have caused me to be late are of little consequence. You should also have a question like: How often have work-related affairs affected your family time? How often have work-related functions caused you to be late or absent from children's formal school functions, parent/teacher conferences, and award ceremonies? (white male middle-level manager)

My boss allows me to manage my work environment, including incorporating my family's needs. Work has interfered with my family a thousand to one over family interfering with work. (white male occupational worker)

But no matter how hard employees try to be effective and make up lost work time, many are only partially successful.

Missing Work

This section shows the correlation among child-care problems, employee absences, and lost productivity. The analyses of missed workdays are similar to the analyses of leaving work early and coming in late; therefore, I will concentrate on missing work.

But first, let's look at how employees explain their lost productivity because of missed work, coming in late, and/or leaving early.

> My day care opens at 6:30 A.M. It's okay, unless the traffic or weather is bad—then I'm five to ten minutes late. I've had to pick up sick children at school and day care. (white female occupational worker)

> I have a 3-year-old who doesn't like to get up early, and her crankiness and uncooperativeness cause me to be late, no matter how early she's put to bed and no matter how early I get up to get ready. (black female lower-level manager)

> As far as missed work, if you have children, they're going to get sick. That's just part of life! It's such a shame that so many good workers are left with no choice but to use up their vacation to take care of sick children. (white female occupational worker)

> I feel that the company is too strict about absences. I have three children, and it's almost impossible to get by missing only two to four days a year before being penalized and probably even fired. I realize people do abuse it, and there have to be rules. However, I think the supervisor/company has to really consider the circumstances and then act. One of the biggest stresses for me, because of my job, is just worrying about missing too many days. I feel that the company needs to realize that a majority of women working for it are raising a family and that there is no consideration made for them in dealing with illness. For example, if my child was to get chicken pox, I would have to take vacation time for a week to be at home with him. If I choose to take 'I' time, it would go against me. Why should I have to take vacation time?! Why is there not a code you could take that would not be penalized . . . other than vacation days? (Asian female occupational worker)

> "Due to a suicidal child, I made myself available at all times to

police, doctors, and therapists." (white female lower-level manager)

A Hispanic female employee summarizes the issue: "Family issues are a part of life. Sometimes it can't be helped to miss, to be late, or to need to leave."

Forty-two percent of the women and 28 percent of the men missed work in the previous year due to personal and/or family matters—and this does not count vacation time that may have been taken for this reason. If we add the vacation days employees took to care for children, the percentage who missed work would be much higher. In 1989, when vacation days were included, the figures were 73 percent of women and 52 percent of men.

Perry wrote of her study's participants that workers at one hospital were penalized for taking time off to care for a sick child. Of the 2,500 employees polled, 66 percent of those with children missed work to care for their children who were ill. Thirty-six percent of them called in absent without pay; 30 percent used personal sick leave; and 24 percent took a vacation day.[9]

With respect to work absence, men and women without children resemble each other much more than they resemble those who have children. Thirty-four percent of the women and 31 percent of the men who were single missed work in the previous year. The large discrepancy in percentages for married couples with children—women (52 percent) and men (31 percent)—provides additional evidence that women are by far the major child-care providers in dual-income families and that many men have wives who either do not work or who work only part-time and handle child care. When we look at children's ages (table 2–4), the numbers reveal that the younger the children, the more problems there are and the more likely the employees are to miss work.

Sick children are a major cause of employee absences. The harder it is to find care for an ill child, the more likely employees are to miss work. For example, 51 percent of the men who said that caring for a sick child is a big problem missed work in the previous year because of personal and

Table 2–4
IMPACT OF CHILDREN'S AGES ON ABSENCE FROM WORK

Respondents were asked: "In the past year, approximately how many times have you missed work due to personal and/or family matters?" (N = percent who have missed work)

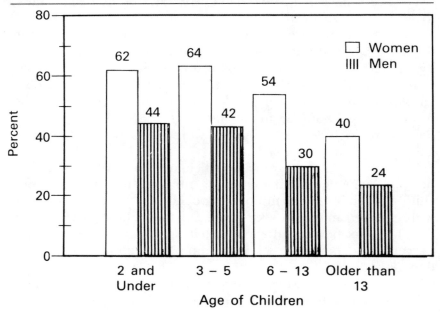

child-care problems, as did 68 percent of the women. One Asian female occupational worker noted, "Managers still frown when workers take off from work due to a sick child or any activities pertaining to children."

Another major cause of employee absence from work is that child-care arrangements sometimes fall through. In 1989, I asked employees how many times their child-care arrangements fell through and special arrangements had to be made at the last minute. Thirty-three percent said never (compared with 26 percent who said more than three times). Fifty-nine percent whose child care arrangements never fell through compared with 89 percent whose arrangements fell through more than three times in the year missed work in the previous year.

Nora W. Wong noted that although an equal percentage of the women and men in her study had their child-care arrangements break down, female employees were twice as likely to have missed work because of this.[10]

The financial cost to companies of employee absence is tremendously high. My calculations suggest that about nine thousand out of twenty-six thousand employees surveyed missed work at least two days during the previous year because of work and family problems. Using an average salary plus benefits of $100 per day, these companies lost at least $1.8 million in the previous year solely through employee absences. If it were possible to calculate the costs associated with leaving early, arriving late, and/or dealing with family issues during working hours, we would see that the cost to these companies is even greater. If we applied those statistics to the workforces of the major American corporations, we would see that the loss amounts to billions of dollars per year.

Summary

The data show that most women and a majority of men have child-care problems. These problems fall into three basic areas: lack of time, limited availability of proper care facilities, and limited ability to pay for quality care. The data also show that large numbers of women who are in the workforce as permanent full-time employees, also maintain a full-time job at home. It is not surprising that married mothers respond like single mothers about child-care problems, missed work days, and lost productivity at work. Many married women are in fact "single" mothers when it comes to balancing work and child-care responsibilities, since they receive only limited help from their partners.

Slowly but surely, more married men are increasing their child-care responsibilities. As a result, the differences in responses between married women and men decreased between 1984 and 1988. Stated one white male middle-level manager, "I believe my wife has had far more instances of missed work, so I believe it is more of a woman's or single father's issue for me." Most single fathers experience difficulties like those women experience in their attempts to be both full-time parents and workers.

As companies try to become more competitive, they demand that their employees work longer hours and weekends and take on more responsibility. But while employers have increased their demands on their employees, they have not taken into account how these demands affect the employees and their home lives.

Child-care problems lead to lost work time, costing corporate America billions of dollars each year. The next chapter discusses the impact of child-care problems on employee stress, both at home and at work, and the resulting stress-related health problems that cost corporate America additional tens of billions of dollars every year.

3

Child Care and Its
Impact on Stress
and Health

C ORPORATE executives are beginning to realize that stress
has negative effects on job performance, corporate productivity, corporate health-care costs, and ultimately, the bottom line. The National Council on Compensation Insurance
reported in 1985 that mental stress accounted for 11 percent
of all occupational disease claims in the early 1980s and represented the fastest-growing type of worker compensation
claim in the 1980s.[1] Rosalind Forbes reported in her book,
Corporate Stress, that American industry loses between $10 bil-
lion to $20 billion annually through "lost workdays, hospital-
izations, and early death caused by stress."[2] Mark McLaughlin
believes that stress may cost U.S. businesses about $75 billion
a year in lost productivity, health-benefit payments, and absenteeism.[3] Finally, Emily T. Smith and Sana Sivolop note that
executives and managers suffering from stress cost their companies $150 billion per year in health insurance, disability, lost
productivity, and other expenses related to stress and mental
illness.[4]

In general, employers say that "good" employees should be
able to control their work/family conflicts and should not allow them to affect their jobs. Family problems should be left
at the corporate doorstep. But when problems with child-care
and work/family conflicts nevertheless result, many employees
themselves erroneously dismiss the problems as "an invalid

justification for work interruption." They have internalized their employer's attitude. Here is how some employees said "good" employees should behave.

> I've developed the ability to leave work at the office 90 percent of the time. The other 10 percent doesn't create stress, but it causes minor inconveniences at times. (white male middle-level manager)
>
> Family problems do not interfere with my job. I won't let them. (black male lower-level manager)
>
> My job has not suffered at all by my family responsibilities. One has to learn to set some priorities, then juggle occasionally. It's called flexibility! (white female officer)

Other employees offered a more balanced perspective, but one that, as we shall see, many employees have not been able to adopt:

> When I get home, I put my work aside. I put in a day's work, and I'm proud of it. But I'm not married to my job, I am married to my family, and it's important to separate the two. (white female officer)
>
> I don't let work and other worries interfere with family responsibilities and enjoyment. (black male lower-level manager)

Others acknowledge the inevitable conflicts and how tightly interwoven work and family lives can become. Their comments are the most representative of the employees as a whole:

> No matter how much you try to avoid it, some family matters inevitably overlap onto work hours. (black female occupational worker)
>
> With sixty-hour work weeks and travel, if I didn't use work hours to tend to family matters, I wouldn't see them. (white female lower-level manager)
>
> There should have been a question in the survey about how increased work loads and stress affect the family, and one on what has happened to family quality in the last two years. I

predict that everyone would have said the family quality is in serious trouble because of work requirements. (white female middle-level manager)

This chapter analyzes the stresses that employees have at home and at work due to work/family conflicts and child-care problems. The health problems created by these stresses and their impact on corporate productivity are also analyzed.

Traditional Values

One of the employees' main sources of stress both at home and on the job is the conflicting social messages about the "proper" roles of women and men. Most of society has finally accepted the idea that women have a right to work outside the home, but the widely held conviction that women should be the primary or exclusive caretakers and homemakers in a family has not changed to any perceptible degree. Social scientists have found that women's work is still considered secondary to—and less important than—men's work. When women employees do give top priority to their families, corporate executives use this as an excuse to relegate them to positions of lesser responsibility and to view them as undependable, noncareer-oriented employees.

The so-called "mommy track," proposed by Felice N. Schwartz of Catalyst, is the limited promotion path for women who put their families before their careers, and it appears to support the traditional notions. But there is considerable evidence that women are at least as ambitious as men (see chapter 4). The real issue at hand is that society places women in a position in which they must constantly juggle—and compromise—their work and family demands. This leads to a catch-22 situation in which neither demand is fully met, and it creates a major source of stress for working women.

After a full day's work, I've run out of steam by the time I get home. This is frustrating for me and my family. (white female lower-level manager)

I'm always wanting to be my best at work but feel unappreci-
ated, yet I'm still trying to be as perfect a mom as I can for a
child with a single parent. (white female occupational employee)

Men also receive conflicting messages, which adds to their
stress over work/family conflicts. Society demands that men
relegate their families to a secondary position. Their jobs are
to have the primary position, jobs that require them to put in
long hours and to bring work home. In addition, a relatively
large number of men still make their partner responsible for
all, or the major part of, child-care and domestic chores. Con-
formity to these male roles can lead to family estrangement
and, for growing numbers of men, a sense of guilt.

One bright spot is that a small but growing number of men
are striving to become more involved in the care of their
children. Some are even trying to become "Superdads"—
fathers who spend a great deal of quality time with their
children and marriage partners, and who share equally in all
household and child-care tasks.

Your family expects and sometimes depends on you at times
when the company is very important and work times are not
flexible. (white male occupational worker)

Time requirements of my position cause problems with the
family, especially quality time that my wife and two young children require. (white male occupational worker)

Let's take a more detailed look at a husband who is attempting to be more involved in parenting. Charles H. is a
black occupational worker in his late twenties. His household
consists of his wife, who works full-time, and two children,
one and two and a half years old. The annual household
income is $39,000. Charles finds his work satisfying, but he
reported that he has problems balancing his work and family
responsibilities. His child-care situation is not as severe as
some other employees' because his mother is willing to care
for his children at home, but he admitted that he experiences
a great deal of stress trying to cope when his mother is unable to care for the children or when she goes to visit her

other children in Chicago. He also has problems getting the children to doctor and dentist appointments.

Charles believes that a big source of his stress is his company's failure to recognize the vital role of the father in parenting. The company's family-leave policy makes this failure clear: "The company does not have a paternity leave for men, so there is no flexibility; if you choose to stay out awhile, it will be counted against you. Since we work for the same company and my wife makes more money than me, ideally, she would have stayed home the first three months and me the second three months."

Charles feels that his company should provide greater child-care assistance and that on- or near-site day care and half-day vacations to deal with family emergencies would be the most beneficial options for working parents.

Stress at Home and on the Job

Although a majority of the fathers in my 1988 (68 percent) and 1989 (73 percent) studies said they share child care equally with their wives, in *reality*, most domestic responsibilities are not equally shared. Studies have shown that the amount of time fathers spend on home and child-care chores each week ranges from fifteen to twenty-five hours, while mothers put in thirty-five to forty-five hours. Given this large discrepancy, it is hardly surprising that women have a higher incidence of family stress.

That women are beginning to expect their husbands to spend more time with their children is a major source of work/family conflicts. Women experience the most stress when they feel their spouses or partners carry less than their share of the family load. This occurs most often in families where the husband holds the traditional sexist views of women's roles and the wife does not. According to Galinsky and Hughes, a good predictor of work/family stress for employed mothers is precisely their dissatisfaction with their husbands' participation with their children. They add that the best predictor of the father's stress level is his satisfaction with his wife's performance of household chores.[5]

Ann C. Crouter found in her studies that the more child-care responsibilities fathers take on in dual-career families, the more marital conflicts they have and the less likely they are to report loving their wives.[6]

Boston University sociologists Diane Burden and Bradley Googins studied sixteen hundred employees in two major corporations in the Northeast and found that working fathers are as likely to get depressed or unhappy as working mothers when they are expected to do a lot around the house.[7]

One does not have to look hard to find sources of stress at home and/or on the job that stem from work and family conflicts. The following employee comments illustrate the stressful daily balancing act. They demonstrate that people of all races, both genders, and all occupational levels are subject to these problems.

My child is nearly through with the eighth grade, but this does not stop me from worrying about her being unsupervised after school and especially during those long summer vacations. Sometimes when children become teens, your problems really begin. (white female occupational worker)

Because my hours begin much earlier in the day than most care facilities open, it is always a race for me to get to work on time. So my day begins and ends stressful. (black female occupational worker)

There is no time for me to relax between job and home due to the long distance between my job and home and the time that I am to pick up my child from day care. (black female occupational worker)

It's always tough to tell your kids no that because you have to work or that because of overtime you will not be home. (white male lower-level manager)

I take out my frustrations on family members by being short with them and ignoring them. (white female upper-level manager)

Knowing I have to be at work during certain times of the month is stressful. I know stress is normal for working mothers. Although my husband has helped a great deal, I know that I will bear the brunt of the stress. When children are ill or have to be somewhere at a certain time, stress occurs. (Asian female occupational worker)

Must be at work—coming in early/staying late—little time for relaxation—too tired to do activities with family in the past. (black female lower-level manager)

Because work takes me away from my children and the time they need me, they hit me as soon as I get home. But I'm usually too tired to give them my full attention, which causes guilt on my part and a feeling of frustration on theirs. (black female middle-level manager)

Working on a stressful job creates tension that pours into my personal/home life. (white female middle-level manager)

My own studies of nearly thirty-five thousand participants over the past six years show that the gap between the amounts of stress that men and women feel at home or on the job is shrinking. This is true for the entire population, regardless of marital or parenthood status. The results of my findings to the two following questions are shown in table 3–1.

To what extent has balancing work and family responsibilities created stress:
  A. On the job for you?
  B. At home for you?

The women's responses changed little over the four-year time span, but there were significant changes in the men's responses. The percentage of men who experience stress at

Table 3–1
FAMILY/WORK STRESS
(N = Percent who say "to a great extent" or "to some extent.")

	1984		1988	
	Women	*Men*	*Women*	*Men*
Stress at Home	44	22	47	39
Stress on the Job	37	16	41	33

home almost doubled, and slightly more than twice the percentage of men experienced stress at work. But although dramatically more men have stress from balancing work and family responsibilities, women are still more likely than men to experience stress.

Let's look at stress at home more closely. (see table 3–2). About the same percentages of women with children report high levels of stress, regardless of their marital status. Married men report a much lower incidence of stress at home than married women.

These facts reinforce the point made in chapter 2 that despite increased stress in men, there is no parity in some homes between men and women when it comes to caring for the children.

> In my previous personal experience, combining local classes and family responsibilities required that I cook, clean up, and parent before I could study. Most men with children don't have this problem; they have a wife to perform these duties. (Asian female lower-level manager)
>
> As a Christian family, my wife quit the company to raise our son. No hardships have arisen due to this. (Asian male lower-level manager)
>
> Family responsibilities are handled by my spouse, relieving me of any job stress. (white male occupational worker)

Table 3–3 illustrates the significant relationship between child-care problems (discussed in chapter 2) and the extent to which employees have stress on the job. Notice that almost three times as many employees with a great number of problems as those with no problems said they have stress to "a great extent" or to "some extent" on the job. As Wong noted in her study, "Breakdown in child care arrangements and missing work due to child care responsibilities were strongly related to both perceived stressors and to health."[8]

Younger children create more stress for both women and men than do older children. For example, 61 percent of the women and 45 percent of the men with children 5 years old or younger have at least "some" stress on the job, but only 43

Table 3-2

STRESS AT HOME BECAUSE OF WORK/FAMILY CONFLICTS

(N = Percent who say they have stress at least to some extent)

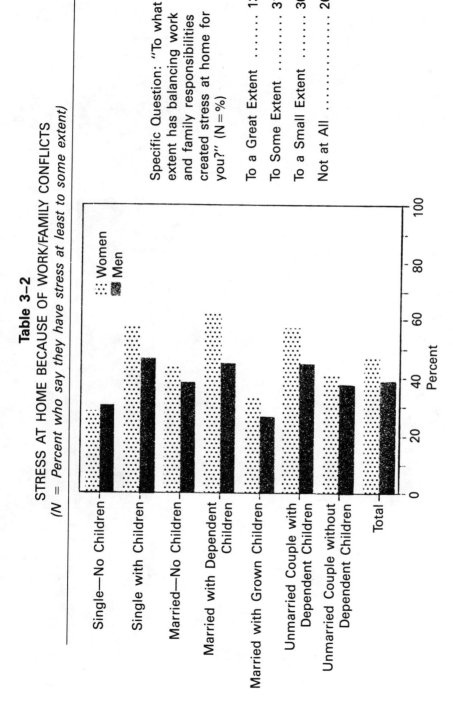

Specific Question: "To what
extent has balancing work
and family responsibilities
created stress at home for
you?" (N = %)

To a Great Extent 13

To Some Extent 31

To a Small Extent 30

Not at All 26

Table 3–3

RELATIONSHIP BETWEEN CHILD-CARE PROBLEMS AND STRESS ON THE JOB
(Respondents were asked: "To what extent has balancing work and family responsibilities created stress on the job?")

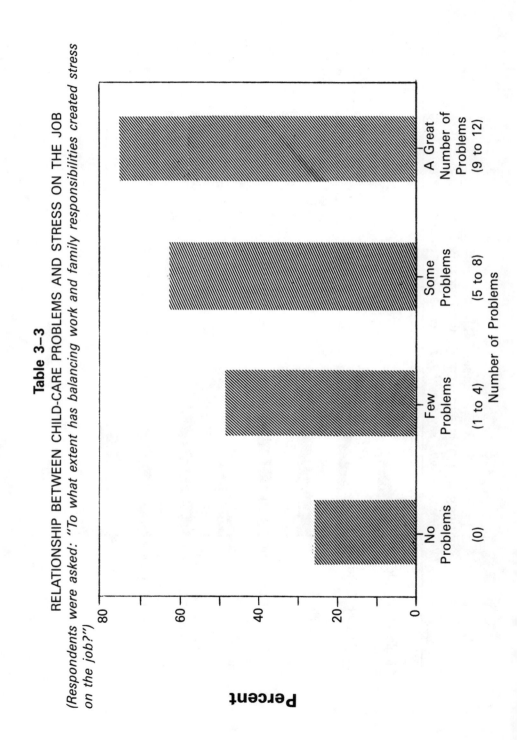

percent of the women and only 35 percent of the men with children thirteen and older do.

Bob G. is a thirty-seven-year-old white middle-level manager. His household consists of a wife who works full-time and two children, aged two and twelve. The family's annual gross household income is $63,000.

Although Bob rated his job content as "very satisfactory," he admitted to feeling a considerable amount of stress—more at home than at work—from attempting to balance his work and family life. Specifically, he works a great deal of unscheduled overtime, and he finds that this greatly interferes with his ability to pick up and drop off his youngest child, who is in day care. Some stress is created at home by conflicts over who will take the day off to care for the two-year-old: "My wife and I are both interested in our careers. It's tough sometimes." He also feels that before-and-after-school care, school holidays, vacations, and closures present "some problems."

"Our twelve-year-old believes he is grown. We trust him to watch himself, but you're always concerned about your children, especially with the drug problems." Bob feels that his company should provide child-care assistance, especially flextime, which would "allow schedule flexibility to meet family needs while still meeting commitment to the company." Before- and after-school programs would also be useful.

Michael T. is a thirty-two-year-old white occupational employee whose wife works full-time. They have an annual household income of $37,000 and a three-year-old child. He wrote of the stress caused by his child-care problems,

> Whose turn is it to stay with a sick dependent? Of all my bills, the child-care ones hurt the most! In order to get to work on time, we have to speed. We're always worried about getting tickets, having an accident or being late. I know of a case where a man was killed by a train because he skirted around the barricades so he wouldn't be late. Stupid? Yes, but people will take risks when their income is on the line.

The consequences of stress for employees are severe. The more stress employees have at work and at home due to work and family conflicts, the more likely they are to miss work, arrive late, leave early, and deal with personal and family issues during working hours. Poor attendance causes additional worry for employees and creates a cycle of stress that is difficult to overcome.

Psychiatrists and physicians who have worked in business report that about 80 percent of all employee emotional problems are stress-related.[9] The American Academy of Physicians says that stress is costing businesses money. A firm of fifteen hundred people that had $40 million in annual sales lost $5 million because of stress. Those employees with high levels of stress had nearly four times as many health problems as those with low levels. One of the most frequently cited reasons for this stress was juggling work/family conflicts.[10]

> We're so pressed for perfect attendance, we're stressed on the job and don't dare miss work. (white female occupational worker)
>
> It's difficult to handle home situations when you're worried about what will happen to your job if you're late or absent to handle personal business. It's almost like you're never relieved of the stress. (black female occupational worker)

Table 3–4 shows the relationship between stress and lost productive time. Notice the dramatic difference in percentages of women and men who have a great deal of stress and those who have no stress at all. Among men who have missed work, the number who said that they have no stress is less than half the number who reported a great deal of stress.

Employees confirmed that productive workdays are lost in their responses to other questions as well. Employees who reported that they have a great deal of stress at work or at home were more likely than those who reported no stress to believe that they are not performing their jobs as effectively as possible. Sixty-two percent of the women who said they have a great deal of stress (compared with 43 percent of those who said that they have no stress at all) believe they are not performing their jobs as effectively as possible.

Table 3-4
STRESS AT HOME AND IMPACT ON WORK ATTENDANCE

(N = Percent who have missed work, been late for work, left work early due to personal and/or family matters, or dealt with personal or family matters during work hours.)

To what extent has balancing work and family responsibilities created stress at home for you?	Missed Work		Been Late for Work		Left Early from Work		Dealt with Personal/Family Matters During Working Hours	
	Women	Men	Women	Men	Women	Men	Women	Men
To a Great Extent	59	39	54	45	73	62	89	87
To Some Extent	59	34	43	37	64	57	86	87
To a Small Extent	49	28	33	31	53	51	83	83
Not at All	39	18	20	17	35	33	64	66

People's morale and motivation affect their work quality tremendously. When emotions are low due to personal problems resulting from lack of concern from employers, it's difficult to perform in positive tones. I personally feel that to invest in the employees is to make an investment back into the business. We must be supportive of one another on and off the job. There are many two-parent families as well as single parents. This causes certain amounts of stress. The stress has to be minimized, and we need corporate America to be sensitive to this. (white female lower-level manager)

My family is my number-one responsibility. It's difficult to concentrate on the job at hand during those times when I feel that I should be with a family member. (white male lower-level manager)

Employers must realize that employees work to live and don't live to work. Conflicts arise, and it's in the employer's best interest to assist in problem resolution. Problems at home can increase stress levels on the job and affect performance. (white female lower-level manager)

For all employees, work and family responsibilities can create an impossible overload—too much to do, and too little time to do it. Ultimately, because of the physical and emotional problems that are by-products of stress, overload leads to less corporate productivity. As one white female lower-management employee noted, "The company is big on physical health, but mental health has just as much influence on the way one performs."

Stress-Related Health Problems

Amelia L. is a white lower-level manager in her early forties whose stress comes both at home and on the job. Her household consists of a husband who works full-time and two children, aged six and thirteen.

Although Amelia enjoys her work, she feels that her supervisor does not support her child-care needs. She has problems in several child-care areas. Traveling overnight, particularly, causes her a great deal of concern: "I am a frequent business traveler, and this is very stressful on my family and me. If I were a single parent, I couldn't do it."

Her travel and work schedule has led to "some stress" at work and to "a great deal of stress" at home. "The stress manifests itself more at home with the family than at work," she explained. The stress also manifests itself in a variety of physical ailments that affect Amelia's productivity—insomnia, morning fatigue, a pounding heart, becoming tired in a very short time, back pains, headaches, and feeling nervous or tense. All are classic symptoms of stress.

Company involvement in family care, Amelia feels, would alleviate some of the stress that she is experiencing: "The company should schedule available or additional days off in case children are sick. We should not have this reflected on our attendance. I end up using many vacation days on this, as I have no other choice. Child care is one of the biggest health care issues not being faced by corporate America."

Stress can be defined as the nonspecific response of the body to any demand. Not all stress is caused by negative changes. Any substantial change in one's life, either good or bad, produces demand and results in stress. Getting a big bonus may be as stressful as not getting one. Regardless of how stress is produced, it increases, among other things, the heart rate and causes rapid breathing, upset stomach, and sweating.

When the amount of one's stress overcomes one's capacity to adapt, stress becomes distress and breakdown occurs. Some of the ultimate results can be heart attack, stroke, hypertension, asthma, tension headache, and migraine headache—in addition to mental and emotional problems. Researchers have found that headaches affect nearly one-quarter of the American population each year and are the leading cause of lost time in business and industry.[11]

J. Grimaldi and B. P. Schnapper have said that the relationship between stress and employee health "is well documented. In fact, high blood pressure, ulcers, and heart disease are examples of stress-related health problems. . . . They also pointed out that lower back pain, colds, and flu can result from stress."[12]

L. Levi has explained the differences in symptoms experienced by workers undergoing stress: he suggested that the body is like a tire—the more stress, the more wear and tear. However, he was quick to point out that each person's genetic makeup and prior condition will affect the symptoms. In other words, some people will get ulcers, others high blood pressure. Some will experience more serious symptoms such as heart attacks. Others will not experience any adverse health conditions.[13]

Several of my survey participants put it this way:

> When my stress reaches its peak levels doing the balancing act, it results in illness and fatigue. (white female lower-level manager)

> Being a single parent and working with outside interests both for yourself and for your children can cause you stress and health problems. (black female occupational worker)

Highly competitive companies are demanding more and more from their employees in terms of time commitment, responsibility, and efficiency. The downsizing of companies, restructuring, and takeovers also produce workplace stress. When these stresses are added to family responsibilities, and when conflicting messages are given to employees—particularly female employees about their proper roles—the total stress level in the lives of many workers is extremely high.

G. Ritzer, writing about the upwardly mobile managers, supports these views. His comments can apply to all workers, especially to women with children and to single parents regardless of occupational status. Ritzer showed a direct relationship between upwardly mobile managers' enormous workload and increased incidence of heart disease, ulcers, arthritis, stroke, and mental illness. Behaviors such as alcoholism and drug abuse were also outcomes of such stress.[14]

Swedish researchers have shown the biological effects of high stress levels on the body's organs. In a series of studies, they demonstrated that the output of noradrenaline and adrenaline (the stress hormones) is substantially increased when exposed to psychosocial stressors. The body's reaction to the increased output of these hormones is to release free fatty acids. Thus, when someone is uneasy or tense, the fat content in the blood increases. That increase in fat content will lead to a buildup in various organs, including the heart.[15]

When work/family conflicts create stress that leads to emotional or physical health problems, companies forfeit a tremendous amount of money, not only in lost productivity but also in increased health-insurance costs.

Most corporations are extremely concerned about rising health-care costs. In a recent union bargaining session, AT&T, for example, estimated that it spends $1 billion each year on the health care of its employees, both current and retired and their dependents. Not surprisingly, we read almost daily that corporations are shifting some of these insurance costs and medical bills to their employees. In 1986–87 General Motors found that it was spending more money on health insurance and sickness than on steel for its cars.[16]

The strikes that have recently occurred in the "Baby Bells" have been primarily over health-care cost issues. NYNEX had asked its employees to pay either $10.27 per week toward their health-care costs or a higher deductible of $500. NYNEX's health-care costs have risen 20 percent since 1986. The union rejected this request, which resulted in a four-month strike. For businesses overall, health-care costs rose an average of 18 percent in 1988—far exceeding the inflation rate. These costs are expected to increase at about the same rate over the next several years.

Rather than passing these costs along to employees, a more effective way to reduce these skyrocketing costs is to assist employees with those family/work conflicts that cause many stress-related health problems.

All employees in my 1988 study were asked how frequently they had experienced each of thirteen stress-related health problems in the past six months. Table 3–5 lists their responses. Recognizing that women carry the greatest burden in the home and report stress more often than men, it is not surprising that a higher percentage of women than men indicated they experienced these health problems often or some-

Table 3–5
STRESS-RELATED HEALTH PROBLEMS

Respondents were asked: "Please check how frequently each has happened to you in the last six months." (N = Percent who responded "often" or "sometimes.")

Stress-Related Health Problem	Women	Men	Total
Finding it difficult to get up in the morning	58	38	49
Feeling nervous, or fidgety and tense	53	41	47
Pains in your back or spine	47	38	43
Overeating	47	32	40
More headaches than usual	48	27	38
Having trouble getting to sleep	40	31	36
Becoming very tired in a short time	37	22	30
Feeling your heart pounding or racing	24	17	21
Smoking more than you are used to	15	13	14
Trouble breathing or shortness of breath	16	12	14
Poor appetite	15	10	13
Drinking more alcohol than you are used to	10	13	12
Spells of dizziness	13	6	10

times in the previous six months. It is interesting to note that, except for having difficulty getting up in the morning, stress-related health problems are not significantly affected by the age of the children.

What does seem to greatly impact stress-related health problems is the number of child-care problems employees report. As we know, the more child-care problems employees have, the more stress they experience, resulting in more stress-related health problems. Fifty-seven percent of employees who had a great deal of child-care problems compared with 33 percent who had no problems reported having headaches often or within the previous six months.

Table 3–6 shows the relationship between the degree of stress and the incidence of stress-related health problems. In

Table 3-6

STRESS ON THE JOB AND STRESS-RELATED HEALTH PROBLEMS

Respondents were asked: "To what extent has balancing work and family responsibilities created stress on the job for you?" (N = percent who responded "often" or "sometimes.")

Health Problems:	To a Great Extent	To Some Extent	To a Small Extent	Not at All
Difficulty Getting Up in the Morning	73	57	47	34
Feeling Nervous	75	59	43	31
Back Pains	61	47	41	33
Overeating	53	44	38	33
Increased Headaches	53	46	35	24
Trouble Getting to Sleep	56	42	33	27
Easily Tired	56	37	26	18
Heart Pounding or Racing	38	25	18	13
Trouble Breathing	26	16	12	10
Increased Smoking	19	16	13	11
Poor Appetite	28	16	10	7
Increased Drinking	23	14	10	8
Dizzy Spells	21	12	8	6

most cases, twice as many employees who had a great deal of stress as those who had none at all reported having stress-related health problems often or sometimes.

Obviously, child-care problems, stress, and stress-related health problems lead to employees who do not perform their jobs as effectively as possible. Seventy-five percent of the men who said they often have a difficult time getting up in the morning compared to 50 percent who say they never have difficulty getting up believe they are not performing their job as effectively as possible. (For women, the figures are 63 percent and 42 percent). Seventy-three percent of the men feel nervous and fidgety often and 52 percent never believe they are performing their job as effectively as possible. (The figures for women are 63 percent and 44 percent respectively.)

These health problems lead to missed days of work and other unproductive time. Fifty-one percent of the employees who said they often become tired in a short period of time and 30 percent who said they never become tired have missed work in the previous year. Obviously, the most detrimental effect of health problems for companies is the loss of employees. Table 3–7 shows the strong relationship between the incidence of stress-related health problems and those employees who are seriously or very seriously considering leaving their jobs.

Vignettes

Leslie T. missed work four to six times in the previous year for doctor visits. She has been plagued by health problems that "mainly stem from trying to be the best at my job—which causes stress."

A white occupational worker in her late thirties, Leslie has four children, aged two, six, seven, and nine, and a husband who works full-time. Their family income is $44,000. She is primarily responsible for her children's care and said balancing her dual role as parent and employee is a "big problem": "When you're worrying about your kids, because of inadequate care, you may not perform your job as well." Finding and affording quality day care are big problems for her, par-

Table 3-7

STRESS-RELATED HEALTH PROBLEMS AND INTENT TO QUIT JOB

Respondents were asked: "How seriously have you considered quitting your current job?" (N =
Percent who responded "often" or "sometimes.")

Health Problems:	Very Seriously	Seriously	Not Very Seriously	Not at All Seriously
Difficulty Getting Up in the Morning	53	37	28	27
Feeling Nervous	56	37	28	28
Back Pains	46	37	31	31
Overeating	46	34	32	34
Increased Headaches	53	38	31	29
Trouble Getting to Sleep	55	39	31	30
Easily Tired	55	41	32	30
Heart Pounding or Racing	57	42	33	32
Trouble Breathing	49	42	35	34
Increased Smoking	54	38	33	34
Poor Appetite	63	47	36	31
Increased Drinking	60	45	35	33
Dizzy Spells	60	42	36	34

ticularly because her hours are irregular. The lack of flexibility or inconsistency in her work schedule "confuses Mom, Dad, kids, school and sitters."

Leslie's supervisor is completely unsupportive of her family situation, which compounds her stress and related health problems. In the last six months, she said, she frequently suffered back pain, insomnia, morning fatigue, and excessive nervousness. She said she also has had more headaches than usual and is smoking more: "I work hard, get sick (pressure at work causes sickness to worsen), and the company kicks me down for being absent so much." Because of the unsupportive work environment, Leslie said she has seriously considered quitting her job to stay home with her children. She has also considered quitting her job to work for another company with better child-care assistance.

Amy W. is a white single occupational worker with two school-age children, seven and ten. Working full-time and balancing the needs of her children is particularly stressful for her because she has no support network:

> My main problem is when my children are sick. I am a single parent with no family in town. All my friends work the same hours I do. I am the only one who can watch them when they are sick. Even if I had someone, they would need to come to my house because my children are usually too sick to go out. The cost of a second sitter plays a part, too.

Overnight travel, late hours, and children's doctor and dentist appointments are also big problems for Amy. In the past year, she has missed work or left early from work several times to take care of family matters. "Single parents have it the worst," she explained. "All people, married or not, have personal things to take care of that can only be done during working hours due to circumstances beyond their control."

In the previous six months, Amy has suffered from a number of stress-related health problems. She said she frequently has spells of dizziness, a pounding heart, fatigue, back pain, and feelings of excessive nervousness. She said she is also smoking more than she used to and is overeating:

The only way the company can help is to reduce stress and change their absenteeism policy. They make you feel so guilty when you have sick kids, but what's worse, if you get three days of absences in a year's time, you are rated unsatisfactory. So you come in to work sick as a dog and spread it around, and it goes around and comes around. This provides the company with a very unhealthy workforce and low production. Does this make sense? Can you really expect every employee to stay healthy 365 days a year or else punish them? Illness is not always due to employees' lack of good health habits!

Amy would like to see her company take a more active role in assisting employees with family/work conflicts, and with elder-care and child-care needs. She suggests that payroll deductions for child care and employee discounts at local day-care facilities would be useful options. Before-and-after-school-care programs would also be helpful. But she is not optimistic about change: "All this company cares about is money, money, money. And look how they waste money."

Frances J. is an American Indian occupational worker, aged forty-one, with more than fifteen years of service at her company. Her household consists of a husband who works full-time and two children, aged fourteen and sixteen. Their annual income is $47,000.

Frances admitted to feeling a great amount of stress at work, and some stress at home from balancing her work and family responsibilities: "I worry about being available. It's so important to me to check with them—to touch base." Frances's two children have been treated for eating disorders and for drugs and alcohol. She feels strongly that her company should help employees with work/family conflicts and provide assistance with child-care needs. Flex-time, she feels, would help her balance her responsibilities.

The high level of stress under which Frances operates is apparent in the many health-related concerns she has. She stated that she sometimes experiences trouble breathing, shortness of breath, a pounding or racing heart, and feelings of nervousness. She strongly agrees that companies should be more actively involved in assisting employees with health care, adding, "I'd like them to offer a room for relaxation and exercise in the building."

Summary

In this chapter, we have observed that stress is created for employees when they attempt to balance work and family roles and that this stress affects productivity and health.

The "normal" stresses of family life are greatly exacerbated in American society because of the conflicting messages given to both men and women. An impossible standard is set for working women in terms of their disproportionate responsibilities in the home. Many women are made to feel guilty for working and leaving their children. Other women are accused of threatening their husbands' masculinity, especially if the women are more successful than their husbands.

Men are also placed in a no-win situation. They are socialized to be the breadwinner, yet they are increasingly being pressured to take on more family responsibility. Of course, some men have wives who stay home or work only part-time, thus relieving them of many home and family tasks. Men whose wives work full-time are still likely to leave their wives with almost complete responsibility for child care and family tasks.

Additionally, many more women than men are single parents. As a result of this sexist role segregation, women are more likely than men to be tardy, to miss days, to leave work early, or to deal with family issues during working hours. Ultimately, women experience more stress because of child care and hence have a greater proclivity to certain health problems. Wilkins showed that headaches affect three times as many working women as men. In the Gurn Psychosomatic Symptom list of twenty symptoms, women scored higher in all but one. Men experienced more ulcers, but women ranked higher in tiredness, nervousness, feeling fidgety, and tense, among others.[17] Many women try to make up for their lowered productivity by taking work home and working on weekends; but this effort, while laudable, further increases their stress and family/work conflicts and consumes precious family time at home.

Regardless of gender, stress can result in unproductive work time, and if it is overwhelming, an employee may become ill. When family/work conflicts create stress that leads to health problems, either emotional or physical, companies lose money, not only in lost productivity but in increased health-care costs and the possible loss of valuable employees. "If a company expresses concern about an employee on and off the job, that employee is more dedicated, more productive and more healthy," said a black male occupational worker.

In the next chapter, we will explore in more detail the career-decision problems of employees with child-care difficulties.

4

Other Work/Family Problems that Negatively Affect Productivity

SOCIAL scientists have for some time been pointing out that good working relationships are important, if not essential, for employees to function at their most productive level. The most satisfying and productive work environment is one in which employees feel there is a high degree of understanding, supportiveness, honesty, and fairness. Companies that want to provide such an environment must be sensitive to the changing composition and needs of its workforce. Stress and tension will assuredly increase if companies adhere to outmoded employee policies and practices that do not take into account the new realities of women's employment.

This stress and conflict will also increase if companies try to treat everyone the same rather than as individuals. The workforce is becoming more diverse. To treat all employees the same (equitably) is not the same as treating them fairly—that is, differently because of their differing needs and concerns. Even if companies try to implement leading-edge policies but have no firm commitment to the philosophy, the policies will be ignored. This corporate indifference occurs primarily because of sexist attitudes and stereotypes, both subtle and overt, about working women.

Legitimate child-care needs and family/work problems of employees affect the corporate bottom line in ways that often are not recognized either by corporate executives or by child-care consultants.

Supervisors' Impact on Child-Care Problems

One of the most crucial elements in creating an understanding, supportive, and healthy atmosphere for employees is a sympathetic supervisor who recognizes that work and family conflicts cannot be left at any doorstep but follow the employee wherever she or he goes. Throughout my research, I have found that a majority of employees believe that their supervisors are at least somewhat supportive. In my 1988 study, 58 percent of the employees said their supervisors support them and their child-care needs more than "just a little." Women were somewhat more likely than men to say that their superiors support their child-care needs (see figure 4–1).

The importance of a supportive supervisor cannot be overstated. In all the studies I have conducted, I have found that employees who have supportive supervisors are more likely to feel valued, to have better attendance records, to be more productive, and to remain longer with their companies. Seventy-one percent of the employees who believe their supervisors are supportive to "a great extent" compared with 50 percent who believe their supervisors are not at all supportive feel that their companies value them to a "great extent."

Stanley D. Nollen has concluded from his studies that supervisors who try to develop positive employee relations with regard to work/family conflicts might be as helpful as formal work/family programs.[1] Galinsky has consistently found that supportive supervisors have a significant impact on productivity and missed workdays.

> Employees in my department are not discouraged from taking extra time to deal with such matters, within reasonable time limits. We have supportive supervisors and we give them our all. (white female occupational worker)
>
> My supervisor is very understanding when it comes to family

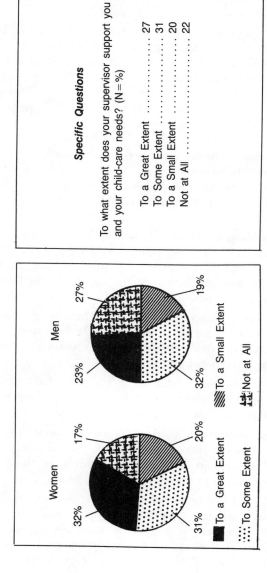

FIGURE 4–1. EMPLOYEE PERCEPTION OF SUPERVISOR SUPPORT FOR CHILD-CARE NEEDS

emergencies. I have telecommunications access from home and utilize it for call-out. I have on occasion, used it when a child is ill and can't go to day care. (white male lower-level manager)

My supervisor allowed me to come in fifteen minutes late and stay fifteen minutes to make up the time to allow me to get my children to day care. It saved me money and stress. (white female occupational worker)

Unfortunately, not all employees have such supportive supervisors.

My husband was in the hospital for surgery, and my supervisor gave me a hard time, even though I took vacation for the time I was out and still was able to keep up my production. If she asks me for anything extra, guess what? (white, female, occupational worker)

You get hassled if you request a day off for a doctor's appointment for your child, so I say I'm sick. They're not concerned with problems—only that you are not at work and not meeting objectives. I do not give my best to my supervisor. (black female occupational worker)

I have a retarded eleven-year-old, and there have been times when I have had to be with her and put her first. Unfortunately, that attitude is not understood by management. (white female occupational worker)

The company seems to state at all levels of management: 'Your children are your problem. Don't let them interfere with your job.' (white male lower-level manager)

I feel that my supervisor could be more understanding about doctor appointments for my children. I'm a single parent, there's no one else who can take my children to their appointments. (white female occupational worker)

Employees should not be criticized for having personal commitments outside normal working hours that may prevent them from doing things that managers or supervisors want done at the last minute. Managers are generally insensitive to the personal time commitments they ask of their employees, and they don't really want to know about the inconvenience they cause in the employees' personal lives. Further, management is often not willing to ensure that adequate time and resources are available to perform various tasks. Consequently, a limited number of people end up carrying loads far greater than they should be expected to carry within the time frames they are given to complete the work. Employees end up having to work evenings and weekends for extended periods of time at the expense of their personal and family lives. (white male occupational worker)

Managers need to be more flexible in allowing flex-time. Stress is added when, even though it is approved, they act as if they disapprove of your request. (Asian female lower-level manager)

They say that no matter what your needs are, you have to be there. What if it is your child? Managers take the morning off to go to a school program. (black male occupational worker)

Sometimes my child will become ill at school and will need a shot for her condition. I leave work, pick her up, go to the doctor and home. I do not need to stay home, as she is in her late teens, and I return to work, but management always says, 'You know this will go on your record,' as if I didn't know. It makes me feel bad, as if I had planned this deliberately. (white female occupational worker)

How do you honestly expect an employee to perform at maximum efficiency when you are having family problems and your employer has an 'I don't care' attitude? (black male occupational worker)

Last Friday, I took a half-day vacation to pick up my husband from the hospital. My supervisor told me, 'I am worried about your job.' At the moment, we were waiting for three biopsy reports to come back. I've taken vacation days every time any of my family is sick, even when my uncles and aunts passed away. I don't abuse the company, and I expect the same treatment. My eight-year-old son comes home to an empty house each day. He went to a stranger's house and called me to say that he had lost his key. My boss answered my phone (I was in a meeting) and told me, 'Your son is too big to get so upset over something so silly as being locked out of his house'. (white female occupational worker)

As demonstrated in chapter 3, supervisors' lack of support for child-care problems leads employees to feel they are not valued. In turn, these feelings can lead to a lack of motivation and a decline in productivity. For example, 21 percent of the employees who say that their supervisors support their needs to a "great extent" (compared with 34 percent whose supervisors respond "not at all") said they are not performing their jobs as effectively as possible because of a lack of motivation. These employees are also much more likely to miss work.

Often, an unsupportive supervisor can influence employees' views about quitting a job. Thirty percent of the employees who said that their bosses are supportive to a "great extent" (compared with 44 percent who said their bosses are "not at all" supportive) are "very seriously" or "seriously" considering quitting their jobs.

As one Asian occupational worker explained, "I nearly had a nervous breakdown because I had to take care of a sick child and work full-time. Sometimes I left my son, age seven, alone at home, but I worried about him at work. My supervisor was not very compassionate about my situation. I was ready to quit."

One employee who works under an unsupportive supervisor is Vincent D., a white occupational worker whose wife stays home with their three children.

> I believe that my wife caring for our children at home is the most important form of child care. The company is making it more difficult with wage freezes and downgrades which have created havoc and stress in my finances and me and my wife's desire to raise our children in our home.
>
> I have trouble dealing with the need to work and meeting the needs of sick children or of my wife when she gets sick or worn out from dealing with sick children. [Two of Vincent's children have asthma.] Especially when you have been up all night with an illness and you call in to take time off, and your supervisor demonstrates a pure lack of concern.
>
> I think that flex-time and half-day options would help relieve some of the stress associated with caring for children and adults. But there is one more thing that might help even more, and that would be for the supervision of this company to develop an attitude that they really do care for the most valuable resource of the company and demonstrate their concern by

being humane when confronted with an employee who has an unexpected illness or circumstances that require unscheduled time off.

Vincent has seriously considered leaving his company to work for one more responsive to employees' child-care needs. I found ample agreement with Vincent's feeling. The more supportive the supervisor, the less likely the employee is to consider quitting to work for a company with better dependent-care assistance. Twenty-eight percent of the employees who believe that their supervisors are supportive to a "small extent" or "not at all" compared with 14 percent who believe their supervisors are very supportive have seriously considered quitting to work for a company that provides better dependent-care assistance.

Supervisors' Impact on Pregnant Women

Supervisors must also address the needs of pregnant employees if they want their companies to remain competitive in the tight labor market. Nearly two million working women give birth each year, and many of them work well into their third trimester. A Rand Corporation study of one thousand eight hundred working women under the age of thirty who bore their first child between 1979 and 1985 found that 45 percent worked into their ninth month. Many cited financial reasons for their decision to remain at work so long.

The Pregnancy Discrimination Act of 1978 forbids employers from treating pregnant women differently from other employees with a temporary disability, but companies do not always comply with it. Nearly three thousand six hundred pregnancy-related complaints have been filed with the Equal Employment Opportunity Commission since 1981. Furthermore, research shows that companies who do little more than the law requires risk losing their employees after childbirth. A 1987 study published by the National Council of Jewish Women found that pregnant women with accommodating supervisors missed fewer days of work, "felt better on the job, did more work on their own time, and worked later into their pregnancies." Follow-up analysis revealed that women whose employers were accommodating during pregnancy were more likely to return to the same employer after childbirth. In addition, having an understanding supervisor was associated with lower levels of stress and higher levels of job satisfaction.[2]

Factors Influencing Employees' Return to Work after Childbirth

Not only can supervisors support the performance of the job, they can also influence how soon an employee returns to work after maternity or paternity leave. The length of time a working parent stays home after the birth of a child has important implications for corporate productivity. Every day that a valuable employee is not working, the corporation operates less efficiently than it could.

Some critics argue that one person missing work does not have a significant impact on overall productivity. But in companies of hundreds to thousands of employees, so many absent workers quickly add up, and costs multiply as well. And for small corporations, the loss of one employee can have an immediate and devastating impact. Despite potential financial hardships, employees stay home much longer after childbirth if they do not have supportive bosses, flexible hours, or affordable, quality child care. The critics also do not recognize that since today's technology is rapidly changing, an employee who is out of the workforce for six months may require an extensive training program to be brought "up to speed."

Kimball found that 52 percent of the participants in her study who were planning to have children would not return to work after maternity leave or were uncertain if they would. But they said they would return if infant care were available at or near the work site. Her study also indicated that a supportive supervisor influenced the decisions of many employees about when they would return to work.

My 1989 study concluded that without convenient, quality child care, only 18 percent of the women *would* return to work within three months after the birth of their child. With convenient, quality care, 47 percent of the women would return to work within the same amount of time. Without quality child care, 20 percent of the women would not return to work at all, while only 2 percent of the women would remain at home if they had quality child care.

Flexibility in work schedules also influences the timing of parents' return to work. Eighty-one percent of the women indicated that their return to work after childbirth would depend to a "great extent" or to "some extent" on the flexibility of their schedules. Of the employees who have children, 53 percent of the women said the flexibility of their work schedules determined to a "great extent" or to "some extent" the timing of their return to work.

Available quality child care was an even greater influence on their decision to return to work. Sixty-nine percent of the women said the timing of their return to work was affected to a "great extent" or to "some extent" by the availability of quality child care.

The more work/family stresses employees experience at home, the more likely their return to work after the birth of a child is affected by the flexibility of their work schedule and the availability of quality child care. For example, 72 percent of the employees who experience a "great deal" of stress said their return to work was based to a "great extent" or to "some extent" on the availability of quality child care.

Another factor affecting employee decisions about whether to return to work is their experience of previous difficulties with child-care arrangements. These difficulties make it harder for employees to return to work quickly. Seventy-four percent of those who had it fall through more than three times compared with 40 percent who have never had their arrangements fall through said the timing of their return to work depended to a "great extent" or "some extent" on the availability of quality child care.

Employee responses to the following question illustrate their growing concern about this issue: "Please explain how the timing of your return to work was affected by the flexibility of your work schedule and/or the availability of affordable child care."

I started to work when children were six weeks old. However, finding someone taking infants early in the morning was extremely hard. (Asian female occupational worker)

I was not able to return for one year because I did not have anyone to keep my baby at a young age; later, I had to have a specific time when I could pick up the child. (black female occupational worker)

I wouldn't take time from work for more than a couple of weeks if the company offered flexible hours and quality child care. (black female lower-level manager)

Knowing that top quality day care is available at the workplace at a reasonable price, I would probably return after six weeks. (white female occupational worker)

I couldn't find quality day care, so I opted to stay home for one and a half years with my daughter. (black female occupational worker)

If it wasn't that my schedule allowed me to work around my child care, it would have been impossible for me to return to this job. I would have to go with a company that had flexible hours. As far as child care, the baby couldn't stay home by itself or in dangerous surroundings. (white female occupational worker)

I was lucky to find excellent family care that helped me to return to work quickly. (Hispanic female lower-level manager)

If quality child care hadn't been available, my husband and I would have made arrangements so I would have been able to stay home. This would have been very difficult for my family. (white female lower-level manager)

These data clearly suggest that corporate America is losing many productive days because employees are postponing their return to work after the birth of a child. With rapid changes in technology and business operations, it takes longer to get them "up to speed" and to regain full productivity.

Child Care and Work-Group Relations

If supervisors do not effectively handle their work group's child-care and family/work problems, these problems can affect not only the employee with the problem but the *entire* work group as well. One Asian female occupational worker stated, "I personally don't have these problems, but it's all around me. I think it would make coworkers' lives a lot better if the company took an interest in it."

In my 1989 study, I found that dependent- and child-care problems affect the attitude and morale of employees. For example, two out of five employees believe to a "great extent" or to "some extent" that they are negatively affected when employees in their work group have dependent-care problems and are absent and/or distracted at work. Only 38 percent of the employees said they are not at all affected.

> I work closely with a woman who has at least one [child-care problem] every day. It disrupts my work schedule along with hers. I feel that you can have a family and work at the same time. But people sure don't understand when you tell them that you can't rely on them because the family gets in the way. (white female lower-level manager)
>
> Employees with children should not be favored or exempt from certain rules over other employees, because the former were aware of the rules before they accepted the job and should have anticipated problems with kids. (Asian female occupational worker)
>
> I do get frustrated with coworkers who are tardy or absent or who spend a lot of time on personal matters. We're supposedly getting paid to work. (white female occupational worker)

The feelings are often mutual: about one in five employees with child-care problems said that their coworkers' negative attitudes about their work/family problems hamper their ability to perform well on the job. The more often employees miss work due to personal and/or family matters, the more likely their coworkers are to express negative attitudes toward them because of their dependent-care problems. Forty-nine percent of those who missed work more than six times said their coworkers expressed attitudes toward them.

Trying to deal with your problems at home and worrying about people's attitudes at work if you need the time off is stressful. (white female occupational worker)

It would be a great idea if my company would help us, as other big corporations help their employees, by providing affordable and quality child care. It would limit the amount of stress and negative attitudes that face working parents. This would help me mentally, and I could return to full-time work. This is a national crisis. (black female occupational worker)

I feel there's a certain amount of resentment from fellow employees who don't have children. I think they feel that people with children get away with things. (black female occupational worker)

The case of Jeffrey N. gives a more detailed picture of the growing awareness, even among the childless, of the effects that child-care problems have on coworkers. Jeffrey is a white lower-level manager in his twenties. He is married and currently has no dependents. His wife works full-time, and their combined income is $56,000 anually.

Jeffrey is one of a growing number of young employees without any dependent-care responsibilities who feel that corporations should become more actively involved in these issues. He realizes that while everyone may not now utilize these services, most will undoubtedly need some or all in the future and that those who do not need the service now will benefit from their coworkers who do because the coworkers will be more productive.

Jeffrey reported that he is very satisfied with his job content and schedule but that he is concerned about his lack of control over his work hours. He and his wife plan to have a child within several years and are apprehensive about the child-care arrangements they will be able to provide for the child. In addition, he works a great deal of unscheduled overtime, which can cause problems if a child is waiting to be picked up at day care. Jeffrey says that his performance suffers when employees in his work group have child-care problems and are absent or distracted from work and that he has considered quitting his job to work for a company with better child-care policies. "A better atmosphere toward child care would help us all," he said.

Jeffrey feels the solution to his coworkers' and his own impending child-care concerns is greater company assistance. He strongly agrees that the company should aid employees with conflicts between work and family demands, with child-care needs, with elderly dependent-care needs, and with dependent-care needs for people who are physically and/or mentally limited.

Enlightened management that creates a positive, supportive atmosphere could do a lot to resolve these problems. Managers who treat these problems as real and know that they will not simply disappear will be able to develop contingency plans for the entire work group when sudden child-care or family problems disrupt the schedule of individual employees. Involving members of the work group themselves in the development of such plans will, in fact, help them to have more cooperative attitudes toward their peers and will aid in bringing about quicker resolutions to problems that call for a redistribution of the workload.

How Child-Care Problems Affect Career Decisions

Corporate leaders are even more remiss in recognizing that child-care problems affect employees' career decisions and that this potentially has a negative effect on the corporate bottom line. *Child Care Action News* reports that changes in the American family have a measurable impact on productivity. U.S. companies lose as much as $3 billion annually because of family-related absences. What's worse, some employees have to leave their jobs because of family pressures.

Labor shortages are already evident in some industries, such as food service, nursing, computer science, and engineering. The statistics point to an ever-shrinking labor pool over the next ten years, which will only increase the problem.

In an increasingly competitive environment with a shortage of qualified talent, it is becoming extremely important for corporations to retain their "good" workers and to be able to place them in the right job at the right time. One white female occupational worker noted, "I refused a transfer into a higher craft position due to hours not being flexible enough for child care. Seventy-five dollars a week upgrade—boy, was I stupid! The kid is better for it, but now I'm locked into a dead-end career with no future." An upper-level black woman said, "I'm seriously considering leaving my company. The job is interfering with my child (four years old) and my husband. We're always rushed to pick her up at the day-care center. They charge $2 per minute after their closing hour, which is 6:00 P.M. . . . I have so much work, I never have time for my daughter or my husband."

In order to evaluate employees' career decisions, the following questions were asked: "Sometimes people make job-related decisions to avoid potential conflicts arising from the demands of work and family. Please indicate to what extent you feel you have personally considered the following to avoid potential conflicts."

- Quitting your job to go work for a company with better child-care assistance?
- Quitting your job and staying home with your child(ren)?
- Turning down a promotion?
- Turning down a transfer to a new geographic location?

Overall, 8 percent of the employees in my 1988 study had seriously considered leaving to go to another company, 16 percent considered staying home with their children, 26 percent considered turning down a promotion, and 43 percent considered turning down a transfer to a new geographic location.

As table 4–2 shows, to all but the question about quitting the job to stay at home, the single women and men responded similarly. The biggest difference in responses be-

Table 4–2

THE IMPACT OF POTENTIAL WORK/FAMILY CONFLICTS
ON JOB-RELATED DECISIONS

Respondents were asked: "Sometimes people make job-related decisions to avoid potential conflicts arising from the demands of work and family. Please indicate to what extent you personally have considered the following to avoid potential conflicts." (N = Percent who respond "to a great extent" or "to some extent.")

	Single		Married Couple		Unmarried Couple	
	Women	Men	Women	Men	Women	Men
Quitting your job and staying home with your child(ren)?	15	5	31	4	23	9
Quitting your job to go work for a company with better child-care assistance?	10	8	11	4	15	3
Turning down a promotion?	29	31	30	22	24	16
Turning down a transfer to a new geographic location?	51	55	48	39	44	43

tween the men and the women came from married couples. Quitting work to stay at home is much more often an option for married women or unmarried women in a couple relationship than it is for single women.

> I have, in the past, turned down positions that had great potential because of the lack of dependable and affordable child care. I anticipate a similar problem in the future because of elder care. (black male occupational worker)

> I turned down a promotion in a city because of child and spouse. Unfortunately, there was no flexibility in doing the job in a distributed location. (white male middle-level manager)

Several employees expressed their desire to change jobs or to leave the company if their child-care needs could not be met.

If the company doesn't offer a dependent-care program by the time I have a child, I'll go to a corporation that does! (black male occupational worker)

If there's no day care provided by the company, if we can make it without my salary, I'll quit. Also, I must be able to have some normal working hours, such as between 7:00 and 5:30, in order to return, so as not to totally take away from my family. (white female occupational worker)

Providing top-quality child-care benefits and facilities is an excellent way for the company to retain valuable employees as they will move or transfer to another company if the job jeopardizes their children's well-being. (Hispanic male lower-level manager)

My wife has quit her job and is now staying home to care for our children. The loss of her income creates some stress, but we feel that this situation is preferable to poor child care. (white male occupational worker)

Overall, more than three in five employees—regardless of gender—had seriously considered at least one of the options.

The age of the child or children directly affects women's career-related decisions; but the age of a man's child does not affect his decision. For example, among the women with children up to two years old, 44 percent considered at least to some extent two out of the four career-related decisions. Thirty-eight percent with children aged three to five did so, as did 35 percent with children aged six to thirteen, and 27 percent with children over thirteen. (For men, the figures are only 22 percent, 23 percent, 20 percent, and 21 percent respectively—further evidence that women are still much more likely to be influenced by child-care needs.) In all, one out of five women and one out of ten men with children five and under said they had considered quitting to go to work for a company with better child-care benefits. In the 1989 study, one out of three employees indicated that they had considered quitting for that reason.

Overall, my data clearly demonstrate that some employees do take their family/work conflicts into consideration when contemplating career moves. The inability of corporate America to transfer and promote employees according to the needs of the business simply because it is not assisting employees in solving their child-care and family/work conflicts is short-sighted. The data also show that some employees will not only turn down a transfer or promotion but will consider leaving their company. Few competitive companies can afford such a loss of talent in coming years, given the labor shortage of talented, skilled people.

Leaving the Company

Thus, the ultimate price that corporate America pays for failing to provide child-care benefits is the loss of well-trained employees. To better understand who might leave their companies, I asked employees how seriously they had considered quitting their current jobs and how likely it was that they would voluntarily leave their company within the next two years for reasons other than retirement. Not surprisingly, employees who said they were "seriously" or "very seriously" considering leaving their company were much more likely to report having child-care problems than the average employee. One white male occupational employee stated it another way: "If you have a family and want to keep it, it becomes more important than work because there are always job opportunities."

Other employees supported this idea:

It is entirely possible that either my wife or I would leave employment to work for a company that offers on-site day care. This is a benefit that the company is long overdue in offering, and the longer it is absent, the less qualified people are likely to hire in—and the more we are likely to lose. (white male occupational worker)

Our children are the workers of the future. We must address these problems now before we lose some valuable people to other companies that have assistance. (white male middle-level manager)

Fifty percent of the employees who have a great deal of child-care problems are seriously or very seriously considering quitting their jobs.

Employees represent a solid dollar value to corporations. On the average, it costs a company $30,000 over the years of each employee's career to train and keep his or her skills current for most jobs, and $50,000 for a skilled professional. The dollar value of a highly skilled, experienced employee approaches—and may exceed—$100,000. Moreover, recruitment costs average about $4,000 per person. Douglas Phillips, director of corporate planning for Merck and Company, has calculated that the average cost of finding and training a replacement for a trained employee is about 1.5 times the annual salary of a salaried exempt (management, professional) employee and about .75 times the annual salary of a nonexempt employee. For example, if an exempt employee's salary is $50,000 per year, it costs Merck $75,000 to replace and train the successor.[3] In the *Philadelphia Inquirer*, Phillips was quoted as saying, "You are losing all the way around." He pointed out how turnover affects not only production but also manufacturing efficiency as well. This in turn can slow down resource development and market penetration.[4]

Judith Auerbach, the sociologist who wrote *The Business of Child Care,* found supporting evidence for this. Auerbach claimed the nursing industry loses $15 thousand every time it loses an employee. Other businesses estimate their losses in terms of time. For instance, it takes one year to bring an employee up to speed. The losses can be calculated in terms of lost productivity, the cost of recruitment and training, and reduced productivity while the new person learns the job.[5] To lose an experienced worker and invest in her or his replacement seems a foolish extravagance since corporations can address many of the child-care problems that cause employees to consider quitting—and for a far lower cost than the cost of training replacements.

Because of the ever-growing shortage of talented people who will enter the workforce between now and the year 2000, corporate America cannot afford to lose high-quality, top-notch employees simply because it refuses to tackle child-care problems. Those corporations that do not address the issue will become training institutions for their competitors that do address them.

Employees Do Want Careers

Recently, the "fast track" and the "mommy track" have been much written about and discussed. Much of this debate has focused on the theory that women with children do not want demanding careers. Some of the information I have presented may seem to support the "mommy track" view, but this would be an inaccurate conclusion. My data suggest that while more women than men are influenced by family matters in making career decisions, women do not have a monopoly on being so influenced. As my data show, it is not that women are less career-oriented than men but that they may have to make practical decisions about family and work if they do not have supportive partners or spouses.

Data about the career aspirations of the survey participants refute the theory that women give up career aspirations to become "mommies." On average, regardless of marital and family status, about half the women and men in my studies said they have career plans with their companies. In addition, regardless of marital status, the women who said they have a personal career plan that they developed for themselves (as opposed to an official company-developed plan) ranges from 73 percent to 78 percent; for men, the range is 75 percent to 81 percent.

Of the more than two out of five employees who do not have careers—except for those women and men with children over eighteen—between 75 percent and 90 percent of the women and 77 percent to 97 percent of the men said that they want to have a career plan. Even if employees consider turning down a promotion because of their child-care needs, this does not mean that they do not want a career. For example, 79 percent of those who said that they had considered turning down a promotion to a "great extent," and 83 percent who said "not at all," want a career plan with their company. Finally, about half of both married and single women with children eighteen and under frequently pursue developmental or training experiences on their own in order to develop their career. The figures for men are also about one out of two.

All this suggests that despite the child-care burdens that women carry and despite their stress and stress-related health problems caused by family/work conflicts, women are as career-oriented as men are.

Summary

This chapter has discussed the impact of child-care and family/work conflicts on employees who are parents and on the companies for which they work. It is evident that employees are productive when their supervisors create an open, supportive, honest environment in which the employees feel free to discuss their child-care problems and when these problems are dealt with in an understanding manner.

Additionally, child-care problems and family/work conflicts influence employee decisions about whether to accept promotions and transfers that might place additional demands on their already-full schedules. Many women decide when they will return to work after childbirth on the basis of available quality child care and the potential for flexible work schedules. Ultimately, good employees will leave companies that do not adequately deal with their child-care problems. But most of these employees will not leave the workforce altogether—having already been trained at great expense, they will go to companies that offer more reasonable child-care policies and benefits. As one black female occupational worker noted, "These items are personal, but if they affect an employee's productivity and attendance, there should be some company assistance other than termination. You could be losing a good employee."

It is crucial for corporate executives to consider how they can retain their employees—and their competitive position in the market—when so many of their workers make career decisions based on family concerns.

5

Child-Care Solutions

WOMEN are in the workforce to stay; they are not on any "mommy track" but on the main track. But most corporations, as well as American society as a whole, are unprepared for this inevitability. This is evident both from the opinions of my survey participants and from the vast bulk of professional commentary in the field.

It is a well-known fact that the United States lags far behind much of the world in offering adequate family care. The United States is the only Western industrialized nation that does not guarantee working women maternity leave. Only about two out of five U.S. businesses offer women maternity leave with job security, and many of these leaves are brief and unpaid.

A recent study by the General Accounting Office shows that American companies lose over $700 million a year because of inadequate parental-leave policies. That study says that it would cost American businesses far less—about half of the $700 million—to give mothers and fathers unpaid leaves with full benefits and a guarantee of their jobs when they return. Progressive parental-leave policies are considered an effective first step in relieving the pressures of child-care demands.

Nevertheless, once an employee returns to work, numerous family/work conflicts arise, including finding affordable, quality day care that fits the employee's work schedule, dealing with children's illnesses and other unscheduled emergencies, working overtime, traveling, attending school conferences, and taking children to doctor and dentist appointments. All these conflicts could be better handled if managers and supervisors were prepared to understand and constructively assist employees who have these problems. They could also be better handled if companies recognized that there is not one single solution to the problem of child care but multiple solutions and options.

> Consideration for children and schedules is my worst problem. 'We want you to go to Minnesota tomorrow at 6:00 A.M., when it's already 5:00 P.M. is difficult to deal with. Just paying for a sitter is not enough. It takes more time to make those arrangements. Also, for overtime, day care closes at 6:00 P.M., *period*. (white female middle-level manager)

Some companies have been responding to their employees' complaints. Over the past ten years, employer support for child-care programs has mushroomed, in both the number and the variety of programs. Some of the more creative approaches are:[1]

- In Orange County, California, eleven developers provided funds to help the local system establish after-school ("latchkey") child-care programs. The Irvine Company donated $250,000 for modular units at four schools, while ten other developers provided $80,000 for water, sewage, and the necessary hookups. Parent organizations have used the space for infant day care during school hours.

- In San Francisco, developers of new office and hotel buildings are required to set aside 2,000 square feet for day care. If they do not do this, they must rent or buy leisure space within one mile of the building, or contribute one dollar per square foot to a child-care fund.

- In Washington State, the Deaconess Medical Center operates a day-care center from 6:00 A.M. until midnight seven days a week because so many of its employees work at night.

- In Mishawaka, Indiana, Nyloncraft, a thermal-molded plastics manufacturer, runs an on-site day-care center that is open twenty-four hours a day and accepts school-age children as well as preschoolers. The center, opened in 1981, began with an enrollment of 50 children and now serves about 150. The cost to the employee for enrolling a school-age child for ten hours per week is $33.25, and the company picks up an additional $28 of the cost per child plus $2 for each trip to and from school. Nonemployees in the community may also enroll their children (space permitting) for the full fee of $61.25 plus transportation charges.

• In South Carolina, the North Carolina National Bank is offering low-interest loans to operators of licensed child-care programs.

• In Iowa, Rockwell International has developed a series of programs to help its employees with their child-care needs. The Rockwell Employees Child Development Center, opened in 1986, is licensed to care for up to 250 children, making it the largest child-care center in Iowa and one of the largest in United States. The center operates infant and preschool programs for children six weeks to five years old; a school-age program that provides before-and-after-school care to first through third graders, with transportation provided; and a summer program that provides activities for youth six through fourteen years of age. Rockwell initially invested close to $400,000 to open the center and currently subsidizes 20 percent of the center's operating budget. After only three years of operation, the company is convinced that the center has had a positive effect on employee recruiting, retention, morale, and productivity.

• Recognizing the problems posed by sick children and child-care emergencies, FEL-PRO, a gasket manufacturer and marketer of automotive products in Skokie, Illinois, operates an emergency service that dispatches a professional caregiver to an employee's home to care for a sick child. The cost to the employee is two dollars an hour. FEL-PRO also operates its own day-care center, which has an enrollment of more than forty children. During the summer, more than three hundred children of employees spend the day at a company-run recreational center. Tuition is $15 per family per week, regardless of the number of children who attend.

• America West Airlines has instituted a progressive policy to accommodate its employees. The company runs a child-care center for children aged six weeks or older. In addition, through a network of thirty-five family child-care homes in the Phoenix metropolitan area (the company's headquarters), it offers seven-day, twenty-four-hour child care for infants and school-age children.

Despite these creative solutions to corporate child-care problems, the vast majority of companies are still unwilling to delve into this relatively uncharted territory.

The companies most likely to offer child-care assistance are those that have a large number of employees of childbearing age, are in an economically stable location, are nonunionized, offer flexible benefits, and have a relatively progressive employment philosophy. Many of these companies are high-technology firms, banks, insurance companies, and hospitals. Increasingly, even retail firms have begun using child-care benefits as a recruitment tool to entice quality workers into jobs.

In my book *Child Care and Corporate Productivity: Resolving Family Work Conflicts,* I presented an array of child-care solutions and discussed both their advantages and disadvantages. (For a list of child-care solutions and their pros and cons, see the appendix.) Since then, interviews with public and private organizations, focus groups, and my survey research have convinced me that certain approaches work better than others. There are still a number of serious flaws in most corporate approaches to child care.

First, when child care is mentioned, many corporate executives immediately assume they are being asked to build an expensive day-care center on or near their premises. They have an aversion to "brick and mortar" and to what they perceive to be "exorbitant cost" and increased liability. They envision the worst—parents leaving meetings early or sneaking out for a short time to take care of the baby. They also have a notion that the employees' children will be running around the halls of corporate America, disrupting the smooth functioning of business.

Second, most corporations consider and/or implement solutions to only one or two child-care problems. They expect these solutions to solve all their employees' various child-care needs. When employees criticize such companies for continued "lack of concern," the companies become frustrated and consider their employees ungrateful.

Finally, very few companies do a serious, in-depth needs assessment before implementing child-care programs. Those that do obtain outside assistance typically hire consultants who have extensive knowledge of child care but who have little experience in developing sophisticated corporate strategies. A needs assessment should measure both short- and long-term employee needs as well as such crucial variables as the company's short- and long-term business plans, the company's human resources plan, an analysis of all these facts for the competitors, and the projected economic growth of the target region. If it clings to common misconceptions about child care and fails to approach the problem systematically, corporate America's solutions will continue to be piecemeal and timid.

What is the correct approach to determining employees' child-care needs? And what are the best solutions to child-care problems? In addition to defining the proper approach, I will indicate what the employees in my studies consider to be the most useful solutions to their child-care problems. I will also discuss the AT&T approach—which is, at this writing, one of the most systematic and creative approaches not only to child-care problems but also to elder-care problems.

Comprehensive Needs Assessment

Before a corporation develops a child-care strategy, program, or solution, it should take the following steps to ensure that the program will successfully address the real needs of the employees.

STEP 1

Focus groups should be conducted with a random sample of employees to gather preliminary impressions about child-care needs. Employee input is a must.

STEP 2

From the information gathered in the focus groups, a survey instrument should be developed and pilot-tested on a hetero-geneous group of employees. (Note: The instrument should have sufficient questions to elicit information about problems *and* solutions, as well as to check the validity of employee responses.)

The survey instrument should be administered to the entire population, if feasible, or to a random sample.

The instrument should have both open- and closed-ended questions. Verbatim questions give life to the statistics.

STEP 3

The current demographics of the workforce should be ana-lyzed. The turnover and hiring trends for the previous five years should be reviewed. Projections of hiring trends for the next five years should be developed. These data will help determine the demographic trends and the needs of the fu-ture employee body.

STEP 4

Employee residence Zip codes should be collected to deter-mine where residences are concentrated. This information can reveal such important facts as which centers the company should subsidize and which school districts the company should assist in developing before- and after-school programs.

STEP 5

The economic, population, and job growth trends in the area should be analyzed. A company's response could be greatly influenced by these growth patterns. For example, in a rapidly growing region into which more jobs and competitors are moving, a company might decide, depending upon employee needs, to adopt a different approach from what it would adopt in a slow-growth area.

STEP 6

The company's employee-deployment plans and real estate plans for the next five years should be examined carefully. A company would not want to build a day-care center or support center in an area where it intends to downsize significantly or to cease operations in the next year or so.

STEP 7

The existing child-care facilities and resource-assistance programs available in the community should be analyzed, as well as the types of programs competitors are providing.

STEP 8

The current and future approaches to child care by federal, state, and local government *must* be taken into consideration.

STEP 9

Commuting patterns in the region should be analyzed in order to determine center location and type of assistance.

STEP 10

All these steps should be viewed together as a comprehensive picture of employee child-care needs before any decisions are made. (Note: This same needs assessment approach also applies to elder care.)

What Employees Want

There is no *one* solution to all employee child-care problems. Rather, there are many possible solutions; each depends upon specific circumstances such as the children's ages, the number of children in the family, any physical or emotional impairments, family budget, and work and school schedules.

The employees with children eighteen and under seem to agree on the following three general solution categories as "most helpful" in dealing with their child-care needs (not taking into consideration the age of the children):

1. Quality day care that provides care for children aged thirteen and under.
2. Financial assistance to pay for child care.
3. Flexible work options that do not decrease pay.

The ages of an employee's children and the number of children significantly affect what he or she believes are the most useful solutions to child-care problems. Many employees list more than one child-care solution because they have more than one child. In addition, the needs of employees change constantly, not only because their children get older but because of the emergencies that are an inevitable part of childhood. Let's look at these findings in more detail.

Table 5–1 shows the most useful solutions to employee child-care problems. If we combine *flexible work options* (without a decrease in salary) such as flex-time or flex-place, 37 percent of the employees select one or the other.

The second most frequently selected broad area, chosen by 25 percent of employees, is *financial assistance* (vouchers, flexible benefits, payroll deduction, employee discounts and corporate contributions). The third most frequently selected area is *day-care centers and child consortia*. This solution was chosen by 19 percent of employees. In the 1989 study, which had a much higher percentage of younger occupational employees (77 percent versus 54 percent), on- or near-site day-care cen-

Table 5-1

MOST USEFUL SOLUTIONS TO RESOLVE CHILD-CARE PROBLEMS

(N = Percent who selected each factor.)

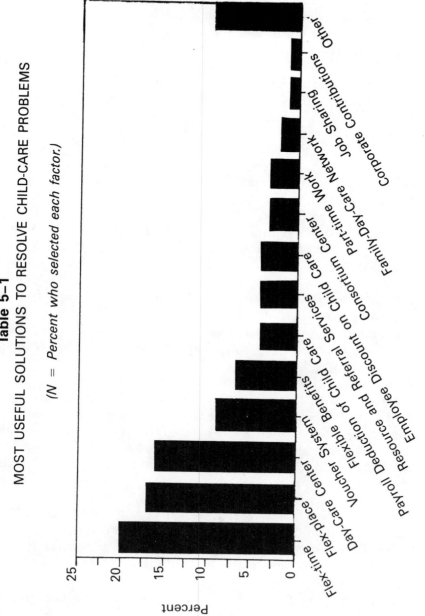

ters were the most popular choice, at 39 percent. Flexible work options were next, with a combined total of 25 percent (this included a compressed work week), followed by various combinations of financial assistance (24 percent).

As table 5–2 indicates, employees with children five years old and younger are by far the most likely to see on- or near-site day-care centers as the most useful solution. But for those employees with children six and older, flex-time and flex-place are the most frequently selected options.

Interestingly, there is a definite break in parental responses among the types of solutions that directly impact the management of the child-care problem versus those that are indirect. Part-time work, job sharing, information and referral, and corporate contributions to local programs rank quite low among workers. Within the limited numbers of companies that offer any of these solutions it is interesting to note the trends that may be developing. According to Sandra Burud's (1988) directory of companies offering some form of child-care assistance, close to half (43 percent) offered flexible spending accounts. Another 27 percent offered on-site or consortia centers (half of these were affiliated with hospitals). Resource and referral (R & R) were offered by 21 percent of the companies.[2]

It is surprising that such a high percentage of companies offered R & R, because no more than 4 percent of employees in my studies who were given this option chose it as the most useful solution to their child-care problems. A white, female, low-level manager said, "We do not need R & R. What good is R & R if there is no supply of quality child care or if you can't afford it."

I believe corporations chose R & R because of its packaging. The companies buy a service, which requires very little effort on their part other than start-up and liaison with the provider. Companies get a lot of visibility for providing R & R and can claim to have made a significant impact on child-care problems.

Employee comments about the various options are insightful, and some are very eloquent:

> Why not a paying, on-the-job child-care center? We work such awful hours for regular child-care facilities or persons. The

Table 5-2

IMPACT OF AGE OF CHILDREN ON MOST USEFUL CHILD-CARE SOLUTIONS

Respondents were asked: "If the company were to offer the following child-care options, which would be the most useful in resolving your child-care needs and conflicting demands of work and family. Select only one that is most important."(N = Percent)

Child-Care Solutions:	Children under 2		Children 3–5		Children 6–13		Children over 13	
	Women	Men	Women	Men	Women	Men	Women	Men
Flex-time	8	10	9	12	22	23	30	23
Flex-place	14	8	17	10	24	15	20	20
On- or Near-Site Day-Care Center	43	32	28	22	13	10	11	7
Voucher System	11	14	14	13	12	9	4	3
Flexible-Benefits Plan	2	4	2	8	4	9	6	16
Payroll Deduction of Child Care	4	6	5	7	4	6	2	4
Resource and Referral Services	3	5	2	4	4	4	5	5
Employee Discounts at Local Facilities	3	4	5	6	3	5	3	2
Consortium Center	2	7	4	6	2	5	3	3
Part-time Work	6	2	7	1	4	1	3	3
Family-Day-Care Network	1	3	1	3	2	3	1	2
Job Sharing	1	0	3	0	2	1	2	2
Corporate Contributions	0	2	0	1	1	1	0	1
Other	3	6	4	7	5	11	12	12

very best would come of relaxed parents with access to children at work. (white female occupational worker)

Child-care facilities at this location would be great. The ability to visit my child during lunch and have her longer in the morning and at night might help alleviate guilt feelings about working and not caring for my child at home. (Hispanic female occupational worker)

During the school year, for an average of 792 hours our teens are left unattended, which leads to major problems. Ironically, the same number of hours are left idle during summer vacation. This totals 1,584 hours during a full year, or approximately 198 eight-hour days, which is 54 percent of a full year. (white female occupational worker)

I think any type of child care would be great, or any subsidy. We plan to have a child in the next few years, and child-care costs are unbelievably high. Help in financing and help in locating good care would be wonderful. Compressed work weeks and job sharing would encourage me to return to work earlier than I would otherwise. I think it's great that the company wants to help in this area. (white female middle-level manager)

It will be good for the employees if the company provided day care near the office (better if at the same location as the office) so the employees can be with their children during lunchtime. If there is an emergency, the employee could be with the child in a minute and bring him or her to the emergency center. Have volunteers to do some errands for the elderly and/or disabled persons. (Asian female occupational worker)

If employers could help with affordable as well as quality day care, the stress on the employee would be diminished to a great extent. Affordable and quality care do not go hand in hand in the metro area. Not only are affordability and quality problems, but most day care as well as sitters will not accept sick children. What is needed is a program by the company that institutes quality day care with at least two nurses who can rotate so that someone is always there on duty. The company can afford this by taking a certain percentage from the parents. Each parent with a child in the program would pay a percentage of his or her monthly gross income instead of a set amount. A minimum and maximum amount should be instituted. I feel that if the company can institute a program such as the one described above, the company would see fewer absences due to child sickness, as well as problems with sitters and day-care centers. This, in turn, would boost productivity levels and the morale of all the company employees. (white female occupational worker)

Flexible Work Options

Many child-care centers do not accept sick children. Many doctors and dentists do not accept appointments outside normal working hours. Many school activities take place during working hours. Overnight travel and overtime hours further complicate these scheduling problems. Given this, it is not surprising that these are some of the most frequently cited problems by employees and that flexible work options are the most frequently cited solution to the problems.

The company could support work-schedule flexibility to allow employees to participate in activities with their families that may occur during working hours. Such time away could then be made up another time. There should be a fair and equitable balance between the company and its occasional personal-time demands. This concept should be supported, not discouraged. (black female lower-level manager)

It would be nice if my manager would allow more work at home on an occasional basis. (Asian female lower-level manager)

Employees need to be allowed to take half-day vacations or 'out early' time (without feeling that they will be in trouble) in order to take care of family responsibilities. Most people are here on the job to do their work as needed, even if overtime is required. Employees would like the same respect when family responsibilities need to be taken care of. These feelings cause stress at work and at home. (white female occupational worker)

The idea of a compressed work week is most appealing. This would give me more time with my child during the week. Consideration should also be given to sick-child facilities provided or referred by my company. This would keep more people on the job. Employee discounts are also appealing. But please try to keep half-day vacations, otherwise there will be a lot of 'out earlies.' My child comes first. (black female lower-level manager)

Flexible work options are a benefit that all employees can take advantage of (whereas some of the others, such as day care, generally focus on parents with young children). They thus eliminate the question of equitability of benefits. Yet although many employees desire these options, and although they are easy to implement and their cost is extremely low, the number of companies that provide them is not as large as one would expect. In addition, I have found that many employers believe that flexible work hours are flexible only as long as the employees are there when the boss is there.

Perhaps one reason that corporate America has been reluctant to offer a wide variety of flexible work options is the old notion, rooted in the puritan work ethic, that a person who does not want to work regular full-time hours is lazy or immoral or both. A second reason is that many corporate executives believe that *good* employees can take care of their child-care responsibilities on their own time, without any help from the company. According to one black male middle-level manager, child-care initiatives are "not needed and inappropriate."

A third reason is that corporate America does not trust its employees; therefore, managers are reluctant to implement an option such as flex-place that would allow employees to work at home to take care of a sick child.

A final reason for the reluctance is that most corporate policies are designed and implemented in large part by men, who have traditionally been able to relegate all child-care and family responsibilities to their wives. There is a complete inability to comprehend and refusal to accept the incursions of family responsibility in the workplace.

One reason occupational employees favor flexible work options more than managers do may be that their jobs are usually more structured, affording them little opportunity to deal with various work and family responsibilities. Even those occupational workers whose jobs are less structured still do not have the same freedom as management to make decisions about how to deal with family/work conflicts.

Flexible work options are not a panacea for all work/family conflicts, especially for workers with young children who need preschool care or before- and after-school care. One employee admitted to experiencing disruptive stress concerning her young, school-aged children's welfare while she is working: "The children are too young to care for themselves. Because I can't afford child care, I have no other choice but to leave them alone." Her well-thought-out reaction shows how very important, as well as how very stressful, child-care problems can be to employees:

> Any company would have a more productive workplace if employees knew their dependents were in the best possible care while they were at work. Times have changed in the sense that women have to work. Any way you look at it, either the company you work for helps you through troubled times, or you have to quit and let the government take care of you. I know this company pays a great deal in taxes. Why not let those of us who can continue to work worry-free with a little 'over' assistance from the company, so we can pay some of those taxes ourselves and at the same time be productive human beings? We should not be punished by society just because we have dependent children. After all, these dependent children are going to make the decisions about elder care for all of us. A child that had a caring, loving, and stress-free childhood grows into that kind of adult. We need to take this issue very seriously now!

Arranging for someone to care for a sick child is expensive—about $35 to $50 per day—and stressful. One permutation on flex-time/flex-place is to modify sick-leave policies. Being able to work at home during childrens' illnesses, having interchangeable sick time, or having additional sick days for dependent illness are all options worth considering. For example, Dominion Bankshares Corporation in Roanoke, Virginia, gives its employees five days of leave each year to care for sick children, in addition to the regular sick-leave policy. The federal government is another example; the Federal Leave-Sharing Act coordinated by the Office of Personnel Management was established on an experimental basis in 1987 through the efforts of Representatives Frank Wolf (R-Virginia) and Gary Ackerman (D-New York). The bill was signed into law for all federal employees in October of 1988. The genesis of this bill resulted from a call to Representative Wolf's office by a federal employee who wanted to donate his leave time to a blind coworker who needed time off to train a new seeing eye dog but had not accumulated enough service time to take an extended leave.

The leave bank created a mechanism for federal employees to donate one day of sick leave or annual leave time to coworkers in hardship such as a personal or family medical emergency. After employees have used up their own various leave time, they can avail themselves of the opportunity presented by the leave bank. Preliminary studies for fiscal year 1988 showed that approximately 2,200 employees from 52 federal agencies have used 270,000 hours of leave.

Extremely small percentages of employees select part-time work or job sharing as their first or second choice. This is due in large part to the fact that many single parents must work to survive and in many dual-income families, both partners must work full-time in order to make ends meet. Therefore, any type of flexible work option that actually reduces the employee's income is not a viable alternative or solution to child-care problems.

As a result of this survey, I began to include the option "compressed work week" in other questionnaires. Since it does not decrease pay, this is a popular option for employees with children, primarily for those whose children are older than six. For example, in 1989 the compressed work week was considered the fourth most useful solution, and when employees selected their second choice, it received the second highest percentage.

The least useful solutions for employees were part-time work, resource and referral (R & R), corporate contributions, job sharing, day-care centers, and payroll deductions. When the age of the children is used as a control, it is obvious how much it impacts on employee responses. For example, on- or near-site day care is least useful for employees with children over thirteen.

To be fair to R & R services, I should point out that R & R in almost every case does an extremely effective job at informing and educating parents about child-care choices, how to recognize quality child care, and how to handle much of the anxiety around the child-care decision. The parent publications produced by Work Family Directions and the Partnership Group are exceptional in this regard.

Resource and referral also has substantially increased communication and networking among local child-care agencies. This has had the beneficial effect of increasing national-information dissemination so that child-care advocacy has been greatly enhanced, and research on regulation or other child-care trends can be quickly identified.

Another significant but "trickle-down" effect of R & R is improved consumer awareness of child-care issues. Even if parents cannot find the provider of choice from among the referrals, they become armed with the kind of information to demand more direct assistance from child-care policymakers and corporate decision makers. These parents now know where to file complaints, how to write to their legislators, and what pending policy changes may improve child-care conditions in their communities.

Finally, R & R does produce informal needs-assessment data to a company that wants to know what their employees with children really need in the way of child-care assistance. While R & R data are no substitute for a formal needs assessment, the case studies and summary statistics do reveal patterns.

Day-Care Centers

The most direct solution to the child-care problem is high quality, affordable child-care space in a conveniently located child-care facility. As mentioned earlier, just over one quarter of the companies with child-care options in place have child-care centers. There is deep corporate reluctance to establish centers because they represent a departure from routine business practice; they are perceived as inequitable, and start up is not a quick or easy process. Moreover, deciding to develop a center is a clear and open acknowledgment that dependent care does, in fact, have an impact on worker productivity and morale.

However, I would like to make a case for corporate America to recognize that developing child-care spaces should be a key agenda item for workforce planning in the 1990s and beyond. Certainly, not every employer is large enough nor has the "corporate birth rate" to justify the dedication of capital and land to this use. However, any company with a thousand or more employees who are at least 40 percent female can support a center with fifty spaces. My research shows that 59 percent of the women and 48 percent of the men would change their current child-care arrangement if their company would establish a quality, affordable, day-care program.

Betsy Richards, co-president of Corporate Child Care Consultants, said that increasing numbers of their R & R clients are becoming interested in developing near-site day-care centers as companies realize they must do more than R & R for their employees. There is increasing evidence that on- or near-site day-care centers bring cost-effective results.[3] Neuville-Mobile Sox, a hosiery manufacturer, credits its on-site child-care center at one of its plants in North Carolina, with a major portion of the savings it realized from reduced absenteeism, turnover, and payroll taxes since the plant opened in 1979. Other benefits to the company are not as easy to measure. For instance, the day-care center was a draw for recruiting new employees. In an area with very low unemployment and keen competition for production workers, the firm received four applications for every opening; 95 percent of the applicants cited the center as the reason for their interest in the company. Since that time, the Neuville-Mobile Sox plant has experienced relatively low turnover—8 percent initially down to 2 percent in the latest reporting year—compared with other companies in the area, which have suffered turnover rates as high as 100 percent. Although the center's subsidy costs the firm $22,000 annually, the firm saves $20,000 to $25,000 per year in payroll taxes alone and has achieved substantial productivity increases.[4]

In the late 1970s, Nyloncraft of Mishawaka, Indiana, found that child-care problems were the reason behind its high absenteeism and turnover rates. This plastics molding company, which employs 350 people, was writing 900 or more W2 forms a year. That added up to as much as $2,000 in training costs per employee. In 1981, it opened Indiana's first twenty-four-hour child-care facility. Six years later, staff turnover is much lower. Today, Nyloncraft writes only twenty-six more W2s than there are jobs.

Stride Rite Corporation implemented one of the first on-site day-care centers in Boston. It has engendered unusual company loyalty, low turnover, and favorable free publicity. The success of this program convinced Stride Rite to establish one of the first intergenerational day-care centers, serving both children and the elderly.

Sandra Burud and associates found that users of the day-care center at the Union Bank in Los Angeles, California, were absent about 1.7 days fewer than parents who did not use the center. She also found that the average maternity leave for parents who used the center was 1.2 weeks shorter than that of those who did not. The bank believes it is saving $63,000 to $157,000 in turnover costs and $35,000 in lost workdays per year. Burud reported that 61 percent of job applicants said the day-care center was a factor in their decision to work for Union Bank.[5]

Near-site centers are also very effective. A Syntex-affiliated center that opened two and a half years ago at a Palo Alto school currently has a long waiting list. The company believes it has decreased stress and has sent a clear message to employees that they are worthwhile.

Another corporate program is the Hacienda Business Park, which developed a model child-care center to serve all the companies there. These developers benefited from their progressive thinking. They have no problem renting units quickly and are retaining their current tenants longer. In addition, the center has served as an excellent public relations tool. According to Joe Callahan, one of the developers of the business park, "We believe that our on-site child-care center gives us a marketing advantage in what is a highly competitive marketplace. This is a win-win situation for us, our tenants, and the community."[6]

These examples are not unusual. A majority of companies that have made the initial investment in a child-care center attribute improved productivity to the service. In a 1984 study of employers who sponsor their own day-care centers, 65 percent believed the center had reduced employee turnover. Fifty-three percent believed on-site day care had lowered absenteeism rates, and 90 percent agreed it had boosted employee morale.[7]

Companies don't necessarily need to run the day-care centers to succeed in addressing child-care problems. There are many other ways to structure the management of a child-care facility. Many companies contract with child-care vendors to operate the child-care facility. This puts the child-care center management in the hands of experts, and the liability for the center's operation is on the vendor. Many companies using this arrangement are named as additional insurers on the vendor's liability-insurance policy. Companies using vendor models are numerous, and include Campbell's Soup, Disney World, the U.S. Government, many hospitals, the city of Los Angeles, and the Miami International Airport.

A second model is for a company to share the burden of the child-care facility with other companies in its geographic proximity. These are usually consortium child-care facilities, and the consortium itself becomes a corporate entity charged with management of the child-care facility. The consortium may bid out to a vendor or directly operate the center. This model has been used successfully in Atlanta; Baltimore; Reston, Virginia; and in three Los Angeles locations.

Sometimes the corporate sponsorship of the center is limited to the physical facility, space, and equipment. Other times the employer may subsidize the tuition as well. A four-year-old day-care center subsidized by Hill, Holliday, Conners and Cosmopolus, one of the nation's top fifty advertising agencies, is an excellent example. Tuition at the center, located three blocks from the company's Boston office, is partially subsidized by the advertising agency according to the employees' family income.

The Stride Rite Center and the Union Bank Center, mentioned previously, as well as the new Genetech Center and Paramount Studios Child-Care Center, offer operating subsidies to keep quality high and parent fees at or below market rates. Stride Rite, for example, does not charge any parent more than 10 percent of his or her income as parent fee regardless of the operating cost for the child-care service.

Other important areas of direct child-care assistance in which corporations can help alleviate the day-care shortage is to support and finance before- and after-school care and to assist in the development of "get well" programs for ill children. These programs require more creativity than on-site centers, mainly because they are either neighborhood based (before- and after-school care) or because no regulation or tradition exists to guide the development of models.

In California, aerospace and defense contractor TRW, established an after-school program for employees' children at a school near the workplace. Parents who did not reside in that district were able to obtain permits for their children to attend that elementary school.

In Chapel Hill, North Carolina, the Frank Porter Graham Child Development Center serves sixty-five children, both sick and well. The operators do not believe sick children need to be separated from healthy children, because they believe that by the time a child exhibits symptoms of an illness he or she is no longer contagious. The center is considered to have one of the most innovative approaches to dealing with sick children.

In some states, regulation does not permit the mingling of sick and well children, and separate programs are developed or health workers are sent to the child's own home to provide care. The oldest child-care program for sick children is in San Jose, California, at the San Juan Batista Child Development Center. This center serves children who are regularly enrolled in the Child Development Center as well as community children who attend only when ill. The program has full-time nursing staff.

Financial Assistance

No matter how many quality day-care slots exist, if they are unaffordable, they are not available to many parents. In addition, the cost of providing day care for sick children is very high, and employee assistance is needed.

There are a number of ways corporate America can assist employees with their child-care expenses, both for the healthy child and for the sick child. (See appendix for the pros and cons of the various options.) One approach is for corporations to negotiate employee discounts with various types of caregivers. Typically, a vendor lowers its fees by 10 percent and the employer contributes 10 percent of the fees, so the employees receive a 20 percent reduction in the costs. In some cases the vendor offers the 20 percent discount directly to the employer in exchange for the purchase of a guaranteed number of slots. Another approach is for employers to offer vouchers to their employees to use at the caregiver of their choice. The voucher provides full or partial reimbursement for the cost of the care. Employers can also obtain employee discounts by offering in-kind services to child-care providers. Possible services might include:

- use of company-owned real estate or storage or office space
- administrative, legal, accounting, technical, printing, maintenance services or management training courses
- office supplies and equipment or products produced by the company, such as computers, paper, lumber, or food
- low-interest loans for construction or renovation
- underwriting staff-training courses at local colleges and universities

Obviously, discounts can be achieved if corporations grant money to child-care providers for discount rates for their employees.

Finally, offering a flexible benefits package would allow employees to make individual choices from a menu of taxable and nontaxable benefits. These benefits may be part of a Comprehensive Cafeteria Plan or part of a flexible-spending account/salary-reduction plan that allows employees to spend pretax dollars on dependent care.

While these various financial approaches are helpful, relative to the high cost of quality child care they are not signifi cant. Thus, as I suggest in chapter 10, the federal government must give substantial subsidies and tax breaks to employees and employers to ensure that their children receive quality child care. Similarly, more corporations must adopt a combination of these financial-assistance programs.

The Leading Edge Approach

Perhaps one of the best approaches to solving employee child-care problems was recently part of a pact signed by telecommunications giant AT&T with its very powerful unions, the Communications Workers of America and the International Brotherhood of Electrical Workers. The package includes sweeping changes in family benefits that take into account the nature of the changing workforce. With passage of the plan, which offers a multitude of solutions to child-care problems, AT&T has moved from the back of the pack to the front in the family-care arena. The plan includes the following:

- *Flex-time.* Employees will be able to take half-day vacations or up to eight hours with pay in two-hour increments. This time does not need prior approval from a supervisor and is intended to be used for child-care (or elder-care) emergencies, doctor appointments, or meetings at school. This is in addition to four paid personal vacation days. A clause stipulates that management and the union will work out flexible ways of dealing with work and family-care issues. The contract provides for a commitment from the unions and management to make the work environment a sensitive, responsive place for employees with family-care needs.
- *Financial Assistance.* The AT&T pact offers a number of financial aid programs. One is a dependent-care salary reduction account that allows employees to pay for day care with pretax dollars. AT&T can withhold up to $5,000 of employees' pay to put aside for dependent care. If that money were spent directly on day care, it would be taxed at about 20 percent, depending on the employee's tax bracket.
- The financial package also sets up a fund for management and for union workers to finance projects and initiatives to

improve the number and quality of child- and elder-care services. Five million dollars will be set aside for the occupational workers, and $3 million to $4 million will make up the management fund. With the interest incurred, these funds could add up to $12 million to be used over the three-year period of the contract. The fund is to be used as seed money for AT&T employees to come up with solutions for their dependent-care problems. In addition, if AT&T staff see a need in one area through Work/Family Directions research, money can be used to address these needs. (I should note that IBM has just established a $25 million fund to be used over the next five years for dependent-care problems.)

AT&T will also provide its employees with a $2,000 adoption-assistance package. In addition, it will offer a national resource and referral program for child care in 1990 and implement a consultation and referral program for elder care in 1991.

Unpaid parental or sick leave will also be expanded. Employees can receive up to one year of leave, with a guarantee that an equivalent job and pay will be there when they return. Currently, there is a six-month guarantee. While on leave the company will pay the premium for the first six months of medical, dental, and vision coverage. The company will continue coverage up to one year of death benefits and basic group life.

"It's a real boost to my morale," said one thirty-three-year-old white occupational woman. "It's nice to know that if you have to go and see about your child in school or if another family emergency comes up, you won't be docked. You don't have to be afraid that you will lose your job," noted a black occupational woman who has been with AT&T for twenty-three years.

The AT&T plan was formulated after an extensive survey of its employees was conducted. The research found that 52 percent of the employees thought child care was an important issue in bargaining; more than one-third called it a high priority. AT&T recognized from other studies and other employee input that one solution was not sufficient. Employees need financial assistance, more flexibility in work scheduling, and affordable child care. AT&T's approach to the last problem truly places it on the cutting edge.

Summary

A growing number of companies now recognize that efforts to help employees solve their personal and family problems can actually increase worker productivity. It is obvious that a broad range of ways exists by which companies can support child care. Each option has its advantages and disadvantages, including cost factors and appropriateness of the solutions. Potential costs must be viewed in terms of potential returns on investments, lower health-insurance costs, increased productivity, reduced stress, improved morale for employees, and an enhanced image for the corporation. "The more an employer helps in these areas, the happier the employee will be, and the more productive," stated a white female occupational worker.

In the next few years, we can expect to see more and more companies consider the work and family needs of their employees. Certainly, those companies who want to have or keep a competitive edge will do so; to do less would be to risk not attracting and retaining a skilled workforce. The question for corporations, it seems, is simple: Will they recognize the tremendous changes in work/family relationships that have occurred in the past twenty years and adopt modern employment policies to accommodate them? Or will they rigidly adhere to outdated practices that reduce their competitiveness—and cut into their profits?

6

Elder Care—The Corporate Realities

THE word *day care* no longer refers only to child care; today it includes caring for senior citizens as well. Five years ago, few people had heard of day-care centers for the elderly. During the past several years however, the media and the public began to pay more attention to the needs of this rapidly expanding segment of our society. The current interest is based on simple demographics; as the American population ages, there are more older people to care for. In the coming decades, experts expect the number of people with elder dependents will outnumber people with child-care responsibilities. Some facts illustrate the magnitude of the change.[1]

- In 1900, only 10 percent of Americans were fifty-five and over and only 4 percent were sixty-five and over. But in 1986, 20 percent were at least fifty-five years old and 12 percent were at least sixty-five.

- The size of the elderly population is growing at a faster rate than at any time in American history. In 1987, the sixty-five-to-seventy-four age group (17.77 million) was eight times larger than it was in 1900, but the seventy-five-to-eighty-four group (9.3 million) was twelve times larger. The over-eighty-five group (2.9 million) was twenty-three times larger. One major reason for this is that medical advances have extended life. But even as the human lifespan has been lengthened, many elderly people spend their extra years with a host of health problems that incapacitate them. They must rely on their children (in most cases) to support and care for them.

• The aging phenomenon is characterized by two distinct groups, the "young old" (sixty-five to eighty-four) and the "old old" (eighty-five and older). Between 1989 and 2000, the proportion of the American population aged fifty-five and over is expected to stay at just over one in five (22 percent); but by 2010, it is projected to have risen to more than one out of four. After 2010, this proportion will rise even more dramatically because of the maturation of the baby-boom generation. By 2030, one in three persons will be fifty-five or older and one in five will be sixty-five or older.

• Demographers classify "old old" age as beginning with the eighty-fifth birthday. This over-eighty-five population is one of the fastest-growing age groups in the United States. The "old old" population is expected to nearly quadruple in size between 1980 and 2030, and to be seven times as large in 2050 as it was in 1980.

While Americans are living longer, they are not necessarily healthier. Many elderly Americans suffer from chronic ailments. The American Association of Retired Persons (AARP) has found that about four out of five persons sixty-five and over have at least one chronic condition, and multiple chronic conditions are commonplace among the elderly.

In 1986, the most common conditions among the elderly were arthritis (48 percent), hypertension (39 percent), hearing impairments (30 percent), heart disease (28 percent), orthopedic impairments and sinusitis (17 percent each), cataracts (14 percent), diabetes and visual impairments (10 percent each), and tinnitus (9 percent). As a result of these illnesses, the elderly spend about 10 percent of the year (thirty-two days) in restricted activity. They spend about half of these days in bed.[2]

Because they suffer from chronic ailments, the elderly are the heaviest users of the health-care system, spending more money on health care than any other specific group. Even though the elderly constitute only 12 percent of the population, they account for one-third of the country's personal-health-care expenditures. According to AARP reports in 1987, these expenditures were expected to total $120 billion and to average $4,202 per year for each older person—more than three times the average of $1,300 spent for younger people. The extent of congnitive impairment diseases, such as dementia and Alzheimer's, among the elderly is just being recognized. A recent study showed that the 63 percent of the elderly in nursing homes have at least a mild form of cognitive impairment. Harvard medical researchers found that Alzheimer's affects four million Americans rather than the two-and-a-half million most researchers thought. Editors of the *Bank Street College Work and Family Newsletter* aptly summarized the multifaceted age-specific problems facing the elderly. These problems included failing vision or hearing, infirmity, death of family and friends, loneliness, financial insecurity, fears of dependency, and the loss of control.[3]

Not only do the elderly face these problems, but the employee caregivers who must assist them face them too. Studies show that caregivers begin to develop problems such as increased stress, lost productive time, and stress-related health problems. Elder care restricts the caregiver's time and freedom. It creates conflicts among competing demands and reduces time for social and recreational activities. These restrictions are the precursors of mental and emotional symptoms such as anxiety, increased drinking and smoking, sleeplessness, back pain, and emotional exhaustion.

Differences between Child and Adult Care

The fundamental difference between child care and adult care is that child care usually involves the delivery of a single service to increasingly independent children, whereas adult care involves the multifaceted coordination and distribution of multiple services to increasingly dependent adults. Simply stated, adult care is far more complex than child care. In most cases, *adult care* refers to the care of the elderly, but it also encompasses dependent adults who are temporarily or permanently disabled because of trauma, cognitive impairment, congenital disease, or emotional limitation.

Other differences between child care and elder care:

- In most child-care situations, the range of needed services is more finite and is typically predefined upon seeking the services, requiring less problem definition and consultation.

- In most elder- and dependent-adult-care situations, the range of needed services is broad and complex, requiring more problem definition and consultation.

- For all types of family care—including elder, dependent adult, and child care—the adult employee is the one who decides whether consultation or referral services will be sought. But in elder and dependent adult care, the *recipient* of the services is also usually involved in the decision-making process, as are other adults (siblings, for example). These additional parties in the decision-making process make the referral situation for dependent adults more complicated than that for children, who are not involved in decision making about child care.

- In most child-care situations, once the issues and referral needs are clarified and a referral is made, the situation tends to stabilize quickly and is maintained for some period. That is, a preschool child will usually enter a full-day school program by the age of six or seven. But given the fluctuations in adults' health problems, elder- or dependent-adult-care situations can and do change rapidly, are unpredictable, and tend to be less stable.

- Further complicating the adult-care scenario is distance. While parents seeking child care normally live with their children, adults and their dependents frequently live apart, often at a distance, which makes caregiving more difficult.

- Most children's health problems are well known, routine, and manageable, but the health problems of most elderly and dependent adults are more complex. The health of these individuals is usually more frail and chronic.

Finally, while we have numerous books about how to care for a child, very little exists on how to care for the impaired elderly. An elder-care expert told the author, "A great deal of information exists on how to change a diaper for the child, but what information exists on changing the diaper for an adult?"

Who Are the Caregivers?

Women bear the burden of caregiving responsibilities. They constitute 75 percent of all caregivers. The typical caregiver of disabled persons aged fifty and over, according to the American Association of Retired Persons, is a woman in her mid-forties who is married, lives in a household with an average income in the mid-twenties, and has at least a high school degree. More than half of all caregivers are employed—42 percent full-time and 13 percent part-time, primarily in white-collar, professional sales positions, and blue-collar occupations. About 16 percent of all caregivers are retired, and another 28 percent are unemployed.[4]

A substantial amount of research has documented the fact that older Americans prefer to remain in their homes and to avoid institutionalization for as long as possible. Many older people can do so because they receive personal care and/or financial assistance from their family. According to one report, for every older American in a nursing home, four others who suffer from physical or mental ailments that impair their ability to function independently avoid institutionalization through such assistance.

Caregiving responsibilities often include providing personal services. On average, caregivers provide assistance with two activities of daily living (ADLs), i.e., eating, transferring, toileting, dressing, and bathing. More than two-thirds (68 percent) of the caregivers surveyed provide assistance with one or more ADL; 19 percent provide one, 15 percent provide two, and 33 percent provide three or more. Almost all caregivers assist with instrumental activities of daily living (IADLs) primarily grocery shopping (82 percent), transportation (79 percent) and housework (75 percent).[5]

Because of the complexity of caregiving, it is not surprising that, on average, caregivers provide almost thirteen hours of care each week. The time devoted to caregiving increases with the age of the person receiving the care. Elaine M. Brody showed in a study of caregivers that caregivers between the ages of forty and forty-nine provided an average of only three hours a week of care to their elderly mothers; those who were fifty to fifty-nine years old averaged 15.6 hours weekly; and those who were over sixty averaged 22.7 hours. In addition, the older the caregiving woman, the more likely she was to reside in the same household as her mother: 9 percent of women under age fifty, compared with 34 percent of those fifty and older, lived with their mothers.[6]

A Review of Key Research

When employees are responsible for providing elder care, they almost always encounter conflicts with their job needs. Increasingly smaller family size, frequent job-related moves, and the growing number of women in the workforce mean that family members may be too few or too far removed to effectively provide care for their elderly relatives. Employees' struggle to balance work and family needs can affect their performance and morale, so that the stress of caregiving often manifests itself in the workplace.

In addition to the emotional strain, the day-to-day tasks also take a physical toll. The employee may be responsible for transportation, housekeeping, bathing and personal care, shopping, cooking, and record keeping. Although some of these duties can be done before or after work, many are likely to take up company time, such as researching and conferring with doctors, finding home health care, visiting nursing homes, and applying for Medicaid. Government offices, of course, are open only during normal working hours. In addition, emergencies do not conveniently happen outside working hours.

Numerous studies have discussed the stresses of caregiving. Let's review some of the current literature that sheds light on the types of stresses experienced by caregivers.

Marcie Parker, senior research consultant for the Senate

Special Committee on Aging, reported in "Overview of Respite and Adult Day Care in the United States" that most caregivers said they were only moderately to mildly stressed because of their caregiving responsibilities, but 80 percent in her study reported that there were aspects of caregiving that are "difficult," "trying," or "emotionally damaging." In addition, more than half said the person they were caring for was very demanding of the caregivers.[7]

Like child-care problems, worrying about elder-care problems can affect work performance. The impact of such worrying on work performance has been reported in a number of research projects. Dana Friedman, in her article "Elder Care: The Employee Benefit of the 1990s?" concluded: "the emotional and financial toll of caring for an elderly relative often has negative effects on an employee's work."[8]

The New York Business Group on Health surveyed a group of management employees about the effects of elder-care responsibilities on the careers of workers. The managers cited unscheduled time off the job (75 percent), lateness (73 percent), absenteeism (67 percent), and excessive use of the telephone while at work (64 percent). Not surprisingly, 46 percent of the corporate respondents reported decreased productivity or quality of work performance.[9]

Robert B. Enright and Lynn Friss reported that 58 percent of the caregivers in their Family Survival Project study indicated that they sometimes work more slowly because of worry or feelings of being upset. Fifty-five percent of those working more than half-time also reported missing time at work, losing an average of twelve days per year. The study also found significant health-care costs associated with caregiving. Caregivers for the elderly were 20 percent more likely to have seen a physician recently than noncaregivers were. Caregivers also had much higher rates of classic stress-related illnesses such as depression, sleeplessness, and weight gain and loss.[10]

Robyn Stone and Pam Short found that caregivers who assist elders with behavioral problems are 18 percent more likely to alter their work schedules. In their study, holding all other factors constant, 65 percent of the caregivers had to accommodate their schedules; the average for their entire sample was 47 percent. Stone and Short cited research on the economic costs associated with caregiving: A study of 1,445 primary caregivers in the National Hospice Study found that 33 percent of the employed caregivers in the home-based hospice setting ceased working to assume caregiving responsibilities. Of those who remained at work, 60 percent lost income directly because of absenteeism. These employees lost an average of 43 hours of work time during their caregiving tenure.[11]

A 1989 study by John Hancock Financial Services and *Fortune* magazine found that six in ten corporate executives are aware of the effects that employees' elder-caregiving is having on the workplace, including specific work-related problems such as employee stress (45 percent), unscheduled days off (38 percent), late arrivals and early departures (37 percent), above-average use of the telephone (32 percent), and absenteeism (30 percent). Those who work in service companies (which have more female employees) were more likely than those in industrial companies to report these problems.

In the same study, employees with elder-care responsibilities were most likely to report emotional stress (51 percent) as a work-related problem associated with caregiving. In addition, 32 percent came to work late or left early, 31 percent took unscheduled time off, 24 percent said they were less productive, and 21 percent missed work because of their caregiving responsibilities. Female and lower-income employees were more likely to report stress and anxiety as side effects of elder-caregiving than male and higher-income employees. Taking into account the high stress of simultaneously working and caregiving to the elderly, the vast majority of employees (70 percent) stated that it is "very difficult" to be an employed elder-caregiver, and 77 percent stated that taking care of elderly relatives or friends interferes with their jobs.[12]

Finally, Michael Creedon found in his study that employee caregivers were more likely than other employees to report having health problems. For example, 21 percent of the caregivers—compared with only 12 percent of the non-caregivers—reported frequent headaches. Twenty-two percent of the former but only 8 percent of the latter experienced frequent anxiety or depression.[13]

These findings suggest that elder-care costs are showing up in employer health-benefit costs, in productivity losses, and in the ultimate loss of good employees. Ten to 20 percent of employed caregivers leave their jobs to become full-time caregivers. The studies also support the notion that elder care is a serious problem for many employees, and that elder care is a bottom-line issue for corporate America.

My Research

While some studies have concluded that as many as 30 percent of the workforce currently has elder-care responsibilities, my 1988 study found that only 8 percent have such responsibilities. When the age of the employees was used as a control, 17 percent of those over fifty say that they have primary caregiving responsibilities for an elderly person. And my 1989 study found that only 9 percent of employee respondents have primary responsibilities for an elderly person or an adult dependent, however, 21 percent of the women and 18 percent of the men over fifty years of age answered affirmatively.

About one out of every four employees who do have elder- and/or adult-dependent-care responsibilities is responsible for the care of more than one person. These employees often operate under an almost unbearable stress level.

Parents (54 percent) are by far the most frequently looked after, followed by in-laws (11 percent) and spouses (10 percent). Forty-five percent of these individuals live in an employee's residence, 26 percent live in their own residence a distance from the employees, and 18 percent live in their own residences near the employees. Only 8 percent live in nursing homes.

Some of the participants described their current elder-care responsibilities this way:

> My company won't transfer me back [to Kansas City, where this employee's mother lives]. It's just a matter of time before I will have to quit. (white female lower-level manager)

> My mother lives out of state. There are other children, but since I am the oldest and the only one who is not married, I feel it will fall to me to take care of her if anything happens to

her health. The fact that she lives in another state is the problem. (black male lower-level manager)

My mother had a massive stroke in early 1986, which ultimately led to her being placed in a nursing home. She had another massive stroke this past week. Since I am the only relative in this area, I have had to take responsibility for her. (This employee, a black female lower-level manager, has missed work four to six times and made more than six telephone calls on family business during the last year.)

Two years ago, my father was seriously ill and needed twenty-four-hour assistance. My work commitments prevented me from helping my family more than I did. I resented it very much, but there were no options available for me, such as a leave of absence. (black female lower-level manager)

Mother is diabetic and has glaucoma. She has lived with me for years; 73 years old. (white female middle-level manager)

My husband has had bypass surgery twice, and my mother-in-law is over eighty years old. She needs to be looked after. (white male lower-level manager)

My mother is eighty-two and has hearing and mobility problems. Her future does not look good. My mother-in-law has heart problems. My daughter is twenty-four and epileptic, and she cannot hold a job to support herself. (white female lower-level manager)

My mother has Parkinson's and is in a nursing home in Missouri. My cousin had to take over my role as primary caregiver when my husband got transferred here. (white female occupational worker)

The types of care the employees in my 1989 study are responsible for are providing financial assistance (72 percent); filling out legal, insurance, and benefits forms (66 percent); coordinating medical activities (57 percent); providing transportation; (53 percent) providing home care, such as cooking, cleaning, and shopping (44 percent); and providing personal care, such as hygiene, dressing, and bathing (14 percent).

My findings support the conclusions of the *Fortune* and John Hancock study. In that study, 59 percent of the caregivers have transportation responsibilities, 58 percent provide companionship, 56 percent provide emotional support, primarily through the telephone, 47 percent provide shopping, laundry, and other household chores, 31 percent manage personal finances, 28 percent coordinate outside help, and about 20 percent provide such personal assistance as administering medication and various kinds of personal care such as dressing.[14]

Because of the many responsibilities inherent in caring for an increasingly dependent adult, it is not surprising that more than two out of five employees in both my studies have "a great deal" or "some" stress balancing work and family conflicts at work (43 percent) and at home (47 percent).

The employees commented most frequently about their financial difficulties. Only 12 percent of these employees do not pay anything for the care of the elderly; 42 percent pay $1 to $50; 20 percent pay $51 to $100; and 17 percent pay more than $100 per week.

> She [my mother] lives with me, and she doesn't make enough money to move on her own. (black male occupational worker)
>
> My parent lives only on social security, which is not enough for daily expenses. (Hispanic male occupational worker)
>
> I have financial responsibility only to a certain extent. At present, we share in financial needs of home. Sometimes I pay for medical care that Medicare does not provide, such as vision and dental care. (black female lower-level manager)

Providing medical and personal care was cited as a problem by a number of employees.

> My primary responsibilities at this point are to ensure she [my mother] has at least part-time help in the home and to monitor her health care. (white female middle-level manager)
>
> A hired person lives in an apartment with my mother. She does the cooking and housework and watches my mother. My mother has Parkinson's and heart trouble. (white male lower-level manager)
>
> I don't have children, but I do have an elderly grandmother in town who has special needs from time to time, such as operations or going to the hospital. (white male middle-level manager)

> My grandmother is unable to perform the personal hygiene care she needs. (black female occupational worker)

Most of the employees are responsible for more than one type of care.

> My mother has cancer, and my father has bursitis in his arms. I must help them with cleaning, transportation, doctor's appointments, and so on. (black female occupational worker)
>
> There's no way to specify just one type of responsibility. I share financial, medical, transportation, and other responsibilities on a part-time basis now for my blind, elderly mother. My brother lives with her, but I take care of all of the business and some of the other activities. (white female occupational worker)

Table 6–1 shows the employee responses to a list of questions about their elder-care and adult-dependent-care problems. The top four problem areas are transporting the dependent person between scheduled activities and appointments (46 percent), handling the person's medical requirements (45 percent), affording the proper care (43 percent), and understanding the requirements of legal/insurance/benefits (41 percent). Overall, only 21 percent of the men and 34 percent of the women said they have "no real problems" in carrying out their responsibilities. Notice that all the top problem areas, except for financial assistance, are time-constraining.

In analyzing the data, some patterns *seemed* to contradict the findings of other studies. One example is the issue of missed work days. The difference between those who have primary responsibility for an elder and those who do not have such responsibility is quite small. Thirty-eight percent of the employees who have elder-care responsibilities, compared with 31 percent who do not, missed work in the previous year because of those family responsibilities. Moreover, 30 percent of those with elder-care responsibilities, versus 29 percent with none, indicated that they had been late in the previous year.

Another apparent contradiction with earlier studies was my

Table 6–1

INDEX: CURRENT ELDER- AND/OR ADULT-DEPENDENT-CARE NEEDS

QUESTIONS THAT MAKE UP THE INDEX

With regard to your elder and/or adult dependent care needs, please rate each situation below: (N = percent who say "big problem" or "some problem.")

Transporting the dependent person between scheduled activities and appointments	46
Handling the person's medical requirements	45
Affording the proper care	43
Understanding requirements of legal/insurance/benefits	41
Handling dual roles between dependent care and work	35
Handling household maintenance for the dependent person, e.g. shopping, cooking, cleaning, etc.	34
Finding appropriate information about handling your care problems	31
Finding quality adult home care	29
Handling a sudden loss of adult day-care provider, i.e., provider quits, gets sick, goes on vacation	25
Finding an adult care-provider to work evenings or weekends	25
Traveling or overnight trips of the caregiver	25
Finding quality adult day care	24
Finding quality nursing care	24
Handling personal hygiene (dressing, bathing, etc.)	17

findings on health problems. Employees who have primary responsibility for an elderly person are not significantly more likely to have stress-related health problems than those who do not, in my study. Forty-one percent of those who have elder-care responsibilities, compared with 36 percent who do not, have had headaches more often or sometimes in the previous six months.

Finally, I found no significant differences between these two groups and how they perceive their performance. Forty-five percent who have primary responsibilities, compared with 41 percent who do not, said they are performing their job as effectively as possible.

The main reason that I can give to account for this similarity is that until the cared-for elderly becomes moderately to seriously impaired and/or a financial burden, they can be helpful to the employees, especially if they live with the caregiver and can help with household responsibilities such as child care.

Thus, merely having responsibility for an elderly person does not necessarily mean that an employee will experience stress at work or suffer from stress-related health problems. The deciding factor is the degree of difficulty the employee has in handling the caregiving duties. Those employees who are having a "difficult" or "very difficult" time managing their elder-care responsibilities *do* have significantly more stress, stress-related health problems, and absenteeism. The difficulty is affected by a multitude of factors such as the frailty of the elderly person, the health status of the caregiver, conflicts with other responsibilities at home and on the job, and assistance with caregiving from others.

Fifty-six percent of the women who described their elder-care responsibilities as "very difficult" missed work in the previous year. But only 35 percent who said it is "not at all difficult" missed work. The lowest rate of absenteeism (33 percent) was reported by women with no family-care responsibilities. (The figures for men are 44 percent, 27 percent, and 28 percent, respectively.)

On the issue of stress at home, 68 percent of the employees who described their elder-care responsibilities as "very difficult" reported stress at home "to a great extent" or "to some extent." High levels of stress were also reported by 56 percent of the employees with "difficult" caregiving tasks, but by only 22 percent whose duties are "not difficult at all." By contrast, only 30 percent of the employees with no family-care responsibilities reported stress at home.

With regard to health, 39 percent of those who find it "very difficult" to care for the elderly but only 24 percent who find it "not at all" difficult indicated that they become tired in a short period of time. (See table 6–2 for additional results.)

Here is how some employees described their difficulties:

> I lost my first husband to a brain tumor, and my mother was terminally ill at the same time. He was sick two and a half years, and I worked full-time and took care of our daughter. I know firsthand how hard it is to care for people with a debilitating illness. (white female lower-level manager)

> My mother lives in another state 350 miles away. I have to share responsibility with my two sisters, who live there. Also, she needs help with insurance forms and so on. (white female lower-level manager)

> It's difficult to get off to take [my mother] to appointments and take care of her. Also, my mother-in-law is getting more and more incapable of taking care of herself. She will have to live with my husband and me, and we will be responsible for all of her needs. (Hispanic female occupational worker)

> It's impossible to get to my home to give her medications, prepare meals, and other things, and still work. (black male occupational worker)

> The limited salary my husband and I make with no additional income makes it very difficult to care for my parents. (Asian female occupational worker)

> My mother is a strong-willed individual, very demanding. This causes, if nothing else, a high stress level. (white male middle-level manager)

Vignettes

Patricia B. is a forty-year-old black occupational worker who has more than sixteen years with her company. She is single

Table 6-2

THE IMPACT OF ELDER CARE ON STRESS-RELATED HEALTH PROBLEMS

Respondents were asked: "How difficult is it for you to care for elderly persons for whom you are primarily responsible?" (N = Percent who responded "often" or "sometimes.")

Health Problems	No Elder Care	Very Difficult	Difficult	Not Very Difficult	Not at All Difficult
Difficulty Getting Up in the Morning	48	63	49	39	37
Feeling Nervous	46	63	53	43	39
Back Pains	41	57	47	42	41
Overeating	39	51	45	40	36
Increased Headaches	36	53	41	38	33
Trouble Getting to Sleep	36	52	41	33	35
Easily Tired	29	51	35	29	24
Heart Pounding or Racing	20	37	26	20	21
Trouble Breathing	14	19	19	15	15
Increased Smoking	14	15	15	15	11
Poor Appetite	12	15	15	12	11
Increased Drinking	11	15	15	9	8
Dizzy Spells	10	13	13	12	10

and has responsibility for an extended family that includes two of her own children, aged eleven and sixteen, a grandson with Down's syndrome, and a handicapped brother. She is also primarily responsible for her mother. Her gross household income is $25,000 annually.

Patricia reported that she is very satisfied with her job content and work schedule, but she is concerned because while "working hours are good," she has very little say in scheduling emergency time off. Like many other occupational workers, Patricia is forced to use her vacation time to care for sick dependents. Not surprisingly, she feels that balancing work and family responsibilities has created a significant amount of stress at home and at work. On the job, she tries to balance "workload problems while worrying about family problems," and at home she is concerned that she is unable to spend "quality time with the children." As a result of this stress, she said, she overeats and is tired easily. She also said she frequently feels nervous.

Specifically, her problems include handling children during school vacations and closures, locating care for a sick child, and affording child care. Patricia's situation is compounded by her grandson's and brother's handicaps, which require her to find child and adult day care that meet their special needs. This, she said, is a "great problem."

Patricia wrote that although her mother is in fair health, she does not drive. This creates considerable problems, especially when her mother has doctor appointments to check her high blood pressure and arthritis. It is because of these health problems that Patricia, rather than her mother, has responsibility for her brother.

The solution, she thinks, would be an on- or near-site day-care center with a "good facility for caring for children with handicaps." In addition, "an adult day-care facility is a major concern among this company's employees. Attendance and time off-the-job would greatly improve if there was an intergenerational facility on-site or near the work location that was affordable so employees would be able to pay the fees."

Although Patricia's situation is extreme (due to her grandson's Down's syndrome *and* brother's handicap), it is easy to imagine the amount of "free" time that she must devote to her family rather than to her personal needs. Indeed, for many caregivers, the time spent on caregiving means less time for other activities. Half the caregivers spend less time on leisure activities since they took on these responsibilities. About one-third spend less time with their own families than before or pay less attention to their own health. Another 28 percent have been unable to take a vacation. These changes are particularly pronounced among primary caregivers, 58 percent of whom spend less time on leisure activities than they did before.

Between one-fourth and one-third of caregivers reported that limitations on their social life and on their relationships with family and friends pose a serious problem; about half reported having "some" problems in these areas.

William T. is a white first-level manager, aged thirty-seven, who has more than fifteen years of service with his company. He has a wife who works full-time and one daughter under eighteen. Their total annual household income is $51,000. William is responsible for the care of his elderly mother-in-law and his handicapped sister-in-law.

He explained that while he finds his job "challenging and interesting," he is somewhat dissatisfied with the amount of overtime he has to work. He feels that balancing work/family conflicts has created stress for him at home and at work to "some extent." But he has developed no serious stress-related health problems.

Currently, William finds handling the sudden loss of a care provider, affording proper care, and traveling overnight to be "great problems." He does not see these problems lessening in the future and added,

> My sister-in-law will become more dependent with age. When my mother-in-law becomes disabled, all of the finances, cooking, personal care, transportation, and medical visits will be our responsibility. In future years this is a major concern for my spouse and myself. One of us will have to quit work unless options become available. That will create major financial and emotional problems for our entire family.

The most useful solution, he feels, would be an on-site or near-site day-care facility for dependent adults.

He "strongly agrees" that the company should take an active role in assisting employees in meeting their dependency needs: "Employees can't perform their best or travel as freely if they cannot feel good about caring for their dependents."

Shelly J. is a white occupational worker in her late forties. She has one teenage child at home and lives with a partner, who works full-time and offers little assistance at home: "Mine is a new step-family situation and we have recently relocated to another state." She has primary responsibility for the care of her partner's father, who is quite healthy physically but who requires lots of attention emotionally since his wife died a year ago.

Family/work conflicts have created a great deal of on-the-job stress for Shelly, as well as stress at home. She missed work, arrived late, and left work early more than six times in the previous year: "There are only so many hours in a day. . . . It's impossible to be all things to all people and most people put family at the top of their priority list—as is only right."

The stress has begun to affect Shelly's health. She said she often feels nervous or fidgety, has a poor appetite, and tires easily. She experienced headaches, shortness of breath, insomnia, and back pain in the previous six months. She admitted that smoking and drinking too much in the previous six months concerns her.

A strong supporter of greater company involvement in family care and employee health, Shelly thinks flex-time would be the most useful way to resolve the conflicting demands of work and family. She also recognizes the need for child care: "Although my own child-care problems are in the past, they were a big handicap at the time and will be as long as both parents work."

Employee Turnover

Perhaps the most serious consequence of the new pressures of elder care will be the loss of competent workers. As Stone and

Short wrote, "approximately one third of caregivers report either quitting their jobs or accommodating their work schedules in order to assume care responsibilities."[15]

The John Hancock and *Fortune* study showed that female employees are more apt than male employees to anticipate quitting or taking a long period of time off from work (29 percent versus 11 percent, respectively) because of impending elder-care problems. Male employees are more likely than female employees to take a *short* period of time off from work (41 percent versus 32 percent, respectively).[16]

Finally, Gary C. Brice et al. found that 28 percent of non-working caregivers in the study had to quit their jobs to care for their dependent mothers. Of the working women, 26 percent were considering quitting.[17] In my 1989 survey, I found that 29 percent of the women, versus only 19 percent of the men, had considered quitting their jobs to stay home with a dependent adult for whom they have primary responsibility.

These findings for female employees raise some important questions. If close to three in ten women in the workforce today anticipate quitting their jobs or taking an extended period of time off to take care of elderly relatives or friends, as our society ages in the years to come, business in the United States could be considerably disrupted. Women will be moving in and out of the workforce just when they are reaching the peak of their careers and are most useful to corporate America. In addition, they will be doing this at a time when corporate America is faced with skilled labor shortages.

Summary

The responsibility for caring for the elderly most often falls on the family, particularly on the female children of aging parents. How best to meet the needs of aging relatives or parents while also meeting the needs of the employed caregiver has become an important challenge to both employees and employers.

When workers are responsible for providing personal care, transportation, shopping, and other essential services to an aging parent or relative, elder-care needs may conflict with job needs. The struggle to balance work and family responsibilities may affect employee performance and morale. Elder care has become a workplace issue that employers cannot afford to ignore.

While the number of employees who have elder-care responsibilities is currently relatively small, my data indicate that in the next five years, the number will increase sharply, by two to three times what it is now—that is, from 9 percent to 25 percent. About 35 percent of the employees over forty believe they will have responsibility for an elder in this time frame.

7

Elder-Care Solutions

INTEREST in elder care is growing in the corporate sector. This interest stems not from corporations' altruism but from their "enlightened self-interest." Several years ago, fewer than ten companies offered elder-care benefits such as financial assistance, family leave, and adult day health care, according to Angela Heath of the American Association of Retired Persons. Today, she says, 20 percent of corporations with a thousand or more employees offer some type of elder-care assistance. Nevertheless, much of this assistance consists of nothing more than flex-time.

Approximately 13.5 million people are spouses or children of disabled elders and, therefore, have potential responsibility for their care; one out of five are primary caregivers. Almost two-million women are part of the sandwich generation, according to Stone. While child care in most cases consumes eighteen years of an employee's life, elder care could last twice that long, according to the Select Committee's 1987 report, *Exploding the Myths: Caregiving in America.*

To fully understand the complexity of caring for the elderly and the crisis in the current state of care, one has only to peek into the plethora of reports and articles that have recently appeared on the subject.

Randy Rieland noted that while care of the elderly is not a new concept, some "baby-boomers" are having a hard time with it. Their aging parents remind them that the Fountain of Youth that television commercials try to portray really does not exist, which reminds them of their own mortality. In addition, because many baby-boomers have children late, they find themselves loaded down with simultaneous responsibilities of caring for aging parents and for their own children. Finally, baby-boomers were brought up in the "me" generation, characterized by detachment and self-indulgence.[1]

In 1988, the U.S. Senate Special Committee on Aging issued a report entitled *Adult Day Health Care: A Vital Component of Long Term Care*, which pointed out that family-caregivers provide 80 percent of all care to the elderly. This informal caregiving network has been the single most important factor in preventing the institutionalization of senior citizens. The report went on to say that "caregiver burnout, not the physical and health status of the older person is the most significant factor in nursing home placement." Nursing home care is the "choice of last resort" for many families, the most obvious reason being the financial burden. Inadequate care is another reason. As Katherine Bishop pointed out in the *New York Times*, more than 1.5-million nursing home residents are over medicated. Forty percent of the patients who have no signs of mental illness are being given drugs for acute mental problems.[2]

Unfortunately, for those elderly who do have mental health problems, the possibility of getting help at a reasonable cost is almost nonexistent. Julie Johnson wrote in the *Times*,

> "While nearly 7 million elderly need some type of mental health assistance, only a few are receiving that help," says Senator John D. Rockefeller IV. He has introduced a bill to extend medical reimbursement to psychologists. Currently, federal money is only available to pay for psychiatrists and other medical doctors. "Without appropriate care, many seniors are forced to live unhappy, confused or institutionalized lives."[3]

Improperly administered medication is also causing great concern to family members of the elderly. The *Philadelphia Inquirer* called the mismedication of American seniors the "nation's other drug problem." The article gives some alarming statistics: two-million older Americans are addicted to or at risk of addiction to tranquilizers. More elderly die from drug overdoses than any other segment of the population. Americans over sixty account for 51 percent of drug deaths, even though they comprise only 17 percent of the population.[4]

Too much medicine is not the only health problem for the elderly. Too little nutrition can also cause severe impairment. As Marian Burros pointed out in the *New York Times*, studies have shown that a lack of vitamin B_{12} and folic acid may lead to a decline in memory, numbness, and tingling in the lower extremities. Replacing these vitamins has been shown to be helpful.[5]

Health insurance is another problem that the elderly population and their caregivers face. Tens of millions of Americans under 65 are without any health insurance or are grossly under-insured. Even those fortunate enough to have insurance find that their insurance plans do not cover long-term care, but only acute care. AARP has pointed out that the costs of nursing homes alone typically run from $20,000 to $25,000 a year. These costs are not covered by most medical plans or by Medicaid unless the patient has exhausted all other assets. Medicare pays for skilled nursing care only for a limited number of days, with strict eligibility requirements. The elderly person can easily become impoverished the first year of nursing care. This financial picture is probably the most frightening aspect of elder care in the United States today.

What Companies Are Doing

While more than four-thousand companies are offering their employees some form of child-care assistance, a much smaller number are assisting their employees with elder-care needs.

The New York Business Group on Health (NYBGH) has been tracking the corporate response to employee caregivers. A NYBGH survey revealed that while companies may not have a specific policy to address caregiving, many companies have informal ways of supporting caregivers. The most frequently cited activities were personnel policies such as flex-time and information provided through caregiver fairs, pamphlets, and so on.

In a 1989 study, *Fortune* magazine and John Hancock

looked at how corporate executives are helping their employees meet their elder-care needs. The highest percentage of executives indicated that they give their employees personal days to handle emergencies and other elder-care responsibilities (67 percent). Sixty-three percent offer health benefits for other family members, 61 percent offer unpaid leaves of absence, while 60 percent allow sick days to be used for elder care. But far fewer companies offer benefits *directly* related to elder care. For example, only 26 percent offer information and referral for elder care, 24 percent offer employee newsletters focusing on elder-care problems, 17 percent offer employees seminars on elder-care issues, 13 percent offer elder-care management coordinators, 2 percent offer elder-care hotlines, 2 percent offer adult day-care assistance plans, and 1 percent offer subsidies or vouchers to purchase elder-care services.[6] Most of these solutions are merely informational; they do not provide the direct benefits—such as adult day health care, flex-time, and financial help—that employees need.

The *Fortune*/Hancock study also examined what companies are considering offering. Eighteen percent of the corporate executives are studying flexible benefit plans with DCAPs; 16 percent are considering offering information and referral services; and 13 percent are interested in helping out through employee newsletters and seminars.[7]

The National Association of State Units on Aging compiled examples of corporate elder-care programs. Here is a partial list of programs:

- PepsiCo developed an extensive elder-care resource guide, offers workshops, and has developed a reserve account to pay for health and nursing care.
- Travelers Insurance conducts caregiver fairs and lunch-time seminars. It encourages caregivers' support groups and provides counselling on family issues.
- Pitney Bowes, Ciba Geigy, and Mobil Oil provide informational forums on aging, disorders, and services on an ongoing basis. Pitney Bowes also has a flexible leave policy for family emergencies; where appropriate, employees can

change their work shifts as needed to deal with family issues.

- IBM has developed a nationwide elder-care consultation and referral service. (We will discuss this in greater detail later in this chapter.) IBM has also introduced an extremely creative and generous leave-of-absence policy that can be used to deal with family-care problems.
- Ford and General Motors are testing long-term care insurance for at-home custodial care of employees or retirees.
- Stride Rite is expanding its child-care center to accept elderly people, creating an intergenerational day-care center. (We will also look at this option later in the chapter.)[8]
- Proctor and Gamble has the Flexcomp program, a cafeteria-style benefit program that reimburses employees for various elderly-dependent, in-home, and all-day care expenses.
- Campbell Soup has a leave policy that allows workers up to three months off within a two-year period to care for seriously ill family members. The company continues medical and health benefits through this time. It also guarantees employees the same or comparable job when they return.

My Research

In my 1988 survey, 64 percent of the employees agreed or strongly agreed that their company should actively assist employees with their elderly-dependent-care needs. The data show broad employee support for this, from 45 percent of married men with grown children to 80 percent of unmarried women who are living with someone and have children under age eighteen. In my 1989 study, 79 percent of the employees agreed that their company should support elder care.

Company involvement is important for elderly care as well as child care—even more so if they are old. (white female occupational worker)

Be proactive, and be progressive. We are an aging society; the baby-boomers will soon be senior-boomers. (white male middle-level manager)

How come you're more interested in the problems of child care than elders? Is this discrimination? (white female lower-level manager)

What Employees Say They Need

The solutions cited as most useful by the 1989 survey participants who have elder-care responsibilities are flexible work options (31 percent), adult day health care centers (23 percent), and various forms of financial assistance (22 percent). These three solutions are the same three cited for child-care problems. The least useful solutions for adult-dependent-care problems are support groups (15 percent) and work options, such as working part-time and job sharing, that would reduce income. Table 7–1 depicts the most useful solutions.

A lot of elderly are on fixed income. It'd be nice if the elderly could be included for benefits as family, like husband and wife. (white male occupational worker)

While taking care of my eighty-eight-year-old grandmother, I was able to work a night shift for six months. I was home during the day and worked evenings. It would be useful if hours were flexible. (white female occupational worker)

Consulting help for the elderly should be available. These issues are overwhelming. (white female occupational worker)

The company should support adult day-care centers just as it does child-care centers. Where is the equity? (white male lower-level manager)

Flex-time or work at home would help me with my father's medical needs. (black female occupational worker)

The cost of caring for my parents is straining our budget and life. A flexible benefit package or long-term care insurance would be most appreciated. (white female middle-level manager)

Adult Day-Health Care

Interestingly, many of my respondents prefer a solution that is just beginning to be recognized as a way to prevent institu-

Table 7-1

MOST USEFUL SOLUTIONS TO ADULT-DEPENDENT-CARE
PROBLEMS

(N = Percent who selected each solution.)

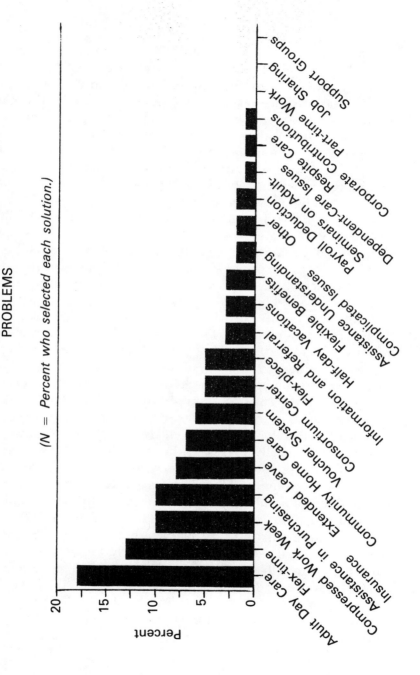

tionalization of the elderly while offering the caregiver some
respite from her or his responsibilities—adult day care. Says
the National Institute of Adult Day Care, such centers provide the elderly with medical and social support while giving
the caretaker some respite. The centers only take the elderly
for a period under twenty-four hours, giving the status of a
day-care center rather than a nursing home.

Seventy-five thousand elderly Americans, many in their
eighties and nineties, attend adult day-health care. Currently
there are approximately fourteen-hundred centers across the
country, an increase from only a dozen centers in the late
1960s. The growth of adult day-health care can be attributed
to the basic recognition among social service providers in both
the community and the government that institutionalization is
often an inappropriate or premature alternative provided at
great financial and emotional cost to the family and the community.

Adult day-health care is generally a less expensive option
than nursing-home care. The average cost of adult day-health
care is $30 to $40 per day, while intermediate nursing-care
facilities average $2,000 per month. It is important to recog-
nize the difference in the delivery of these services when
comparing their costs. Nursing-home care can be primarily a
custodial service that includes room, food, and supportive
services over a 24-hour period. In comparison, adult day-
health care typically shares in the provision of caregiving and
support services to the frail elderly with the family and other
community resources. Therefore, it is difficult to compare the
direct costs of adult day-health care with the comprehensive
costs included in nursing-home charges. However, the therapeutic component of adult day-health care, which greatly enhances the quality of life for the elderly individual and their
family, is generally considered to be its primary value.

Furthermore, adult day-health care centers have been
shown to prevent further medical problems by providing a
caring atmosphere and support staff who monitor and super-
vise the senior's health. This may, in the long run, lower the
costs of care for the elderly by preventing or delaying hospitalization and institutionalization.

Adult day-health care, according to testimony given by Representative Leon Panetta of California before a Senate committee on aging, can

> reduce the incidence of acute illness through ongoing monitoring of symptoms and preventative health care, and has been successful in avoiding or delaying institutionalization. In addition, clients, many of whom live alone, receive the vital psychological benefits of mental and social stimulation not available to them when confined to the home. He noted that a study of adult day-health care centers in California found that "87 percent of seniors who participated in the program maintained or improved their level of functioning."[9]

Adult day-health care has a positive effect on caregivers' ability to cope with their responsibilities. Some of the areas of family functioning most helped by the elderly member's participation in adult day-health care are:[10]

- attending to the older person's needs (83 percent)
- attending to their own needs (72 percent)
- doing household chores (64 percent)
- enjoying being with family (60 percent)
- doing things with family (54 percent)
- making needed purchases (52 percent)
- being with friends occasionally and engaging in recreation outside the home (49 percent each)

The verbal responses to open-ended questions in Zimmerman's study clarify the meaning of her statistics. One caregiver said that adult day care gave her "freedom from her constantly bugging me—I don't have to be her only friend." This type of response was common. Many caregivers appreciate adult day-health day care for expanding the social horizons of the elderly person, which allows the caregiver time to take care of his or her personal needs. As a result of the program, feelings toward the elderly person generally improved; one participant said, "I like her better as a person—

she is more interesting." Another elaborated: "I used to say 'I might as well be alone,' but now we talk. He talks to the kids." One caregiver's terse comment—"it has helped me tolerate her"—shows how strained caregiver/caregivee relationships can become without relief. It also shows how helpful adult day-health care can be in easing strains in those relationships.

Another added benefit of the program was the reduction of intrafamilial stress. Because caregivers were no longer as dependent upon other family members for help in caring for the older person, their relations with other family members improved. Many commented that they were more relaxed. "I no longer fly off the handle with them from holding it in with her," one person said.[11]

One elderly man who attends adult day-health care testified before the Senate Aging Committee about his experiences:

> The center picks me up at my door and brings me home. At the center, we do many different things. We have competitive sports we can play like bowling, golf, volleyball, football and baseball. That doesn't mean the center is merely a social club or recreational club for the elderly. It is much more than that. It is exactly what the name implies with the emphasis on care.[12]

SENIOR CARE CENTERS

Let's look at one company that is trying to address the adult day-health care issue. Senior Care Centers of America is a recently established company whose goal is to provide a timely, creative, and cost-effective solution to the problem of caring for the frail elderly. The company's philosophy is that the elderly and their families should have access to a high-quality adult day-health program that will allow the elderly to maintain a dignified existence, avoid unnecessary institutionalization, and remain in the home setting as long as possible.

Senior Care Centers owns and manages adult day-health care centers in several states throughout the country. These centers provide a comfortable, homelike atmosphere in which guests receive daily supervision, individualized assessment and care plans, health services, hot meals and snacks, transportation, therapeutic and recreational activities, and social interaction. The centers also provide counseling, guidance, and information to assist the caregivers in finding the appropriate services to meet their needs.

Senior Care Centers directly addresses the needs of the employed caregiving population by providing an accessible, secure environment for the frail elderly during working hours. The centers bridge the gap between full-time care by family members and long-term institutionalization, thus making a positive difference in the lives of dependent adults and their families.

According to Robert Willis, chairperson and chief executive officer of Senior Care Centers,

> Adult day-health care has been the step-child of long-term care for years: we intend to legitimize the concept, educate the market and establish adult day-health care as an integral part of the long-term care continuum. The key to our business is not only serving the elderly, but addressing the needs of the care-givers as well.

Senior Care Centers are led by experienced health-care-management professionals who are attuned to the inherent problems in health-care systems. The centers are staffed with a multidisciplinary team, including a registered nurse, a social worker, and activities therapists. This team works closely with the medical director of the center and the guest's own personal physician to ensure quality care. A corporate quality assurance program monitors staff performance, program outcomes, and client satisfaction.

A unique aspect of Senior Care Centers' approach is that many of the centers are affiliated with hospitals and health-care systems. Hospitals are aggressively directing their services to the elderly population because that population represents the only real growth market in demand for hospital services. Thus, hospitals are natural partners in providing day-health care services to the elderly.

Senior Care Centers also operates free-standing centers in the community that serve both private paying and publicly funded patients. The need for adult day-health care is common to all socioeconomic groups.

Senior Care Centers is planning to introduce an innovative overnight respite option as part of its service to families with caregiving responsibilities. Caregivers can employ this option in order to plan a vacation, travel for business purposes, or when they simply need a break from the physical and emotional demands of caregiving. The overnight respite option will be implemented as a pilot program through an in-home care program for guests of the adult day-health program. As the demand for this service grows, Senior Care Centers may eventually provide overnight respite on-site at some facilities.

Senior Care Centers helped Mary S., who had suffered a series of strokes and could no longer live independently. Her children did not want to place her in a nursing home, but they all had work or family responsibilities that made it very difficult for them to provide full-time care for their mother. Private-duty nurses were too costly, and home health aides did not provide the full-time supervision that she needed. The family was referred to Senior Care Centers by the hospital discharge planner. Now Mary is picked up every morning and taken to the center, where she participates in group activities and exercise, maintains ongoing social relationships, and has her health monitored daily by a registered nurse.

Rose M. discovered Senior Care Centers two years ago, when her husband, Walt, was diagnosed with Alzheimer's disease. Walt spends three days a week at the center, which allows Rose to work part-time and enjoy the community and volunteer activities in which she has participated for years.

Last year, Jim and Karen F. were faced with a major family crisis. Jim's mother was the caregiver for their five- and eight-year-old daughters. This arrangement enabled both Jim and Karen to work without concern for their daughters—until Jim's mother fell and broke her hip. Not only did Jim and Karen lose their sole child-care provider, they had to find care for Jim's mother while she recuperated.

Senior Care Centers offered Jim's mother a safe environment during the day and occasionally overnight and has allowed Jim and his wife to regain control of their personal and work lives.

A PUBLIC-PRIVATE PARTNERSHIP

Awareness is increasing in governmental circles that adult day-health care centers are valuable as a cost-saving alternative to nursing-home care and professional in-home care. The clearest reflection of this increased recognition is the continuing efforts of legislators and policymakers to provide for financial support and reimbursement for these programs. The financial impact of adult day-health care on the family and the community has been greatly reduced through the responsiveness of some states, which provide for the reimbursement of adult day-health care through public-funding sources such as Medicaid waiver programs (Title XIX), Social Service Block Grants (Title XX) and Older American's Act monies (Title III).

Another important source of reimbursement and support for adult day-health care comes from the efforts of public charitable and private philanthropic organizations. On Lok, for example, is a nonprofit, community-based, long-term care program that gives the frail elderly a way to continue living in the familiar surroundings of their community. It opened its first adult day-health care center in San Francisco in 1972. Working with teams consisting of health-care professionals, families, friends, and volunteers, On Lok helps about three hundred elderly remain as independent as possible. On Lok provides physical and occupational therapy and in-home training. It develops networks to assist those who are unable to live as independently as they would like. The On Lok team even modifies the participants' homes to make them safe and more accessible to seniors with limitations.

On Lok is unique in that the government and the private sector join forces to pilot a consolidated model for long-term care, like an HMO organization. In this consolidated model, On Lok provides a comprehensive continuum of care that includes both social and medical services. Through the efforts of On Lok and the Health Care Financing Administration, Congress has permitted special waivers of traditional Medicare and Medicaid rules. Under these waivers, On Lok assumes full financial risk for all health and social services. Reimbursement for client care from public or private sources remains constant, regardless of the client's fluctuating health status, and regardless of whether it is chronic or acute.

On Lok is one of the most successful examples of a public-private partnership. The program has been achieved through the pooled efforts by a variety of government entities such as the Administration on Aging, The Office of Human Development Services, and the Health Care Financing Administration; state and federal legislators as well as private nonprofits such as Robert Wood Johnson. In 1987 grants from the Robert Wood Johnson and John A. Hartford Foundations and an expansion of the Medicare and Medicaid waivers by Congress and the Health Care Financing Administration permitted the On Lok model to be replicated in ten sites across the country under the Program of All-Inclusive Care for the Elderly. Such cooperative efforts between the public, private, and professional sectors will be necessary if the United States is to successfully deal with the high cost of and growing demand for elder care.

INTERGENERATIONAL CARE

A brand-new concept in adult day-health care is intergenerational day care, which provides dual programming for both child care and adult care. The idea is to bring together the young and the old in programs that serve the needs of both generations. This solution is particularly valuable to the working men and women of the sandwich generation, who are squeezed between finding care for their children and finding care for their aging parents. In an article in *Pediatric Nursing*, Catharine Kopac and Deborah Price wrote,

> The elderly develop feelings of usefulness as they realize their value to the children; in turn, the children feel valued as they reach out, understand, and encourage the elderly. In conclu-

sion, they wrote, "The physical and mental health of older persons often improves as the result of new relationships with children."[13]

Recognizing a trend that has come of age, the National Council on Aging has created a division of intergenerational care to provide information and direction in developing these programs. Employers can develop an intergenerational program under a variety of legal and financial arrangements such as company owned and operated, independent contractor owned and operated, cooperatively owned by employees, or owned and operated by a separate nonprofit or for-profit entity. Stride Rite will become one of the first employers to open a company-owned-and-operated intergenerational center.

A successful intergenerational program must maintain separate programs for children and adults. Experts suggest that the time the young children and adults spend together should be about two to three hours a day.

Financial Assistance

Since very few communities and even fewer companies make available adult day-health care services, many families must continue to rely on the existing options of in-home-care nurses, nursing homes, and in the case of illness, hospitalization. These solutions are costly and can bankrupt both the elderly person and the caregiver. The House Select Committee on Aging wrote: "According to the committee staff analysis, *7 in 10 elderly living alone* find their income spent down to the federal poverty level after *only 13 weeks* in a nursing home, over 90 percent of these elderly are impoverished."[14]

MEDICARE AND MEDICAID

Government health care includes Medicare, the federal health-insurance fund for all citizens over sixty-five. It has two parts: hospital insurance (Part A), which is automatic, and supplementary medical insurance (Part B), which covers physician and other services, is voluntary, and requires the payment of a monthly premium. Except in a few pilot studies, Medicare is not intended to pay for long-term care or for private-duty nursing. It certainly does not cover social services, which are the most common needs that the frail elderly have.

The other major governmental health-care program is Medicaid, which provides health benefits primarily for the poor and the medically needy. Medicaid is funded jointly by the federal and state governments and administered by individual states. The Medicaid picture for the elderly and their families is also bleak. Because the program is means-tested under current laws, the elderly become eligible for Medicaid benefits only after they have depleted most of their assets and savings. Nursing-home care is expensive and is thus the largest component of Medicaid benefits, accounting for more than one-half of all expenditures.

One solution now being proposed is that states require adult children to pay at least part of nursing home costs, an option the states have because of a 1983 change in federal regulations.

In addition to Medicaid and Medicare, public funding for the elderly is available through Social Service block grants, the Older Americans Act, and food programs.

TAX BENEFITS

Recognizing the problems that employees have with dependent care, the federal government has made a variety of *tax benefits* available to employers for employees. The Economic Recovery Act of 1981 provided tax incentives for employer-sponsored dependent-care benefits. Many states are also implementing programs to enhance tax incentives for employees. At present, the federal government seems to be shifting its emphasis away from direct subsidies and support toward an emphasis on tax credits for caregivers and tax incentives for employers. This trend is expected to continue. While these tax incentives can be viewed as a positive step there are many restrictions when it comes to elder care.

- The employee must provide more than 50 percent of the funds necessary to care for the elderly person.
- The elderly person must be physically or mentally incapable of self-care.
- Both the employee and the spouse must be working or actively looking for employment. Full-time students are an exception.
- In order to qualify for away-from-home care, the dependent must spend at least eight hours in the home of the employee.

The following is a list of provisions set forth by the IRS for the implementation of flexible benefits:

- *Dependent-Care Assistance Program (DCAP).* Employer-provided dependent-care benefits—such as direct payments, services, or vouchers—are sheltered from taxation as part of an employee's gross income. DCAPs must satisfy certain requirements regarding participant eligibility, payments, and notification. Employers receive a tax credit for implementing such programs. The programs may be funded through employer contributions, salary-reduction plans, or both.

- *The Comprehensive Cafeteria Plan.* This plan was created by section 125 of the IRS Code (1978 Revenue Act), allowing employers to offer a choice in benefits. Employees receive a core set of benefits and the use of flexible credits to purchase more of the core benefits or optional benefits that are either taxable or nontaxable. A DCAP may be, but is not required to be, one of the benefits offered in a Comprehensive Cafeteria Plan.

- *Flexible-Spending Account/Salary-Reduction Plan.* This plan allows employees to make a pretax contribution to the flexible-spending account of up to $5,000, which reduces the amount of salary subject to income and social security tax. Employees must determine at the beginning of each year the amount of salary reduction they wish to contribute to this spending option, and they must forfeit any spending dollars unused at year end. These leftover funds become available to the employer for program management.

Another tax option is the *Dependent Care Tax Credit for Workers*, which can cover expenses not covered by a DCAP. Eligibility is the same as for DCAPs. The maximum amount of the deductible under the Dependent Care Tax Credit is $2,400 for one dependent and $4,800 for more than one. Since the Dependent Care Tax Credit is 30 percent for incomes under $10,000 and gradually decreases to 20 percent for incomes over $28,000, the credit is generally more beneficial for low-income employees, while a flexible spending account tends to benefit those with higher incomes.

Even with these tax options and the current government programs, public assistance will still not meet the needs of our elderly population for long-term care. Several bills have been introduced in Congress to rectify this situation, but in the meantime, this funding gap will have to be filled by the private sector.

MEDIGAP

Medigap, or supplemental health insurance, does not generally cover additional services that are unpaid by Medicare or Medicaid. Rather, it pays the costs for services unpaid by Medicare, such as hospital deductibles and physician copayments. Some plans may pay for drugs or services, such as private-duty nurses. The AARP, in an excellent publication, has cautioned about medigap insurance. They noted that medigap does not cover chronic ailments, only acute diseases, which means most elderly people aren't covered. The Alzheimer's victim, the person suffering from arthritis, stroke victims, and people losing their eyesight due to diabetes are not typically covered under this plan.[15]

LONG-TERM-CARE INSURANCE

One of the newest elder-care benefits being offered by some employers is long-term-care insurance. These policies are designed to cover nursing homes, adult day care, personal care, medical care, in-home care, and help with chores. This benefit would go a long way toward meeting the needs of the estimated millions of Americans who are at risk for the cost of long-term care.

But AARP has also cautioned buyers to beware before buying long-term-care insurance. The policies vary greatly in what they cover, such as the amount of daily benefits, restrictions, or lack of restrictions prior to institutionalization; length of benefits; waiting or elimination periods; preexisting health conditions; types of facilities; the excluded coverage; the cost of the policy; and the age at which one can obtain the policy. AARP concluded, "To adequately protect a person from long-term care expenses, insurance policies should be flexible and provide protection for all levels of nursing home care and for care in the home without severe restrictions."[16]

Financial planners, too, caution that these plans are not panaceas. They are expensive, and they often carry riders that require persons to undergo medical exams before they are eligible. A senior may be rejected because of a prior condition. And inflation can reduce the level of coverage over the years.

In the John Hancock/*Fortune* magazine study, 8 percent of corporate executives reported that their companies currently offer long-term-care coverage. This statistic may be misleadingly high, however, because only a handful of companies across the country are actually offering real long-term-care insurance. The researchers believe that the corporate executives were confusing medical-care benefits with this new type of insurance for the chronically ill. But when asked if they were considering long-term-care insurance, 18 percent responded positively.[17]

The Ford Motor Company is already offering long-term-care insurance. On April 1, 1989, sixty-six hundred active and retired employees became eligible for a program in which Ford pays the costs of nonmedical custodial care at home or in a nursing home. The program particularly benefits the victims of Alzheimer's disease. It provides help with the costs of activities of daily living such as eating, bathing, dressing, preparing meals, and house cleaning. Employees of several other large companies, including Procter and Gamble, American Express, and General Foods, can also purchase long-term-care insurance at special group rates.

In addition to the solutions discussed in detail here, several of the financial options for child care discussed in chapter 5 can be easily adapted to people with elder-care needs. These are corporate discounts, vouchers, flexible benefits, and corporate in-kind services.

Flexible Work Options

One of the biggest problems that caregivers face is finding the time to take care of such things as their elderly person's doctor visits, insurance problems, and financial problems— problems that generally must be dealt with during the day. Emergencies can arise anytime, so flexible work options, such as those discussed in chapter 5, are very helpful. These options include a compressed work week, flex-time, half-day vacations, job sharing, and part-time work. Remember that few employees are interested in job sharing or part-time work because it lessens their pay. (For a detailed look at each of these solutions, see appendix.)

Consultation and Referral

Like other aspects of elder care, the possible sources of financial support are complex, and the employee must determine which ones he or she is eligible for. This problem often confuses the caregiver. Caring for the elderly has multifaceted solutions. Consultation and referral may be useful to employees to help sort through the complex types of services available. (While R&R, I&R, and C&R supposedly are different, as of this date those distinctions are not significant.)

There are basically two consultation and referral systems in this country: the public, nonprofit system (which is forty years old and free to all Americans) and the newly emerging private, for-profit system.

The public system was mandated by the Older Americans Act, and is funded, in part, by the U.S. Administration on Aging. Members of this network include 57 state units on aging, 672 area agencies on aging, 721 state and local advisory councils, and thousands of service providers at the community level (see figure 7–2).

In the past few years, thirty-two states have implemented "800" numbers at the state level, and twenty-eight states now offer consultation and referral services on such issues as finding appropriate care, elder abuse, nursing home complaints, Alzheimer's disease, and filling out Medicare forms. But former U.S. Commissioner Carol Fraser-Fisk, now editor of *Aging Network News*, points out that this network is limited because of lack of adequate funding, and because there are no standards for quality. For instance, if a person seeking information calls the public agency, he or she may get lucky and reach a professional, or he or she may reach a volunteer with little knowledge about elder care. Fraser-Fisk believes the public I&R system should be upgraded and that the staff should meet specific standards to minimize confusion and increase its efficiency and effectiveness.

To add to the confusion, a number of private, for-profit companies have sprung up, ostensibly to assist corporate employees with elder-care I&R needs. One of the first companies to use a private elder-care R&R service was IBM. The computer giant set up a private referral service for its 220,000 employees through Work/Family Directions. IBM decided to go this route because it felt that one contractor would be able to guarantee some degree of standardized responses.

In the first year, nine-thousand employees used the service, which provides general information on aging and specific details about elder-care programs in the senior's hometown. While the costs cannot be confirmed, several experts in the elder-care field believe that IBM spends over $2 million per year on this I&R service.

Companies such as IBM like this approach because it offers the employees an array of solutions, from which they can personally choose the one that is most appropriate. But it has problems; one is that most for-profit companies heavily rely

FIGURE 7–2. THE NATIONAL AGING SERVICE NETWORK

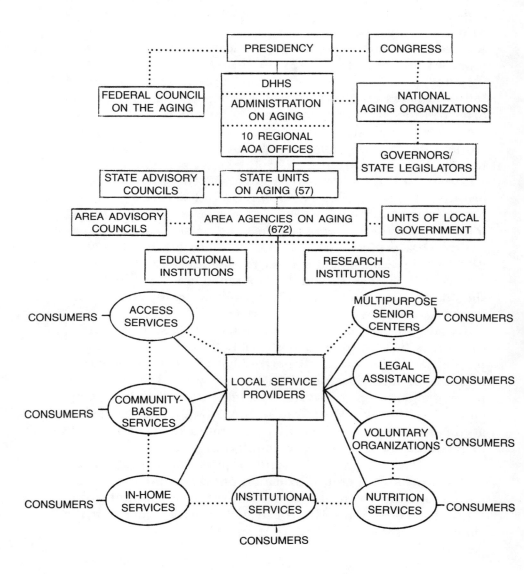

Source: *An Orientation to the Older Americans Act*, Revised Edition, National Association of State Units on Aging, Washington, D.C., 1985.

upon the existing public information and referral system to assist corporate clients. Former U.S. Commissioner Fisk doesn't believe the private resource and referral companies enhance the quality of the public system. The National Association of State Units of Aging chimes in on the criticism: "The private companies only contribute to the confusion of an already fragmented I&R system."

In an ongoing discussion with the Administration on Aging, some questions have been raised about the legality of area agencies on aging (AAAs) contracting to work for private, for-profit R&R companies.

John E. Hansan, publisher of *Aging Network News*, has pointed out some of the serious deficiencies of elder-care I&R services, calling the I&R specialists simply "brokers between the employer and what is already available in the community. The elder care contractor is paid to provide information and materials about local services and programs available to help older persons, many of them organized and funded by State and Area Agencies on Aging." Hansan wrote that access to this information could be improved by an infusion of money into the public programs and more education among corporations. He doesn't believe we should reinvent the wheel by creating a private I&R system.[18]

AAA staffers are now receiving numerous calls, and I&R is adding to the already-long waiting lists of elderly who need assistance. The staffers argue that for I&R to be an effective elder-care solution, more money should be spent in increasing available services.

Elder-Care Management

Given the high cost of I&R services (over $2 million for IBM), this money might be better spent on upgrading the public system and/or on helping to subsidize the cost to employees of more comprehensive private counseling services specializing in geriatric care, such as Aging Network Services (ANSER).

ANSER was established in 1982 to provide quality, personalized attention to families with older relatives in need of assistance. As the oldest national geriatric-care-management network in the country, ANSER pioneered long-distance care-giving for families living apart. The company is currently a leader in care management.

ANSER provides a comprehensive set of services that are available nationwide to employee caregivers and their elderly parents. It's four discreet kinds of *caregiver services* provide support to individuals.

- Telephone *consultation* makes available, toll free, ANSER's skilled counselors, who assist employees in identifying care-giving needs and supplying elder-care information.
- Specific *resource referral information* identifies sources for the broad range of services, from homemakers to nursing homes to physicians, that may be needed by older persons in their own hometown.
- The *assessment and care plan* is for parents of employees regarding their current functioning. This multidimensional evaluation identifies service needs and recommends ways to address them with the goal of maintaining the parent's independent functioning.
- Continuing *care management* is a comprehensive service designed especially to meet the needs of families with aging parents and adult children living apart. This service continually updates its care plan. The local ANSER affiliate links the older person to necessary services, taking into account a supportive environment and cost factors. Affiliates maintain close touch with families through this process.

These four caregiver programs represent a range of services, from the least to the most intensive. They cover the range of needs of family caregivers, helping with questions such as whether to place a parent in a nursing home or whether to move a parent into the home of an adult child. Such issues require the involvement of a professional counselor. Information and referral services fall short of providing these types of answers.

A unique element of the ANSER service is its national network, a membership organization of approximately two-hundred-fifty geriatric-specialty social workers in all parts of the country. Network members are highly qualified and trained to provide assessments and care-management services as well as referrals for elder-care services. All are MSW social workers, with state professional licenses (or Academy of Certified Social Workers licenses if their state does not have state licensing). They have postgraduate clinical experience with older persons. They are available for twenty-four hour service or arrange for professional coverage when they are unavailable. Applicants for membership go through a standardized screening process, including submission of written credentials and a personal telephone interview.

Value for the dollar invested is a major advantage of ANSER's services. The full range of its services is available to the employer for a price comparable to that offered by I&R vendors. I&R vendors say their services are inexpensive but they are limited. With I&R, the caller still has to contact and select a source, often from a distance, and pay out of pocket for those services. Such an approach misses the mark for an employee caregiver who is either facing a crisis and needs immediate help or is caring for an elderly person with deteriorating health. For an equivalent price, you get much more than access to information or sources of service from ANSER.

To summarize, for a price comparable to that of a simple I&R service, ANSER can structure an elder-care program, including professional counseling and asessment, that directly addresses employees' needs to respond to crises and to deal with the complex social and health-care problems of caring for elderly parents. ANSER's value both to the employee and to the employer is enhanced by its ability to target resources and services more effectively and directly to solve elder-care problems.

ANSER services can be financed in a variety of ways, including employer-paid and employee-copaid options. Its services can be combined with a company's existing EAP program and/or corporate health units, or it can stand alone and be accessed by its nationwide toll-free number.

Another elder-care management organization worth mentioning is Pathfinders/Eldercare. It provides a centralized system of elder-care service. In contrast, most other elder-care management organizations subcontract to agencies or individuals for services.

There are many advantages to providing services from a centralized location rather than subcontracting them. For one thing, there is a greater consistency and uniformity of the quality of the services delivered. For another, there is greater quality control. In addition, professional standards and qualifications are maintained because of close supervision. By eliminating both layers of administration and subcontracting, Pathfinders/Eldercare is also cost effective.

Pathfinders provides employees with toll-free access to a counselor. These counselors are master's level social workers with extensive knowledge of community resources for the elderly. The counselor develops an action plan and then aggressively researches available and affordable services anywhere in the United States. The counselor continues to follow the case until the employee feels the problem has been resolved. The personalized service includes counseling, consumer education, and aggressive resource finding.

The professionally trained counselors are also available to help with questions about health, living arrangements, legal and financial issues, entitlements, home care, and nursing-home placement, to name a few. As part of its program, Pathfinders/Eldercare also offers hour-long workshops and maintains a library of videos for distribution to employees and field staff.

The elder-care referral services are paid for by the company. The employee or elderly relative pay only for the elder-care program or provider they select. From the standpoint of management, Pathfinders is beneficial because it keeps employees off the telephone. Phone calling is done by Pathfinders.

Let's look at a typical case to see how Pathfinders works:

An employee contacted Pathfinders/Eldercare through its toll-free number. The employee had recently returned from a visit to Miami Beach, Florida, where her mother, who is suffering from Alzheimer's Disease, lives. She was very concerned about her mother's increasing forgetfulness, her verbally abusive behavior, and her inability to shop, cook, and take care of herself. To make matters worse, her mother continued to drive and refuse all help.

When the employee's initial call was received, a counselor was assigned who listened sensitively to what the employee said, clarified the needs of both the mother and the employee, and identified possible types of care.

Once a plan of action was developed, the counselor researched available resources in the area where the mother lived. The counselor telephoned each resource to be certain of its appropriateness and affordability. The employee was telephoned and given the names of agencies, the people to call, and their telephone numbers. The counselor also discussed with the employee the pros and cons of each referral, and the criteria for selecting a particular program or provider, including the financial aspect. In addition, written material related to Alzheimer's disease was sent to the employee. The employee was also referred to an Alzheimer's support group.

The counselor continued to maintain contact with the employee until there was a satisfactory resolution of the problem. As the condition of the employee's mother deteriorated, the employee touched base with the counselor to discuss the situation and explore alternative solutions.

As corporate America comes to understand the complexity of elder care, services like ANSER and Pathfinders/Eldercare will be a crucial part of elder-care packages.

Summary

It is critical to maintain an awareness of the difference between the problems of elder care and the problems of child care so that one solution is not considered the solution to all dependent-care problems. For example, many corporations that offer resource and referral (R&R) for child care and find it successful are also offering R&R for elder care.

But a public system of information and referral exists, administered by the Older Americans Act. The dollars spent on the elder-care R&R could be used more effectively either by funding the public system or by assisting employees with financing more in-depth professional consultation services. This could ultimately save the caregiving employee money, time, and trouble, especially the long-distance caregiver.

The federal government, in cooperation with NASUA (The National Association of State Units on Aging) and the State of Illinois Department on Aging, has recently installed Elderlink, a toll-free system to assist caregivers living outside of Illinois to obtain services for elderly family members living within the state. The program will match information, referral, and support services for elderly relatives. In addition, Elderlink will contact a local agency that will visit with the elderly family member, do an assessment of his or her needs, determine eligibility for benefits, and help arrange services. For Illinois residents who have elderly reponsibilities living in other states, Elderlink will assist the caregiver in plugging into the state's network of services for older people. There are hopes that the Elderlink program will be implemented on a national level.

Corporations also need to recognize that the dependent-care industry is fragmented. Nationally, elder care has been regulated by the mandates of the Older Americans Act, but there are numerous players in both the public and private sectors, and the quality and range of services vary greatly from location to location.

In order to assist corporations in understanding many of the confusing aspects of elder care, I strongly urge them to contact NASUA, which represents the fifty-seven states and territorial government agencies. The State Units on Aging are responsible for planning and coordinating statewide systems of community-based services for the elderly. NASUA has the ability to refer employees within a state to the appropriate state agency. For companies with employees in multiple states or with long-distance care needs, NASUA can provide direct access to all state aging systems. The State Units on Aging have the unique capacity to act as liaison for employees. NASUA can currently be contacted by calling (202) 785-0707.

Recognizing that elder-care needs are dynamic, changing, and complex, and recognizing that corporate America is only beginning to address these needs, I conclude with a very general, but crucial suggestion for corporate America: that corporations create a pool of money to be used for family dependent-care assistance.

The money should be used to make needs assessments, to evaluate the services offered by different vendors, to generate recommendations for different approaches, and to fund a number of different trial programs over a two-to-three-year period. After the testing period, companies will be in a better position to select the solutions most appropriate for meeting the elder-care needs of their employees.

Although child care is simpler and more predictable than elder-care, any needs assessment should address family care as a whole rather than address elder care and child care separately. Remember that the number of employees who have dependent-care responsibilities will increase most among the sandwich generation, those with dual responsibilities for child care and elder care.

The demographics, the responses of employees in surveys, and the advice of industry experts all make it clear that elder care is increasingly the responsibility of corporate employees. Corporations must begin addressing these needs while the numbers are small enough. This will allow them time to conduct adequate trials of the many various approaches to elder care so that they can arrive at the correct mix of services and providers in the most cost-effective manner.

The problems of dependent care will not go away. Policy-makers need to take this step *now*.

8

Triple Responsibilities— The Sandwich Generation

WITH the graying of America, more and more people in the workforce have an added responsibility. In addition to doing their jobs and caring for their children, they must care for their aging parents. People who are caught in this triple bind are often referred to as the "sandwich generation." Workers squeezed between caring for their parents and their children are a growing problem for corporate America.

During the next twenty years, as the baby-boomers swell the ranks of the elderly, an increasing number of people will be saddled with triple responsibilities. The baby-boomers' children will become parents. However, the "Boomers" have given birth to fewer children. There will be more older people and fewer younger people to care for them. This increases the likelihood that more workers will be caught in the triple bind. Robyn Stone recently reported that 1.8 million women are already part of the sandwich generation.

In 1988, the House Select Committee on Children, Youth, and Families heard these pertinent observations:

The new generation of caregivers is different from any other in American history. Healthier lifestyles and lifesaving medical technologies have lengthened the lifespan of aging adults as well as children with severe disabilities and chronic illnesses. At the same time, fewer family members are available to provide care. The growing participation of women in the workforce, greater separation of extended families, and the increasing numbers of single-parent families have affected the ability of families to take care of their own.[1]

Another reason that the sandwich generation will grow is that more women are postponing childbirth. A recent government report said that the number of women bearing their first baby while in their thirties has quadrupled since 1970. The Census Bureau noted that women in their thirties account for one-third of new mothers. The birth rate overall is 70 births per 1,000 women and has remained constant over the past decade. The rate for women aged thirty to thirty-four rose to 81.6 births per 1,000, up from 56.4 in 1976. For women aged thirty-five to thirty-nine, the birth rate in 1988 had risen to 33.8 per 1,000 women from only 22.6 in 1976. Obviously, the longer a family waits to have children, the more likely they are to have elders to care for as well.

In 1985, the Travelers Insurance Company studied employees aged thirty to forty in the sandwich generation. Of those who had children under six, 29 percent had triple responsibilities. Of those who had children six to eighteen, 43 percent were sandwiched. In the age group forty to fifty, the figures were 4 percent with children under six and 37 percent with children six to eighteen.[2]

While I will focus on employees with children eighteen and under, it is important to recognize, as Dorothy A. Miller, a professor of social work, points out, that many members of the sandwich generation have adult children for whom they are still responsible along with their aging parents or relatives. Miller noted that just when the middle-aged sandwich generation has reached relative equilibrium in the financial, marital, and personal areas, just when they are ready for relaxation and self-indulgence, they find that their grown children are not quite independent and their parents have moved from autonomy to a degree of dependence.[3]

More generations are living in a single home. The nuclear-family household is giving way to the extended-family household. Researchers attribute this trend to the fact that the elderly are living longer, to the increase in divorces, to the increase in teenage pregnancy rates and to the fact that younger adults are remaining in the family nest longer. Alan L. Otten has discussed the proliferation of extended families living under the same roof, pointing out the negative side of the trend: "In contrast to the idealized image of joyous multigenerational coexistence, many of these extended families are doing all they can to just cope."[4]

Otten cited a number of case studies about families grappling not only with dual but with triple and quadruple caring responsibilities.

A 60-year-old woman, Jeanne Pejeau, has four generations living in her home. They are her 85-year-old mother, who has Alzheimer's disease; her stroke-impaired husband; and two daughters, one who has a 10-year-old son, and another who has a husband and two young daughters. "When you think of a grandmother, you think of someone who adds to your surroundings," Mrs. Pejeau says sadly. "I'm afraid my mother doesn't add anything; she's just a burden."

Kathleen Hoban is a 60-year-old who lives in a small northeast Philadelphia row house. She gives round-the-clock care to her 85-year-old mother, who has Parkinson's disease and a variety of other physical problems that keep her confined to bed. "There are days when I could put my fist through the wall," Mrs. Hoban says. In addition to caring for her mother, she frequently babysits her 3 grandchildren, because her son is separated from his wife.

Despite this problem, our more basic analysis here is of employee caregivers who have responsibility for children eighteen and under and for the elderly. Even for this group, the stresses and strains are grave. In 1988, testifying before the House Select Committee on Children, Youth, and Families, one man spoke about the emotional strain he felt in attempting to deal with two sets of fragile elderly parents and children.

In 1986 we learned of my mother-in-law's cancer. We were trying to give care and solace to her and my father-in-law during her surgery and radiation therapy and her intense pain when my father suddenly died. What is double duty—life in the sandwich—like now? My wife and I have not yet been able to mourn our lost parents and put our grief to rest properly—we had been repairing and selling my mother's house and managing her complex financial affairs instead. . . .

Paying bills for two households, time for my older son, and care for the baby leave little conjugal time for us. My mother seems settled now, but is volatile and has had two incompatible roommates and enough friction with the staff to warrant a multidisciplinary conference. . . .

When we were both working, it was a child's illness that would suddenly wipe out our precisely orchestrated schedules; now it is specialized medical care for my mother. . . . My wife has sacrificed the satisfactions and income from an established professional career for our children's welfare. . . . I have sacrificed rapid career development because I must take frequent annual leave to attend to my mother's needs and cannot undertake necessary further academic training at night. . . We are heavily in debt and cannot adequately save for our son's college education. Any inheritance for the grandchildren from my parents will likely have been used up by my mother's nursing care.

Our son's last year in day care, 1987, was marked by the effects of an apathetic and negative primary caregiver. . . . He had behavioral difficulties in kindergarten serious enough for us to consider taking him to a psychologist to help improve his self-esteem.[5]

And a woman testifies,

When grandma is having another of her multiple heart attacks and my son's cardiac monitor begins beeping, I know what my responsibilities are. And what is really poignant about this job is that I cannot fail. . . .

The dream of an extended family unit, taking care of themselves, for us, is dying. My 68-year-old father is cleaning cars in a car rental business to put food on the family table, as our income is insufficient. My husband's blood pressure skyrockets. I am no longer gainfully employed. I no longer hold a position or a title. I no longer have credit. My financed downstairs apartment was sold at a quick sale and the funds used to live on and pay debts. . . . We have gone from Yuppies to major financial burdens. . . . I am not alone. Many women in varying socioeconomic strata are in my position.[6]

These testimonies may seem extreme or unique, but the reality is that more and more employees will eventually face some combination of these very problems.

Researchers Arthur C. Emlen, Paul Koren, and Dianne Louis surveyed employees at the Sisters of Providence Hospital in Portland, Oregon, to determine the level of stress experienced by women workers who are squeezed between caring for children and caring for their aging parents. They found that comparing the sandwich generation with other women caregivers, the former reported somewhat more difficulty, worry, stress and time lost from work. For example, they found that 73 percent of women with dual-care responsibilities reported stress and worry about family finances, compared with 64 percent of mothers with child-care needs only and 59 percent who provide adult day care only.[7]

Elaine M. Brody has extensively described the negative consequences of dual-caregiving, including the emotional strain that can lead to depression, anxiety, frustration, helplessness, and guilt over not being able to do more.

My Research

In my 1988 survey, about 2.4 percent of the 26,000 employees had both child- and elder-care responsibilities. Ten percent of them had children two and under, 8 percent had children three to five, 29 percent had children six to thirteen, and 54 percent had children over thirteen and under nineteen. In 1989, 3.3 percent of the employees were members of the sandwich generation.

My findings reflect the difficulty that employees have in caring for the elderly, difficulty that is largely determined by the frailty of the elderly and by the difficulty of caring for the children, which is usually related to age. Older parents with more medical problems are harder to care for. Younger children require more care, are more prone to illness, and typically create more stress.

In some families, the elderly are not impaired and are not hindered by a chronic illness. In these cases, they are assets, not liabilities, to the caregiver families. They can assist the family by caring for the children and the home. This idea is supported by the fact that employees who are responsible for child care alone are more likely to have more child-care problems in some areas than employees who have both elder- and child-care responsibilities.

For example, 33 percent of the employees who have only child-care responsibilities said they are having a difficult time finding quality care for their children, compared with only 25 percent with dual-care responsibilities. Fifty-one percent of the women with children only, versus 41 percent of those with both children and elderly, said that it is a "big" or "somewhat of a problem" to find care for a sick child. Similar differences occur on such issues as handling child-care responsibilities during vacations and holidays, handling sudden losses of child care, affording child care, finding overnight and evening care, and handling doctor and dentist appointments.

There were no significant differences between the two groups in handling the dual roles of parent and employee, in going to school conferences or programs during work hours, or in telephoning and transporting children. This suggests that some elderly are helping families with child care.

Another factor that could alleviate stress in dual-dependency families is that many employees who have elder-care responsibilities also have children who are older and generally less difficult. If these older children live at home or nearby, in some cases, they could assist with care for the elderly.

Vignettes

In some situations, elderly dependents help care for dependent children. Julia E. is a thirty-five-year-old black in a lower-level management position. The combined annual income of her and her husband is $58,000. To pursue her career, Julia postponed having her first child until two years ago. About a year ago, her father died without leaving much money to her mother to subsist on. As a result, her mother, who was in good health, came to live with Julia to care for her grandchild.

Since her mother has moved in, Julia said, "having my mother live with me has been great. I no longer have to worry about my child getting quality care, or missing work when she gets sick. I am much more able to concentrate on my job and career."

Her mother's excellent health does not create any additional care, except that her mother does not drive. Still, "my mother not being able to drive is a slight burden, but the benefits of her living with us and caring for the baby far outweighs her transportation needs."

In the opposite type of situation, elders must be cared for by the employee. Jack and his wife both work in nonmanagement positions for the same company. They have a combined annual income of $42,000. Their three children are four, six, and thirteen. While both sets of grandparents are alive, both grandfathers are in failing health, and the grandmothers are finding it hard to cope with caring for them. Jack's father-in-law has had several heart attacks, and Jack's father is somewhat immobile because of arthritis and failing hearing and eyesight.

Jack said that his life seems to be just "one big crisis." When a problem with one of the dependents ends, another is certain to arise:

> Our stress level is about to bust. We are having a difficult time dealing with each other. We both try to support one another, but at times you are so tired, you will jump on the next person who says Hello!
>
> We're both concerned with our mothers' health. They both help with the kids on occasion; but our fathers are very demanding and our mothers are always tired. . . . We wish we could afford to help our mothers with some professional care, but child care is $400 a month for our three-year-old, and we give our parents a few dollars here and there.

Jack hopes his wife's sister, who lives in a town eighty miles away, will move closer to help with her parents. Jack has no brothers or sisters to assist him.

There is the single parent who is in the sandwich generation. Elizabeth W., a black occupational worker, is a single mother of four. She makes about $20,000 per year but feels that her company does not support her child-care and elder-care needs. Along with her responsibility for her children, she is responsible for her aging mother. In the previous year, she missed work more than six times, left early and arrived late five times each, and dealt with personal or family-related issues numerous times.

> I have problems as far as attendance, which in turn makes it harder for me. I'm trying my best, but when you have four kids, you can't say 'okay, everybody has the chicken pox this week, so I won't have to stay out next week.' It's uncontrollable, but it's still held against me. So I end up in attendance arrears as soon as a child is sick at day care or if I schedule regular doctor appointments for the kids, such as physicals every year.
>
> It's hard to look into the future. My mother isn't totally dependent on anyone. She does get a check from my father's death in 1986. She is still able-bodied, although she's becoming very forgetful, and her eyesight is fading rapidly. I just can't let anything happen to her. I have brothers and sisters, but they can't or won't be able to help her. I send what I can to her, and I do her correspondence as well as possible on a long-distance basis. I'm trying to get her to move up here. But she is old and set in her ways and doesn't want to be a burden to me.

Despite Elizabeth's work/family conflicts, she feels that there is "no better company" to work for. She is a productive employee who saved her company $2 million last year by spotting an account oversight, and yet she concluded her survey response by writing, "P.S. Please help! The stress is getting worse." Corporations should carefully consider this dilemma and become more aware of the numbing burdens that can be placed upon valuable, productive employees.

Mary L. is a white occupational worker in her early thirties. She earns $24,000 per year and has three children, aged four, seven, and ten.

I answered your questions as well as possible, since my main concerns are related here as indicated by my answers. I am single, and I depend greatly on my mother for care of my children. However, this situation could change at a moment due to the serious health problems my mother has. She cares for my children before and after school, and I, in turn, attend to her needs—medical appointments, transportation, filling out forms, and so on. As she grows older, the bulk of the responsibility for child care and adult care will shift toward myself. While I see no indication that this shift will affect my job performance, I do see a need for more involvement from the company in assisting with employee needs and outside responsibilities to dependents. More than anything else, employees need an understanding and supportive attitude from employers regarding these issues.

Finally, one future sandwich-generation person has a child with a severe learning disability. Betty K. is an American Indian in her early thirties. Although she and her husband both work full time, Betty has primary responsibility for the care of their two teenaged children. An occupational worker, Betty has a very inflexible work schedule, which creates many conflicts with her child-care needs.

The children are unable to participate in any scheduled activities due to my schedule. I also have a very big problem with school conferences and with getting them to dentist and doctor appointments because of my schedule. Handling dual roles as a parent and an employee is a big problem for me. It creates at least some stress on the job and at home.

Betty indicated that the most useful child-care option for her would be a compressed work week, and the second most useful, a half-day vacation.

She anticipates having more problems in the future because her daughter has a severe learning disability, and her mother will become more financially dependent upon her. She expects that these responsibilities will greatly impair her effectiveness as an employee. In order to deal with her emerging problems, the company would be most helpful by providing a compressed work week and a voucher system for dependent care.

These vignettes illustrate the stress and productivity problems caused by changes in American family structure.

Let's look more carefully at how the various groups responded to the same questions on stress and lost productivity. It is important to remember that neither having children nor caring for the elderly is in and of itself very stressful; the stress is more directly related to the age of the children and to the health and financial situation of the elderly.

The following data indicate that dual-caring responsibilities are taking a greater overall toll on employees than either child care or elder care alone. Employees who do not have any responsibility to care for either children under nineteen or the elderly are less likely to miss work, leave early, or come in late because of family responsibilities, or to deal with family issues during working hours. Only 31 percent of those with no family-care responsibilities missed work in the previous year due to family matters. But 38 percent with elder-care responsibilities, 41 percent with child-care, and 44 percent with both child-care and elder-care responsibilities missed work.

These general figures mask crucial differences, such as the gender of the employee. Table 8–1 shows employee responses by gender. Among men with different care responsibilities, the differences are not large, but among women there are significant differences. Women who have no responsibilities (33 percent) are much less likely to have missed work than those with elder-care (45 percent), child-care (51 percent), and dual-dependent-care (55 percent) responsibilities. These statistics clearly demonstrate that women assume increasing role burdens as their caring responsibilities increase, while men's responsibilities don't seem to increase at the same rate.

The difference in responses between men and women is smallest between those who have no care responsibilities. The biggest difference is between those who have dual responsibilities—again demonstrating that women are more likely than men to pick up the additional burdens of caring.

Table 8–1

RELATIONSHIP BETWEEN CAREGIVING RESPONSIBILITIES AND LOST
PRODUCTIVE TIME

(N = Percent who have missed work, left early, etc.)

| | Type of Responsibilities | | | | | | | |
| | Elder Care | | Child Care | | Dual Care | | No Care | |
	Women	Men	Women	Men	Women	Men	Women	Men
Missed Work	45	28	51	30	55	28	33	25
Arrived Late	33	25	42	32	41	27	33	25
Left Early	54	46	65	53	63	47	46	42
Dealt with Family/Work Issues during Work Hours	81	82	86	85	87	83	74	74

Table 8–2 shows that employees who have no caregiving responsibilities are much less likely to say they have stress "to a great extent" or "to some extent" at home or on the job because of balancing work and family responsibilities. It clearly demonstrates that caregiving responsibilities significantly affect employees' perceived stress level both at home and on the job. It also highlights the fact that dual-caring responsibilities create more stress than either elder care or child care alone. Even if the elderly are healthy and help around the house with the children, the fact that they are the employee's primary responsibility still adds stress to the relationship.

The stress level and stress-related health problems of the sandwich generation are greater than those of employees who are not sandwiched. For example, 45 percent of those in the sandwich generation had more headaches than usual in the previous six months, but only 41 percent of those who have elder-care responsibilities, 39 percent who have child-care responsibilities, and 36 percent who have no family-care responsibilities did.

Table 8–2

RELATIONSHIP BETWEEN CAREGIVING AND STRESS AT HOME
AND ON THE JOB

(N = Percent who say "to a great extent" or "to some extent.")

	Elder Care	Child Care	Dual Care	No Care Responsibility
Stress on the Job	43	45	51	26
Stress at Home	47	51	59	30

There is some evidence that men who have dual-caring responsibilities are more likely to make career decisions in light of those responsibilities than are men who have only child-care or elder-care responsibilities. Specifically, 30 percent of men with dual responsibilities—compared with only 22 percent of those with only child-care responsibilities—have seriously considered turning down a promotion. In addition, 10 percent of the former versus only 4 percent of the latter said they "seriously considered quitting their current company to work for a company with better dependent-care assistance."

Among women, the differences aren't as great. For example, 52 percent of women with dual-caring responsibilities—compared with only 48 percent with child-care responsibilities—had seriously considered turning down a promotion. Sixteen percent of women with dual responsibilities but only 10 percent of those with child-care responsibilities alone had considered quitting to go to another company.

George Miller, chairman of the House Select Committee on Children, Youth, and Families, summed up this issue this way.

As a result, family members are often compelled to juggle careers, nursing duties, housework, and the nurturing of two sets of dependents. This "double duty" takes its toll. Family care givers who work full-time frequently spend more hours every day providing care than they do at their job. Emotionally and physically, they pay the price in depression, anxiety, fatigue, illness, isolation, fear of the future and guilt over not doing more. The financial toll can also be particularly steep. A significant proportion of family members are forced to quit their jobs to fulfill their duties at home.[8]

Summary

In the coming years, more and more employees will become part of the sandwich generation, squeezed between responsibilities of caring for young children and elders. This dual-caring responsibility is not inherently stressful; rather, the degree of stress depends upon the age of the children and on the health and financial situation of the elderly. Those who have young children (which means more problems) and are caring for an ailing and/or financially needy elder are more likely to miss work, have a greater degree of stress, and have more stress-related health problems than employees who have only child-care or elder-care responsibilities.

More and more employees will face the dual-caring responsibility, and corporate executives will have to address their problems. Considering the age trends and the smaller number of children to care for the elderly, the majority of employees may be in the sandwich generation in the not-too-distant future. The next chapter discusses why corporate America has not moved ahead at a rapid rate to address family-care issues.

9

The Politics of Corporate Dependent Care

FAMILY-CARE issues and work/family conflicts are taking a tremendous toll on corporate America's productivity. Yet few companies are responding to these problems. The executives will tell you that the main reasons they don't are equity, cost, liability, lack of need, and lack of knowledge. Most of the arguments I discuss in this chapter are arguments against child-care assistance. The issue of elder care is relatively recent but I suspect that many of the arguments against child care will reappear to oppose elder-care assistance. Let's examine the corporate arguments against including family care in companies' human resource policies and practices.

Equity

Many corporate executives do not offer child-care benefits to employees with children because they feel this may be construed as unfair to those without children. "The perceived problem is that employees without children will want a fringe benefit of equal value," says family-care expert Dana Friedman. In my survey, a small group of employees did voice this resentment.

> The company didn't help me with my four kids. Why should it help people now? (white female lower-level manager)
>
> I'm tired of hearing these people cry about their child-care problems. Why should the company help them? It isn't helping me. (Hispanic male lower-level manager)

I stayed home and raised my children before I came to work. Let them do the same sacrificing I did. I don't think the company should do anything for one it won't do for another. (white female occupational worker)

A divorced black male occupational worker who doesn't have any children complained, "It's unfair! Just because you have kids doesn't mean the company should help you."

It is true that some child-care solutions will not be needed by all employees all the time. But consider this concern in the context of other employee programs, such as drug and alcohol treatment programs. Corporate drug and alcohol treatment programs are used by only 10 percent to 15 percent of the workforce, but there have been few complaints about equity. By contrast, child-care problems affect most employees at some time during their working lives. At any given time, one-third to one-half of a company's workforce has children eighteen and under. If you add the number of employees with elder-care and adult-dependent-care problems (approximately 15 percent to 20 percent of the workforce), you are talking about services that would actually be used by a majority of company employees.

Moreover, many of the child-care solutions, such as flexible work options, flexible benefits, and supportive supervisors, can in fact be used by all employees.

Finally, any family-care assistance given to employee caregivers will benefit not only the caregivers but also noncaregiving employees. This is because the caregivers will experience less stress, miss fewer days of work, and be more productive on the job, all of which directly affect the work group. As employees who support the notion of family-care assistance said:

Our supervisors have decided to give employees flexible work hours, and it has helped my coworker tremendously. She's able to stay at home with her seven-year-old child until the bus picks her up for school. She's much more relaxed, and so am I. (white female occupational worker)

If the company helps people with family issues, it helps us all. (white male middle-level manager)

I don't have any children right now, but my group includes four parents of little kids. When they're having problems with child care, we all feel it. (Hispanic male middle-level manager)

Even though I'm single and have no dependents at this time, I can relate to having family problems and can understand how at times, working hours can be a conflict in some situations. I believe it would be a good initiative for my company to have some kind of day-care facility to aid those working parents with needs. It's convenient to the parent and will limit being late or leaving early due to problems with various day-care centers. It also shows a sense of understanding, care, concern and realization on the company's part to see the need of accommodating their employees to help productivity in all areas. . . . The less worry one has at home/work, the better job one can perform. (Asian female occupational worker)

Another perceived inequity is that building an on- or near-site day-care center would help only those employees with children (or with elderly dependents, if the facility provides adult day care). In other words, it is difficult to administer a program that will be fair to all employees with dependents. In this case, many researchers, including myself, suggest that the company offer a wide variety of solutions, as AT&T did in its recent labor contract (see chapter 5). For example, flexible benefits (cafeteria plans) should be made available to all employees to give them the option of choosing child care, elder care, enhanced retirement, longer vacations, expanded health benefits, or an enhanced savings plan. A multi-site company might find that a day-care center is the best solution in one area, but in another site a before-and-after-school-care program is preferable because of the workforce demographics and the age of the employees' children.

The equity argument, according to Friedman, is usually raised by parents whose children are on waiting lists for day care, but I have not found this to be the case. Rather, I have found that the equity argument often comes from older employees with grown children who believe that because the company didn't help them when their own children were young, it should not help employees now. One white upper-level manager said, "Early in my career (over twenty-five years ago) my wife, who has a degree, and I decided that she would stay home to raise the family. That was and is the right way to go. Children need their mother." In his response to the question about company involvement in child care, he strongly disagreed that firms should assist employees with child care. A white female occupational worker concurred: "I had to stay home to care for my children until they were old enough to watch themselves. The company did not help me." She also strongly disagrees with company-assisted child care.

Growing numbers of employees are also complaining that helping employees who have children neglects the needs of employees who have elder- and adult-dependent-care responsibilities. An American Indian female lower-level manager wrote, "Why doesn't the company help employees who care for old people? (I have no children, but I have my parents to care for.)" Her point is well taken, but she and other employees should be urging the company to provide family-care assistance that addresses most employees' needs rather than to stop helping employees who do not have their own care responsibilities.

Finally, we should remember that nothing in corporate life is fair and equitable. Numerous distinctions and perks come with the various levels of the organization. The higher you go, the better it is. There are far greater equity issues facing corporate America than the issue of family care, such as discrimination against people of color and women. It's time for this equity issue to be addressed in a more realistic perspective.

Costs

Many corporate executives contend that they would help their employees with their family-care problems if only the solutions "just didn't cost so much." The cost of family care is a serious issue, but many companies do not look at the total financial picture: they look only at the cost and not at the return on the dollars spent. The real question is, by ignoring the problem, what will it cost the company in lost time, productivity, turnover, health care costs, and competitiveness? My research indicates that the expense of offering child-care assistance is a short-term cost for long-term savings. Argues Ellen Galinsky, "Studies have shown and companies have reported paybacks in terms of increased productivity and employee job satisfaction. It also helps keep and retain valued employees."

Ironically, many of the solutions that have very low costs also happen to be some of the most sought-after benefits. Flexible work options, payroll deductions, flexible benefits, supportive supervisors, and an accommodating work environment are inexpensive solutions that many employees in my research said would help them solve their family-care problems and be more productive employees.

Doug Phillips of Merck and Company, has estimated that for every dollar it spends on family care, the company gets about three dollars in return. John Harrigan, chairman of Union Bank in Monterrey Park, California, says that the child-care center the bank opened several years ago will actually save the bank four dollars for every three it invests.

Isaac Heller, the president of Heller Construction Company, in Edison, New Jersey, pointed out in a letter to the *New York Times* that his company had built an $800 thousand quality day-care center. His employees had to pay only half the actual cost (about $50 per week). In order to reduce his company's subsidy, he leases a parking lot to the center near a commuter rail line, which produces a steady stream of income. He wrote,

> Quit talking about day care and do something about it. . . . It will cost you some money. But so does health care and life insurance for your employees.[1]

For smaller companies, the cost of opening an on- or near-site center may be too burdensome to consider. Nevertheless, executives of these companies could consider less expensive alternatives such as child-care consortia, vouchers, DCAPs, flexible work options, and progressive leave policies.

Family-care expert Karen Hill-Scott has noted that ultimately, the issue of costs will be seen in the larger context because the "primary barriers to increasing the availability of child care . . . are the lack of funds for capitalization . . . and lack of funds for subsidy." In other words, the biggest obstacle to providing child care is not any lack of knowledge of child development but financing and securing a broad social commitment to resolve the crisis.[2]

Although Hill-Scott was referring specifically to child care, her comments also apply to elder care. Through the combined efforts of public and private financing, the costs of day care could be greatly lowered, while at the same time the quality of dependent care could be vastly improved.

In sum, while short-term cost is a real issue for some corporations depending on the type of assistance they provide, it is not an insurmountable obstacle. In fact, most companies that do assist their employees with child care say the benefits of the programs outweigh the costs. American companies should conduct sophisticated needs assessments and compare the cost of ignoring family-care problems with the costs of providing assistance. They would see that family care offers a significant return on the investment.

Liability

Liability is another argument that many corporations raise against providing family-care assistance. But there are a wide variety of child- and elder-care solutions that have very low or no additional liability costs to employers, solutions that employees want and need. In fact, two of the three main solutions add little, if any, liability risks to the company: flexible work options and financial assistance (in the form of vouchers, payroll deductions, flexible benefits, and the like). Nor does creating a supportive, responsive work atmosphere pose any liability problems, and in fact, it can decrease the likelihood of lawsuits based on gender discrimination.

Despite this, liability is considered the second leading deterrent (cost is the first) for most companies considering child care. A wave of child-abuse cases in the early 1980s drove up the cost of liability insurance for day care and left much of corporate America scared to death to enter the business of child care. But like the issue of child abuse itself, the liability issue has been blown out of proportion. Galinsky, Hill-Scott, and others have said that they are not aware of any lawsuits against a corporate-sponsored day-care center. Galinsky has written that the child-care industry has received an average of one claim per thousand child-care centers. Of those claims, the majority are for trips and falls and are settled for less than $300. Most insurance policies today do not cover child-abuse claims; but contrary to popular belief, most insurance carriers *are* willing to write policies for corporate child-care programs. Friedman studied the liability issue and concluded, "The cost of liability insurance is far less than the insurance a corporation needs in order to cover someone who slips in the lobby and breaks a leg."

The liability risks of elder care are less than those of child care since an elderly person or their guardian can sue for only limited damages one time; the parent of a child, by contrast, can sue a provider on behalf of the child, projecting averages based on the child's potential earnings. Later, when the child becomes an adult, the child can sue for further damages. For employers concerned about liability, plenty of information is available on how to reduce the risk.

The Bureau of National Affairs has put together a publication on limiting employer liability.[3] Here are some of its suggestions:

- Employers should not run day-care centers themselves; subcontract the center out to family-care experts, or create a separate nonprofit corporation to run it.
- Employers should make sure the outside day-care centers that they support are insured, and ask for indemnification.
- When providing information and referrals, the employer should be careful that the information includes no recommendations. They should allow their employees to make up their own minds; include disclaimers, and carefully select the referral service.

- Dependent care assistance plans (DCAPs) and flexible hours are the least risky of all the family-care options. Businesses should help employees by lobbying the government to limit liability for day-care centers.

Another expert on liability, James Strickland, president of Human Services Risk Management Exchange, believes that liability risks can be minimized by "implementing and enforcing strict internal loss control and risk management." This can be accomplished through intensive training programs for employees of company family day-care programs and through constant monitoring of the quality of both the environment and the standards. In other words, the best way to reduce the risk is to make sure the program is of top quality.[4]

Isaac Heller noted about the liability question that there are potential liabilities in anything a company does—from building a sidewalk on which someone might fall to installing a new machine by which someone could injure a hand. He wrote:

> If companies take the same precautions about child care—and preponderantly these precautions are in quality of personnel—then the costs of liability really are not as fearsome as they imagined.[5]

In brief, the liability issue applies only to a few family-care solutions, and there are a number of creative ways that corporate America can limit its liability. The issue of liability should be broadened so that stockholders regard corporate executives as liable if they lose billions of corporate dollars because they have not instituted progressive family-care policies and are consequently losing their competitive edge. They are liable because they are not providing the stockholders with the best return on their investment.

Lack of Knowledge

Some companies argue against assisting employees with family care because information on it is unavailable. The Massachusetts Industrial Finance Agency surveyed sixty-four companies about their interest in assisting their employees with child care. Thirty-two companies said they weren't interested, but many of them said they had too little information on child care to start a program. The study concluded, "Child care for many companies is an undefined issue." The corporate executives did not believe there was a readily available method of delivering child care (and probably elder care as well).[6]

As I have shown throughout this book, unavailability of knowledge is simply a negative myth. The information exists, not only for child care, but also for elder care, and there are hundreds of experts who are willing to provide corporations with it.

In addition, the federal government funded the Women's Bureau, in the Labor Department, to set up the Women's Bureau Work and Family Clearinghouse.[7] The clearinghouse was designed and established to help employers identify the most appropriate policies for responding to the dependent-care needs of employees seeking to balance their dual responsibilities.

Information and guidance are available from the clearinghouse in five broad option areas: direct services, information services, financial assistance, flexible policies, and public-private partnerships. The technical assistance it provides includes national and state information sources, bibliographic references, conference information, research, and statistics. Among the specific materials available to employers are "Program Profiles" that describe employer-related child- and elder-care systems already in place. Approximately a thousand employer programs are highlighted in the computer file.

How-to guides are available to employers in about twenty-six areas. These include "On/Off Site Centers," "Family Day Care," "Resource and Referral," "Contributions to Community Resources," "Flexible Leave Policies," and "Maternity Leave." Assistance is also available through telephone discussion and written materials, including a Work and Family Resource Kit and a publication on employer-sponsored child-care programs.

The clearinghouse's phone number is 202-523-4486. It will

set up facilities in all ten Women's Bureaus over the next two years. The information is there both on a private and public level—all corporations have to do is pick up the phone.

Lack of Demand

Another argument that companies raise against helping with family care is that there is no need for it—"there is already enough day care in this community." These executives fail to realize that there is actually a great shortage of quality day care, and most of the day care that exists is unlicensed. Karen Hill-Scott believes that 75 percent of all family day care is unlicensed. Day-care centers are usually of higher quality than family day care, but licensing requirements and quality vary greatly from state to state.

In addition, the available day-care centers are often unaffordable for many people. The average cost is $3,000 per year, making day care the fourth largest household expense, behind housing, food, and taxes. Executives who say there is enough day care have tunnel vision; not only do employees need more day care for preschoolers, they need more before-and-after-school care programs, more summer and vacation care, more sick-care programs, flexible work hours, and financial assistance.

The shortage of affordable, quality day care in the United States is a well-publicized fact. Hill-Scott estimates that in the Los Angeles area, there is a shortage of more than 100,000 slots for preschoolers. In addition, very few programs are available for the 11 million school-age children who must care for themselves before and after school.

- In Washtenaw County, Michigan, the demand for infant care exceeds the available supply by as much as three to one.
- In Seattle, Washington, licensed day-care facilities have space for only 8,800 of the 23,000 children who need it.
- In Des Moines, Iowa, 47,000 children need care, but existing child-care facilities accommodate only 12,076.[8]

Playing the day-care roulette wheel leaves many employees spinning and wondering where to turn for help. So far, very few employees have been able to look to their employers.

My extensive research shows that between two-thirds and four-fifths of all employees believe that companies should be actively involved in both child care and elder care. But over and over again, I hear corporate executives say, "We aren't doing anything about dependent care because employees don't ask for it." It is true that employees are only recently beginning to speak up about their family-care problems. But those who have spoken up have received no or very little positive response from corporate executives, many of whom have wives who stayed home to care for their families. The wives of corporate executives who did work outside the home were able to afford quality day care for their children.

Corporate Sexism

"Its almost as if companies have been caught in a 1950s time warp," says David G. Blankenhorn, executive director of the Institute for American Values. Blankenhorn says that this 1950s way of thinking is one reason that only a small percentage of companies have so far taken steps to help parents with family care. I would go further and say that corporate sexism and outdated stereotypes are the main culprit, even though these issues are rarely discussed in corporate America. Until corporate America truly stops believing that a woman's place is in the home and that a man need not worry about child and dependent care, there will always be obstacles to addressing these needs.[9]

The roots of corporate gender discrimination, as we know it today, can be traced back to the late eighteenth century. Before the Industrial Revolution, little differentiation had existed between men and women's work, except among the wealthy. Many jobs were performed by both sexes, and all members of the family had to work. In the late eighteenth century, the notions of maternal love and maternal instinct came into vogue. By the time Sigmund Freud popularized the mother-child bond theory, many women had already been literally shut out of the productive workforce. In modern times, functional sociologists have attempted to explain role allocation between mothers and fathers in biological terms: "Mothers take care of children because they naturally produce and feed them and men do not." These theories helped popularize the Ozzie and Harriets and June Cleavers in the 1950s. They came to represent the ideal mother.[10]

Judith Auerbach wrote, "The dominant American ideology of mothering holds that children need the nurturance of their mothers at home to ensure proper physical, emotional, psychological, and moral development. Any mother who does not stay home and care for her children is a bad mother who wants to 'get rid of her children,' "[11]

Economics and biology have historically been used to explain role differentiation, but many sociologists, including myself, believe that the current insistence on gender discrimination is better understood in terms of the power structure. According to Margaret Polatnik, "The allocation of child-rearing responsibility to women . . . is no sacred fiat of nature, but a social policy which supports male domination in society and in the family." Polatnik discussed child rearing as a set of tasks that offer low status and low or no pay. These tasks are assigned to women by men who don't want to do them and who wish to preserve their monopoly of the higher status and prestige that come from being the breadwinner in this society.[12] In short, Polatnik argued, women are assigned the job of child-rearing as a means of keeping male power intact.

Over twenty years of research, I have documented the existence of sexist stereotypes in the majority of American society. My 1988 study shows just how prevalent these gender stereotypes are. In that survey, I asked the employees to respond to a series of statements of stereotypical views of women. In table 9–1 are the employees' responses. Profound differences exist between the female and the male views.

Different groups held different views about women. Black men responded very much like women themselves when it came to stereotypes, while white men and American Indian

Table 9–1

THE RELATIONSHIP AMONG RACE, GENDER, AND NUMBER OF SEXIST STEREOTYPES

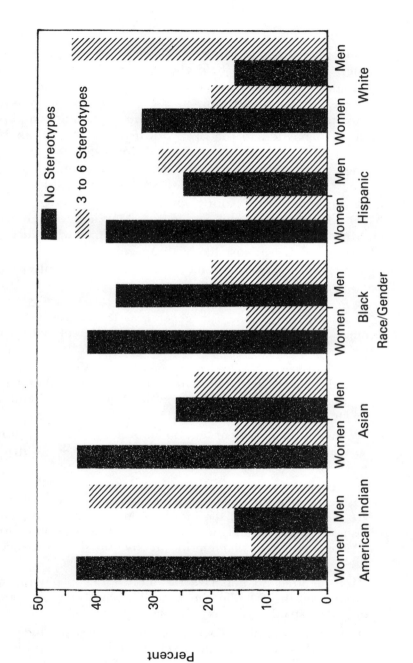

men displayed the most stereotypical views of women. Among women, white females held the most stereotypical views.

Of all the positive responses to the stereotypical roles of women, the most alarming in the context of this book were the responses to the statement, "The increasing employment of women has led to the breakdown of the American family." Overall, 38 percent of the employees—29 percent of the women and 49 percent of the men—"strongly agree" or "agree" with this statement. Men with grown children (55 percent) and men with young children (51 percent) were most likely to agree with this statement. Married women with no children (24 percent) and unmarried couples without children (24 percent) were least likely to agree.

Some of the sexist comments expressed by employees who participated in the survey are:

> "I tend to view women, in general, as less aggressive, and all other things being equal, slightly less competent than a male counterpart." (white male middle-level manager)

> "I grew up in a family where women were subservient. These attitudes and expectations are deeply rooted within me. As hard as I fight them, I'll never be free of those attitudes." (white male occupational worker)

> "Women in management tend to be overaggressive. Much more so than men in a similar position." (Hispanic male occupational worker)

> "My experience in the short five years I have been in the business is that the majority of women that I have worked with are too emotional and too hung up on petty bickering, gossip/fashion/cat fights, and not focused on their jobs and careers. The remaining small minority are the finest professionals in the workplace." (white male lower-level manager)

> "Women often do not have the mechanical or physical background or the 'rain in the face' discipline to get some jobs done." (Hispanic male occupational worker)

> "I have seen some women promoted because of their after-hours behavior with upper-level supervisors." (Hispanic male occupational worker)

"Women can't do jobs like men. They don't have the physical strength." (black male lower-level manager)

"You and your entire group can't change the fact that a woman belongs in the home, no matter what -ism you dream up." (white male occupational worker)

These views clearly show a lack of understanding of current demographics. Working women constitute 45 percent of the workforce; by the year 2000, they will constitute 47 percent. Anyone who believes that working women are a significant factor in the breakdown of the American family or who believes in any of the other stereotypes will not give women a fair and equitable chance in present-day corporate America. In addition, they will not be supportive of corporate involvement in family-care matters.

Another underlying factor that is reflected in the biases of the business world is the old-fashioned belief that corporate involvement in the private lives of employees is comparable to mixing church and state:

> The family in American culture has long been viewed as a private realm, a haven from the rest of the world and one ideally free from outside influence. . . . The decision about how to raise a child is considered to be a private one, based upon the experience, culture and style of parents themselves, and carried out in their own manner in their own homes.[13]

This is why government has been reluctant to intervene in family-care matters, and it could also explain some of the hesitancy of corporations to step on this sacred territory.

Some employees also hold these biases.

"It's not the company's role to meet the needs of my family's care. As long as I am paid fairly, I can best meet these needs myself." (black woman middle-level manager)

"Working women are taking jobs away from men and destroying American families. We are headed toward Communism." (white male lower-level manager)

"Women should be home raising children. Look at the high rate of illiteracy." (American Indian male occupational worker)

"I am a father who has sole financial support for my wife and four children. Most of the women working outside of the home here don't need to. They should be home. I support many of things for those men and women who are single parents or sole support." (white male occupational worker)

One employee, Linda J., is not very sympathetic to the issue of corporate support for family care. She raised her three children on her own while working full-time. Linda is married, but she also considers herself the primary person responsible for raising the children.

"This is not a new problem. I personally resent some of these 'career people' who feel it is the company's obligation to see that they have adequate day care. There are thousands of us who have managed, and they could too, if they would try. Employees need to take care of family/work conflicts themselves. To do it for them denies their basic freedoms."

"Babysitting is not a company responsibility," argued Barry G., a white occupational worker in his forties. Barry's wife stays at home to care for their one child. "My wife is at home, where a *mother* should be. After the child leaves home, then if the wife wants to work, okay." Barry strongly opposes company involvement in family/work conflicts and child care. "A family's children are their responsibility. The company is not responsible for their daily care. If the company must babysit, then it should have the say whether to have kids or not."

A white occupational woman who is from a dual-career family and who has two children aptly summed up the current situation in corporate America:

"I think all persons should be treated as individuals. Unfortunately, we have been socialized to believe females are more emotionally out of control and less strong than males. 'Home is where they should be.' There has been a lot of effort to correct this mistaken concept, but we have a long way to go, and presently, I see us backsliding."

Summary

Sexist attitudes among corporate executives, both male and female, remain the greatest obstacle to corporate involvement in the family-care problems of employees. One of the overall strategies that those who support corporate involvement in family care must undertake is to get the corporations to recognize the sexist stereotypes that are still held by the majority of Americans and to make an effort to dispel the myths. They must recognize that underlying all of the rational "reasons," such as cost and liability, is the irrational "reason" of sexism.

As long as family care is considered to be a women's issue and the private responsibility of the homemaker, little more than lip-service will be given to employees' dependent-care problems. Corporate executives should focus less on the "obstacles" to family-care assistance, such as cost, liability, knowledge, and equity, and realize the enormous benefits that result from a comprehensive program. Not only would they see a decrease in employee absenteeism and turnover, they would also see an increase in productivity and a decrease in their health-insurance costs. An added bonus would be positive publicity and goodwill.

10

A Marshall Plan for Family Care

AMERICANS like to think of their country as the most advanced nation in the world. But when it comes to caring for their children and their frail adult and elderly dependents, they fall short of many industrialized nations.

The U.S. government does not offer job protection for maternity leave; nor does it provide monthly or weekly cash benefits to families with children. But sixty-seven industrialized nations do. In Europe and elsewhere around the world, single mothers frequently receive additional payments. Several European countries provide maternity grants to reduce the expense of supplies and equipment for the new baby.

Let's briefly review what several specific countries provide to families.[1]

- In Sweden, public child care is available for children as young as six months and as old as seven years. The system includes an independent preschool run by the state, which subsidizes 90 percent of the cost. It also allows for one year of parental leave. The mother can take the first nine months off and receive 90 percent of her pay.

- In Denmark, parents are offered twenty-four weeks off; the first fourteen weeks are reserved for mothers. Day care costs only $119 per month, so 44 percent of Danish children under age three and 69 percent of children aged three to five are enrolled.

- In Israel, new mothers are given twelve weeks of paid leave and an additional forty weeks of unpaid leave. There are more than nine hundred subsidized day-care centers throughout the country, and nearly one-quarter of Israeli children are enrolled. The cost is only $27 to $90 per month, based on family income.
- In France, working mothers are given sixteen weeks of maternity leave with 90 percent of their pay. Government-subsidized day-care centers care for more than seventy thousand children. These centers are open up to fifteen hours a day and cost only $3.00 to $17.50 daily if employees use them outside regular working hours—otherwise they are free.

But Europe, the Soviet Union, and the Far East are also facing a crisis in day care. In Japan, the number of working women quadrupled during the past twenty years. There are long waiting lists at the twenty-three thousand licensed day-care centers in Japan. In the Soviet Union, nursery centers are poorly run for the most part; most working mothers who take the four months of paid maternity leave and the additional eight months at one-quarter pay prefer to give the care of their child to their *babushkas* (grandmothers) when they return to work.

In West Germany, women's advocates contend that the most significant factor contributing to the low employment rate of West German women—about half—is the shortage of child care. Only 16 percent of women with infants and toddlers are employed. (In the United States the figure is over 50 percent.) Of those who are working, many are employed only part-time. Comparing West Germany with France, one can see the extent of the problem: only 3 percent of toddlers in West Germany are enrolled in day care, compared with 33 percent in France. Another problem with West German day care is that the vast majority of day-care centers close at noon.[2]

Even as most of the industrialized world is coming to terms with the need for child care, a new problem looms on the horizon—care of the elderly. In Western Europe and the Far

East, corporations and governments are realizing that the graying of the population is affecting the national economy.

Across Europe, some employers are desperate to recruit young workers as older ones retire. Conflicts are cropping up between those who want a comfortable old age and the shrinking number of young people who must subsidize the escalating cost of caring for the elderly.[3] For example, in France, the overall population will increase by only 5 percent between 1980 and 2000, but the over-sixty age group will increase by 19 percent, the over-seventy group by 10 percent, and the over-eighty group by 5 percent. West Germany will experience a 3 percent decrease in its overall population, but the over-sixty group will increase by 17 percent, the over-seventy group by 1 percent, and the over-eighty group by 13 percent.[4] With the recent changes occurring in East Germany, the West Germans' population problems could be solved because of an influx of young, educated East Germans.

Japan is aging more rapidly than any other country. Jeff Ostroff has noted:

> . . . Between 1970 and 1996, the percentage of Japanese citizens sixty-five and over will double, jumping from 7 to 14 percent of the population.[5]

Not only is the industrialized world aging, but Third World countries such as Brazil are too. The over-sixty population in Brazil will increase by 86.7 percent between 1980 and 2000; the over-seventy population by 100 percent in the same time period; and the over-eighty population by 11 percent. Economic conditions in Brazil are already poor; the country is facing high unemployment and soaring inflation rates. Given these conditions, experts believe, there is no hope of financing the elderly services needed. Another obstacle to the proper treatment of the elderly in Brazil is the low level of education, especially regarding health. Experts in Brazil say that many older people are living in conditions "inconsistent with dignity." Between now and the year 2000, experts expect the situation for the elderly to worsen.[6]

What are some of the creative ways that countries are dealing with the aging issues? Most Western industrialized nations provide families with an allowance to help pay for a caregiver to come into the home to care for a disabled person. Qualifications and allowances vary greatly. Mary Jo Gibson observed that in West Germany

> the Federal Public Assistance Law permits the reimbursement of relatives or neighbors who provide nursing care to the low-income infirm and elderly.[7]

Recognizing the extreme stress caused by the responsibility of caring for an elderly adult, some nations, such as New Zealand and Denmark, have developed unique approaches.

> In New Zealand, persons caring for disabled elderly persons are . . . entitled to four weeks' holiday. While on holiday, the carees [sic] are housed in quality accommodations or a qualified caregiver comes to his or her home. . . . Denmark also provides short-term stays in nursing homes.[8]

Burton Reifler, director of Dementia Care and Respite Services, has noted that because of its cultural bias against placing the elderly in nursing homes, Japan builds geriatric hospitals (or so called "medical nursing homes") as an alternative. This is to "reduce the use of expensive hospital beds."[9] In contrast to the United States, where the cost of care is born by the elderly or their families, in Japan the cost of nursing homes depends on the financial status of the elderly person and his or her family.[10]

Sweden has one of the most comprehensive approaches to elder care. The main tenet of its approach is to make it possible for the elderly to stay in their homes. Such services as the following are provided to achieve this objective: delivery of meals, transportation, night and weekend care, and caregivers who cook and do chores. These services are paid for by the government.[11]

Many social scientists believe that the United States is five to ten years behind Western Europe and Japan in facing the elder-care crisis. Because we lack some of the features of many European elder-care systems, which allow them to deal effectively with the special concerns of the elderly, we are less prepared to take the necessary steps to move into this new world. The twenty-first century will be an era in which more older people will live longer, more women will choose to have fewer children later or not at all, and labor shortages combined with greater technological developments will demand a highly skilled, highly motivated workforce.

Jeff Ostroff describes how the United States will look in the early twenty-first century. He feels the country will mirror Florida, with an elderly (fifty +) population that makes up more than one-third of its general population. Seventeen percent of the population is older than sixty-five. The rest of the country should catch up by 2020.[12]

The Social Costs

Throughout this book, we have looked at the corporate costs of failing to deal with family care, but there are social costs as well. Social scientists agree that the first five years of a child's life are the most formative in terms of educational and psychological development. Without proper care, according to Child Advocates, "many of these children will have difficulty in school, in finding and holding jobs, with the law and managing their personal lives."

We can make our children liabilities, or we can make them assets. Studies of poor children who have attended such preschool programs as Head Start show that they have more self-confidence than those without preschool experience. The House Select Committee on Children, Youth, and Families found that each dollar invested in preschool education returns $4.75 by saving special education and welfare costs. The Children's Defense Fund says that for every dollar invested in high-quality preschool programs, six dollars are saved because of less need for "special education, grade retardation, public assistance and crime." Investing in our children will go a long way toward meeting future demands in our labor force and toward increasing the United States' economic viability.

The fate of children who are left in the care of unfit parents is another problem that society must address. Do we do nothing and allow these children to become a liability, or do we intervene and develop support systems that will ensure that they become assets? Margaret Beale Spencer, a renowned Emory University developmental psychologist, believes that:

> As we approach the twenty-first century it is very clear that parents have multiple demands with which they must cope and few supportive resources available to them. In order to maximize the developmental outcomes of children, we have to work through the parents. The changing nature of the family and the increased stress of modern society together undermine effective parenting. Ideally, what quality child care does is promote and reinforce resilience, diminish vulnerability, and offset the adverse effect of at-risk situations. These supports are vital to the maximization of effective parenting.[13]

Should the Government Act?

Recent public opinion polls show that more than half the population believes that family care is a public responsibility, not a private matter. A Washington Post/ABC News poll showed that the public wants the government to help both low- and moderate-income parents with their child-care expenses (73 percent). This sharply contrasts with the mere 34 percent of the population ten years ago who said they wanted the federal government to spend more money on day care. People are increasingly looking for assistance through employee benefits (57 percent) or through guaranteed time off from work for newborn or ill dependents (74 percent), or through financial assistance for nursing homes or long-term-care expenses (71 percent). Today nearly everyone (87 percent) agrees that it will take a joint effort between private employers and the government to meet this country's family-care needs.[14]

In case U.S. government officials aren't listening, the public says it is willing to put its money where its mouth is. Two out of three voters have said they would support a candidate who supports child care. Eighty-eight percent of voters have said they would support a presidential candidate who supports long-term care and nursing-home assistance, and a third of voters said they were more apt to vote for a senator or representative who favors parental leave. Only 7 percent said they would regard them less favorably.[15]

Women are an increasingly integral part of the workforce and are becoming even more important as the "baby bust" hits the marketplace; but these women are also becoming more politically active—9 million more women than men voted in the last election. In the Senate, seventeen Democrats lost the men's vote but won because of the women's vote. Women, in general, want a greater role in government on issues such as family care, and they are increasingly voting their "needs."

Elinor Guggenheimer, president of Child Care Action Campaign, summed it up this way:

> This country will not continue to tolerate the neglect and abuse of children, nor are citizens willing to pay the cost of such neglect. These costs, she claims, include more prisons, more educational failure, and a labor force that will lack the skills to be competitive in a global marketplace. She urges our governmental leaders to wake up and get in synch with their constituencies.[16]

Principles to Operate By

The Child Care Action Campaign would like the government and private sector to keep in mind the following principles when approaching child-care policies and programs. I have modified some of them slightly, and I have added the care of elderly people and other adult dependents.[17]

- All children should have access to affordable, quality child care. Child care must be of quality sufficient to ensure that children get the educational, social, and health benefits that are essential to growth at each and every stage of development. All elderly and physically or emotionally impaired adults should have access to affordable, quality care. The care must be of sufficient quality to ensure that they are receiving proper assistance with respect to their personal dignity and specific multiple needs.

• Every sector that benefits from family care should make an investment in it. The federal, state, and local governments and employers must invest additional resources to expand the supply and improve the quality of care available to families at all income levels. We must avoid a two-tier system that maximizes the choices of middle- and upper-income families based on their ability to pay, while leaving low-income and poor families to "warehouse" their dependents.

• Caregivers should have access to adequate professional information about existing resources, various alternatives, and the components of quality care in order to be able to make informed choices for their families.

• Parents must be an integral part of any child-care program so that their values are communicated to their children. Programs must respect cultural differences. Parental involvement also allows parents to feel confident about their child-care choices. Caregivers for the elderly and adult dependents, to the extent that the recipients are able and willing to participate, should be encouraged to be an integral part of the multifaceted decisions affecting their care. Programs must be respectful of cultural differences so that the elderly, adult dependents, and their caregivers avoid unnecessary and uncomfortable conflicts.

• There should be a variety of quality, affordable options for family care so that caregivers anywhere in the nation can choose the type best suited to their needs and values and to those for whom they are caring.

• Family-care funding should be administered in a manner designed to maximize coordination and efficient use of resources. Duplications of programs and turf battles must be eliminated or minimized.

• Resources for family care must be planned for and coordinated through a partnership of different levels of government: federal, state, and local. The state level should ensure that there is a continuum of care, that caregivers can make informed choices among a variety of options, and that the resources invested are efficiently used. This does not mean that the federal government does not set standards or act as a facilitator and clearinghouse.

- The federal, state, and local governments must create plans and strategies to develop public-private partnerships to resolve the family-care crisis.

- Because family-care providers are the most essential component of quality; training, wages, benefits, and working conditions must be improved so that competent and caring providers are attracted to the profession and are able to remain in it.

Government's Role

Pressure from the public and from family-care advocates is having an effect on the federal government. In the 100th Congress, more than a hundred bills were introduced to address the problems of child care, parental leave, and elder care. The 101st Congress is seeing a continued increase in interest in family-care bills. Unfortunately, the bills that have any chance of passage don't go far enough to address the family-care crisis. The most ambitious would spend about $2.5 billion on child care, but Los Angeles County estimates that it needs that much to meet its child-care needs alone. Compare that amount with the $72 billion cost of the Stealth Bomber program, or with the $42 billion that the Defense Department wastes each year because of inefficient procurement practices, and you get the picture of our government's priorities. The current Medicare and Medicaid laws are limiting and restrictive, leaving many caregivers without the means to provide proper quality care.

Many family-care advocates—including myself—believe this inequity is a direct result of the composition of American leaders. Congressional and state legislators mostly consist of men from the middle and upper classes, most of whom have not played any significant role in caregiving. In addition, their views reflect the views of their constituencies, and the majority of the people they represent hold sexist stereotypes of women. These views hinder the ability of legislators to understand the urgency of the need to enact comprehensive family-care legislation.

To effectively deal with the nation's family-care problems, the U.S. government should take the following steps. First of all, it must pass a comprehensive family-leave law. AT&T's family-leave policy is a model to follow; as discussed in chapter 5, it gives either parent one year of unpaid leave, which can be used during the course of twenty-four months. The company pays the premiums for medical, dental, and vision coverage for the first six months. It also covers death benefits and basic group life insurance for one year. The employee is guaranteed a job at the same level without a reduction in pay when he or she returns.

The American Agenda Report, co-chaired by former presidents Ford and Carter, calls for a $2 billion increase in funding in each of the next eight years for programs such as Head Start, prenatal care, and preventative care. The Children's Defense Fund's 1989 Preventative Investment Agenda calls for $4.3 billion per year. In their excellent 1988 book *A Vision for America's Future: An Agenda for the 1990's; A Children's Defense Budget*, the fund came up with some "painless" ways of raising the necessary money. They pointed out that the U.S. Energy Department requested $50 billion to increase the nuclear-weapon capacity of the United States. The Defense Department requested $5 billion a year to fund the Strategic Defense Initiative (SDI) and $72 billion to build the new Stealth Bomber before the Air Force could make the old B-1 bombers, which cost over $30 billion, work. The bankers requested—and got—over $100 billion to bail out the poorly run savings-and-loan industry. They concluded, "Do not tell us that this nation is unable to afford to lift its thirteen million children out of poverty."[18]

I recommend that Congress budget an appropriate yearly sum to build day-care centers both for children and for elderly and impaired adults, to assure before-and-after-school care programs, to provide financial assistance to low- and middle-income families with real needs, and to assist caregiving companies so that they can attract qualified care providers with an attractive salary and benefits. I would suggest an annual budget allowance of a thousand dollars for each child needing care, a total of about 25 million children, and an additional thousand dollars for each frail elderly or impaired adult and for the healthy but poor elderly.

Currently, the turnover rate among child-care providers at day-care centers is 40 percent, and the turnover in family day-care homes is 60 percent. The figures on elder-care providers in nursing homes range from 65 percent for nurses to 103 percent for nurse's aides. Child-care providers are paid an average of $9 thousand to $12 thousand a year, even though the average educational level of most child-care workers is fourteen years. Sandy Lutz noted that the average pay of a nurse's aide working in a nursing home is 47 percent less than a hospital nurse's aide, and a registered nurse is paid 13 percent less. The federal and state governments must make certain that these caregivers are paid adequately.

The following approaches will make more money available for the caregivers. Congress should reform the tax codes to increase the limits on the tax-free set-asides used to defray costs of dependent care and remove current severe restrictions on paying for elder care. Also, employees should be allowed to increase or decrease the amount quarterly, according to their needs, instead of once a year. Unused money should be saved for the following year. If it cannot be used at that time, the money should be spent to increase the supply of quality care in the community.

The Dependent Care Tax Credit doesn't do much to help those with low incomes because their tax liability is not high enough. Of the 4.6 million people who claimed the credit in 1981, 64 percent were above the median income level. Since the 1986 Tax Reform Act, even fewer low-income people can take advantage of the tax credit. Irwin Garfinkle, professor of social work at the University of Wisconsin, explains that poor families will not benefit from an increase in the value of the child-care tax credit because of the 1986 Tax Reform Act. The personal tax exemptions of nearly $2 thousand per dependent adult and child knocks out most poor families because "even if they fully utilize the earnings capacity of all adult family members, the income would not be enough to incur substantial tax liabilities.[19]

I believe that direct, up-front subsidies to families and/or to the care providers would be a better use of federal money. Poor and middle-income people need the money when they spend it, not next year. In addition, governments should provide employers with tax credits up to 50 percent to defray the costs of establishing day-care centers (both child and elder) at or near the workplace, before-and-after-school programs, vacations and summer programs, and sick-care programs. Tax credits should also be used to entice employers to offer flexible schedules, compressed work weeks, and working at home.

The government should provide guaranteed low-interest loans to companies so that they will adopt comprehensive family-care programs. They should also provide guaranteed low-interest loans to operators of licensed family-care centers and programs for both children and the elderly. Those states that adopt this approach will find it an economic boon, because businesses and people want to live in states that promote progressive family-care policies.

The California legislature is in the forefront of tax efforts to assist in child care. In 1988, California passed Bill 722, which allows employers to take a 39 percent tax credit not exceeding $30,000 (in 1989 a proposed bill sought to raise this figure to $50,000) for startup costs in the establishment of a child-care program or the construction of a child-care facility for use by company employees. The bill also allows a tax credit for employees who want to use a care plan. The amount is 50 percent of the cost, not to exceed $600 per year for full-time employees and $300 per year for part-time employees. One hopes California will pass similar legislation regarding elder- and adult-dependent care.

In addition, Congress should take several steps to directly address the needs of elder care. For one thing, the federal government should allow Medicare funds to be used for adult day-care centers. At this writing, there are bills in both the House and the Senate to amend Medicare regulations to include reimbursement for adult day care. More money should be given to the Administration on Aging in order to upgrade the existing public information and referral system. Some of this money should go to expand services and improve the quality of the programs run by the government's aging network. Lastly, Congress should pass a long-term-care bill to provide financial assistance to the elderly as well as to other people inflicted with chronic illnesses. This bill should include nursing-home care, in-home care, and adult day-care centers.

Because of the federal deficit and the government's continued insistence on overfunding the Defense Department and expensive weaponry, Congress may be reluctant to enact any of these measures. In that case, Congress and the state and local governments may be forced to try an approach that was recently offered to the people of Freemont, California. The Freemont child-care bill would have taxed residents and businesses to help pay for day care for all children. The only change I would have suggested is expanding the measure to include money for the care of the elderly and impaired adults. The measure was soundly defeated, but the concept may not be dead. Under the measure, households would have paid $12 and businesses a 20 percent surcharge on their local taxes to raise $1 million annually. An additional $800,000 would have come from general funds and fees from developers. The money would be used to train child-care workers, provide vouchers for low-income residents, and build portable classrooms. Karen Hill-Scott suggests that bond issues are another finance method, and we should not exclude "sin" taxes as a source of revenue to be specifically used for family care.

Most states and some cities are moving ahead with measures to help people with family care. For example, California has allocated money for school-age child-care programs. California also has the largest state-funded resource and referral network program around the country, and it funded its own version of Head Start to the tune of $35 million in 1987–88. In 1988, Virginia governor Gerald Baliles created a child-care agency that provides day care to four-year-olds of low-income and single-parent families. The cost of that program was $40 million. Oregon is offering communities grant money totaling $29 million to come up with child-care solutions.[20]

Pomona, California, has one of the most diverse child-care programs in the nation. Its fifteen child-care centers serve nine hundred children in twelve different programs. Some of the programs deal with infants, toddlers, preschoolers, Head Start, abused children, and sick children. At least one center is open every day during the year, from 6:00 A.M. to midnight, for children six weeks to fourteen years old. Not only is the program diverse, it is a top-quality program. Pomona spends an average of $4,500 per child on child care. The average staff member is paid $26,000—almost three times the national average. As a result, the turnover is very low.[21]

There is also movement on the elder-care front. In Iowa, Governor Terry E. Branstad has made elder care a top priority. Key points to his program are:[22]

- increase funding for local public-health nursing to provide an additional 7,700 elders with home nursing care
- expand the well-being clinics to all parts of the state
- increase support to the Retired Senior Volunteer Program
- provide support and assistance for Alzheimer's disease victims and their families
- increase the state's Medicaid funding by $11 million to provide catastrophic coverage
- provide funds to assist the Iowa Veterans Home to open a new sixty-bed unit
- increase the elderly-property-tax and rent-reimbursement credit, at a cost of $2.6 million to the state treasury

In the letter describing his program, the governor summed it up: "All of these efforts are designed to help elders in Iowa maintain their involvement as active and involved citizens in our communities. The goal is to help the elderly stay in their homes as long as possible."

West Virginia is participating in a trial program funded by

the U.S. Administration on Aging to address the housing needs of the elderly. The state initiative will concentrate on developing a range of culturally and financially acceptable housing alternatives and social-support agencies to serve West Virginians who are most at risk of being institutionalized.[23]

In Delaware, the division on aging is working on a program to expand long-term-care services offered in the home and community for elderly and disabled persons. The plan has two unique features. One is that it deals specifically with persons with physical disabilities. The other is that it fully involves the private sector and places significant emphasis on case management.[24]

Local governments also have a role in the advancement of elder care. Janet Sainer, commissioner of the New York City Department on Aging, has been a pioneer in demonstrating how a city can mobilize to help the elderly. She and her predecessors have developed an efficient network of more than three hundred community-based volunteer agencies to assist not only the elderly but the caregivers to the elderly. She has also worked with corporations to form public-private partnerships. American Express and Sainer's department have developed the extremely successful City Meals On Wheels, a program that has been copied in twenty other cities. In 1988, Sainer formed partnerships with American Express, Philip Morris, and J. P. Morgan to conduct two-year demonstration projects to assist working caregivers.[25]

Corporate Answers

Meaningful government policies and programs would go a long way toward encouraging the private sector to take up the ball and run, not crawl. In this book, I have detailed the costs of inadequate programs and the benefits of taking action to address family-care needs. AT&T's family-care package is a good working model because it addresses a multitude of problems with a variety of solutions (see chapter 5).

Models, policies, and practices are only part of the corporate solutions to family care. The other important part is changing corporate culture and philosophy. It must be proactive toward family care.

> Organizations of all sizes must begin to develop a family friendly culture which encourages the exchange of information between employees and their managers, so policies and programs can be developed and refined to meet the needs of both.

So says Chase Manhattan Bank's vice president of employees services, Bill Craig. Chase has made it okay for employees to deal with family matters at work. Currently, Chase Manhattan Bank offers moderately progressive dependent-care assistance. The Employee Assistance Program has organized a range of services to assist employees with dependent-care needs such as information and referral for child care, free of charge to Chase employees, and a Dependent Care Reimbursement Account available to employees who have either child-care or elder-care expenses. In addition, Chase makes every effort to work with employees who want to use personal-leave time for the management of family responsibilities.

The manifestation of Chase's attitude is that it permits employees to use various leaves of absence, personal leave, and vacation days to attend to family matters. Most companies tend to discourage or eliminate discussion of the use of vacation or leave time for dealing with family issues; but Chase recognizes that all employees must balance work and family obligations. At Chase, there is no stigma attached to the employee who, for example admits that he or she needs time to make arrangements for a parent who recently had hip surgery. The company realizes that, sometimes, a modified work schedule or leave arrangement can facilitate an employee's ability to care for a dependent. Managers are encouraged to find ways to adjust an employee's work schedule if it can alleviate time conflicts.

An illustration of the Chase & Family approach to elder care, Corporate Counseling Associates (CCA) of New York provides elder-care counseling and assistance. The elder-care information service can be accessed through a 24-hour hotline, seven days a week. The following initial information services are provided free of charge: a telephone needs assessment to determine required services, which might ease the burden of the elderly person and the caregiver; eligibility for entitlement to services provided in the community and through Medicare and Medicaid; and recommendations to preferred providers who can offer the more extensive services often required in these situations, such as legal counsel and geriatric-care management. For employees who have more extensive needs than can be provided through telephone counseling, CCA enlists the services of a geriatric-care manager; in these cases, the employee pays an initial $50 copayment while Chase picks up the remainder of the charges.

Chase has made a long-term commitment to family care. Everything they add to their benefits program reinforces family-care needs and their long-term effect on employee careers. As an example of the company's understanding of the ongoing and multifaceted nature of family care, Chase allows employees to mix sick leave and vacation options to get maximum time off after childbirth. This allows the employee, who has put in several years of service, to come back to work in the same position or one with comparable pay. Chase is an example of a company that fully recognizes the interconnection between work and family.

If the government moved forward on any of my family-care suggestions, I believe AT&T, Chase Manhattan, and other companies would take the next step in increasing the supply of quality care for children of all ages and the elderly. Federal encouragement is also needed for more companies to offer long-term-care insurance.

While growing numbers of corporations are offering resource and referral, most shy away from establishing or supporting child-care centers, sick-child-care programs, before-and-after-school programs, summer programs, and vacation programs. This is ironic, because most families need these other programs more than they need I&R. Diane Levitt, director of Head Start in Pasadena, believes that "there is little point in providing information about child care if that care is limited in both quality and quantity, and all the child care in the world is useless if one cannot afford to pay for it."

Hill-Scott found a great shortage of affordable child care in Los Angeles County. First she noted a shortage of 155,539 slots. Over nine-thousand children needed some level of subsidy, resulting in a cost of $290 million. She wrote, "The cost of financing capital outlay for approximately 1,200 centers and 5,000 homes at current reasonable costs in Los Angeles County totals over $1 billion."[26] Using a fifteen-year capital amortization for day-care centers would cost only $567 per child per year in present-rate dollars. Because family day-care homes have a higher turnover rate, only about half the costs for homes would recur. Over fifteen years, the cost per child would be $337 per year. As one can see, the total costs are higher but the cost per child is relatively low.

Some of my survey participants agreed:

"Any company that will be successful in the future will protect its people, investments, and future resources (children) and reap the efforts of its former resources (elderly) understanding their value to the current workforce." (Hispanic female low-level manager)

"Working women are here to stay. It's an economic reality. Our company needs to deal with this to attract competent women to work with." (Asian female middle-level manager)

Education

The subject of education is too broad to be fully dealt with in this book, but it is worth mentioning because it is intrinsically related to the crisis in child care and to the future of the American labor force.

Current funding of education is abysmally low. Our educational institutions are suffering, and so are the children who are depending on them to be prepared for the future. According to the Child Care Action Campaign, we need to start making certain our children have a quality education. The campaign believes that quality day care can ensure a future supply of able workers, because the first five years are crucial in giving children the ability and desire to learn.[27]

More money should be spent on teachers' salaries and on building schools so that classroom sizes will be dictated by the best interests of the children, not by space and dollars. In addition, our educational institutions need enough money to operate year round.

It is a waste of good space to close schools from 3 P.M. to 9 A.M. each day and all day for three months a year. Year-round schools would be an ideal location for day-care centers, before-and-after-school programs, vacation programs, and summer programs.

And there would be an added benefit to providers. As the Child Care Action Campaign noted, California, which has school-based child-care programs, pays their day-care workers an average of $21,600—much more than the average salary of child-care employees elsewhere. The proponents of this plan say that the better salaries are a direct result of locating the centers within the schools because it puts the child-care workers on par with teachers.[28]

Putting more money into the school system will go a long way toward solving some of our child-care problems. But the content of the curriculum also needs to be changed to better prepare these children for their future caregiving responsibilities. A systematic approach should be taken to teach children about family care, including the responsibilities and problems of becoming a parent, the importance of nurturing children, and the difficulties of balancing work and family responsibilities. In this way, we could break some of the myths about parenting that are constantly being presented to our children through the mass media and perhaps reduce the incidence of illegitimate births.

The Family Caregiver's Role

Society's responsibility to its children and its seniors cannot be overstated. Yet no legislation, corporate programs, or educational reforms will solve the crisis in family care without the consent and assistance of the family itself. American families must take a hard look at themselves and see if they are living up to their modern potential or operating under outdated, unworkable stereotypes. Men must become more actively involved in child rearing and caring for aging parents, and women must put their foot down and demand that their partners share this responsibility. There must be a concerted effort to change the "family task norms." Families must be willing to spend money for quality care if they can afford it. I have often heard parents complain about spending a hundred dollars a week to care for their most precious resource, their children—yet they think nothing of dropping the same amount of money on a fancy dinner. Parenthood is not a right—it is a responsibility to ensure a strong future.

Summary

American businesses are at a crossroads. They are faced with an increasingly competitive global economy, an aging workforce, a shrinking labor pool, and an increasing number of working women. Between now and the end of the century, women will make up 65 percent of the new entrants into the workforce. They will bring more of the skills employers need. Among new graduates, women already account for 13 percent of all engineers, 39 percent of all lawyers, and 31 percent of business administrators with MBAs. Whether corporations will choose to recognize these changing demographics and enact policies to attract and retain highly qualified employees is up to them. But if they do not, these working women will go elsewhere—and so will their spouses.

To society as a whole, there is more at stake here than the corporate bottom line. If the United States is to remain prosperous, competitive, and free, American lawmakers, institutions, and families must understand the importance of dealing with family care. The quality of the U.S. workforce will depend on its skills, education, and health. Providing appropriate child care will improve the skills and educational level of our future workforce, while implementing programs that address work/family conflicts—such as elder care and family leave—will improve the adaptability and morale of the workforce.

None of the solutions I have presented in this book are, in and of themselves, a panacea. But taken in combination, they provide an array of choices for families. Let's go to work on changing policies and attitudes toward our children, our seniors, and perhaps most important, our working women. Let's develop a Marshall Plan for family care.

Notes

Introduction

1. U.S. Department of Labor, *Child Care: A Workforce Issue*, Report of the Secretary's Task Force on Child Care (April 1988).

Chapter 1
The Changing American Workforce

1. Interview conducted by the author, March 20, 1989.
2. U.S. Department of Labor, *Child Care: A Workforce Issue*, Report of the Secretary's Task Force (April 1988).
3. D. E. Bloom and T. P. Steen, "Why Child Care is Good for Business," *American Demographics* (1988): 22–77.
4. U.S. Department of Health and Human Services, *Aging America: Trends and Projections* (1987–88); American Association of Retired Persons, *A Profile of Older Americans* (AARP, 1988).
5. Interview conducted by the author, January 6, 1989.
6. Ibid.

Chapter 2
Child Care and Corporate Productivity

1. G. Kimball, "Dual Career Couples," unpublished results, 1988.
2. A. C. Emlen, "How Do Variations in Child Care Arrangements Affect Employed Parents?" presentation at the Symposium on Workplace Research on the Family (Harriman, N.Y.: Arden House, March 23–25, 1988), 48.
3. K. S. Perry, "Conflict Between Work and Child Care Responsibilities," presentation at the Symposium on Workplace Research on the Family (Harriman, N.Y.: Arden House, March 23–25, 1988), 97.
4. E. Galinsky and D. Hughes, *The* Fortune *Magazine Child Care Study*, unpublished paper, 1987. Overview provided to the author by Galinsky.
5. A. G. Dawson et al., "An Experimental Study of the Effects of Employer Sponsored Child Care Services on Selected Employee Behaviors" (Chicago: CRS, 1984), 5.
6. M. S. Kraukopf and S. H. Akabas, "Children With Disabilities: A Family

Work Place Partnership Problem Resolution," 21 (Los Angeles: University of Southern California, 1988), 28–35.

7. E. Galinsky et al., *Work and Family: Research Findings and Models of Change*, (Ithaca, N.Y.: New York State and Labor Relations, Cornell University, 1987), 13.

8. Perry, "Conflict Between Work and Child Care Responsibilities," 97.

9. Ibid., 96.

10. N. W. Wong et al., "Child Care Patterns Stress and Job Behaviors Among Working Parents," presentation at the Symposium on Workplace Research on the Family (Harriman, N.Y.: Arden House, March 23–25, 1988), 74.

Chapter 3
Child Care and Its Impact on Stress and Health

1. L. R. Murphy, "Workplace Intervention for Stress Reduction and Prevention," *Causes, Coping and Consequences of Stress at Work*, ed. G. L. Cooper and R. Payne (New York: John Wiley, 1988), 302.

2. R. Forbes, *Corporate Stress* (New York: Doubleday, 1979).

3. M. McLaughlin, "Stress Audit of Employees May Help Business Solve Costly Problem," *New England Business* 8 (April 21, 1986), 32, 34.

4. E. T. Smith and S. Sivolop, "Stress: The Test Americans are Failing; The Crippling Ills That Stress Can Trigger," *Business Week* (Industrial Technology Edition, April 18, 1988), 74–78.

5. D. Hughes, "The Work and Family Life Studies: An Overview of Ongoing Research and Selected Findings," presentation at the Symposium on Workplace Research on the Family (Harriman, N.Y.: Arden House, March 23–25, 1988), 9.

6. A. C. Crouter, "Spillover from Family to Work: The Neglected Side of Work-Family Interface," *Human Relations* 37 (1984), 442–45.

7. B. Googins and D. Burden, "Vulnerability of Working Parents: Balancing Work and Home Roles," *Social Roles* 32 (July/August 1987), 295–300.

8. Wong, "Child Care Patterns, Stress and Job Behaviors," 74.

9. Forbes, *Corporate Stress*, 51.

10. Ibid., 53.

11. Ibid., 55.

12. J. Grimaldi and B. P. Schnapper, "Managing Stress: Reducing Costs and Increasing Benefits," *Management Review* (August 1981), 24.

13. L. Levi, *Stress Industry: Causes, Effects and Prevention* (Stockholm, Sweden: International Labour Organisation, 1984), 11.

14. G. Ritzer, *Working: Conflict and Change* (Englewood Cliffs, N.J.: Prentice-Hall, 1977), 114.

15. Cited in Levi, *Stress Industry*, 13.

16. D. Norfolk, "Putting A Price on Stress," *Chief Executive* (October 1987), 57.
17. M. Davidson and C. Cooper, *Stress and the Woman Manager* (Oxford, England: Martin Robertson and Co., 1983), 137–50.

Chapter 4
Other Work/Family Problems

1. S. D. Nollen, "Answers to Research Questions," presentation at the Symposium on the Workplace Research on the Family (Harriman, N.Y.: Arden House, March 23–25, 1988), 93.
2. T. Bond, "Job Factors Predicting Work-Family Conflict," presentation at the Symposium on Workplace Research on the Family (Harriman, N.Y.: Arden House, March 23–25, 1988), 88.
3. "More Corporations are Focusing on the Hard Reality of Bringing Up Baby," *The Philadelphia Inquirer* (September 5, 1989), 1E.
4. Ibid.
5. J. Auerbach, *In the Business of Child Care: Employee Initiatives and Working Women* (New York; Praeger, 1988), 75.

Chapter 5
Child-Care Solutions

1. The U.S. Department of Labor, Women's Bureau Work and Family Clearinghouse, Washington, D.C., has information on about one-thousand companies' involvement in family-care issues: *Child Care Challenge: Report on Employer-Sponsored Child Care Services, Congressional Caucus for Women's Issues* (May 5, 1988); *Child Care: the Bottom Line; A Guidebook for Employers and Developers*, State of California Commission for Economic Development, 1986; *Employers and Child Care: Benefitting Work and Family*, U.S. Department of Labor, Office of the Secretary, Women's Bureau, 1989.
2. B. A. Nye, "Employer-Sponsored Child Care: A Topic for National Research," unpublished paper.
3. Interview conducted by the author, March 20, 1989.
4. See note 1.
5. Information received from S.L. Burud, 1989. *The Productivity Impact Study of On-Site Child Care* (Pasadena, Calif.: Burud and Associates): 1–3.
6. State of California, *Child Care: The Bottom Line*, 6.
7. S. L. Burud, et al. 1984. *Employer-Supported Child Care: Investing in Human Resources* (Dover, Mass.: Auburn House).

Chapter 6
Elder Care—The Corporate Realities

1. U.S. Department of Health and Human Services, *Aging America: Trends and Projections* (1987–88).
2. American Association of Retired Persons, *A Profile of Older Americans* (AARP, 1988).
3. "Work and Family Life: Balancing Job and Personal Responsibilities," 2 (September 1988), 5.
4. AARP and the Travelers Foundation, "A National Survey of Caregivers," (November 1988), 5.
5. Ibid., v.
6. E. M. Brody, "Women in the Middle and Family Help to Older People," *The Gerontologist* 21 (1986), 476.
7. M. Parker, "An Overview of Respite Care and Adult Day Care in the United States," prepared for the U.S. Senate Special Committee on Aging (June 14, 1988), 108.
8. D. Friedman, "Elder Care: The Employee Benefit of the 1990s," *Across the Board* (New York: Conference Board, June 1986), 45.
9. L. J. Warshaw, Barr, J. K., Rayman, I., et al., *Employer Support for Employee Caregivers* (The New York Business Group on Health, 1986), 9.
10. R. B. Enright and L. Friss, *Employed Caregivers of Brain-Impaired Adults: An Assessment of the Dual Role* (Family Survival Project, February 1987), 4.
11. R. I. Stone and P. F. Short, *The Competing Demands of Employment and Informal Caregivers to Disabled Elders*, unpublished manuscript, 5.
12. *Corporate and Employee Response to Caring for the Elderly, A National Survey of U.S. Companies and the Workforce* (Sponsored by *Fortune* magazine and John Hancock Financial Services, 1989), 116.
13. M. A. Creedon, *Issue for an Aging America: Employees and Eldercare* (Southport, Conn.: Creative Services, 1988), 28.
14. *Fortune* and John Hancock report, 111.
15. Stone and Short, *Competing Demands*, 3.
16. *Fortune* and John Hancock report, 136.
17. G. C. Brice et al., "A Profile of the Travelers Insurance Company (Buffalo Office) Employee Caregivers to Older Adults," presentation at the Symposium on Workplace Research on the Family (Harriman, N.Y.: Arden House, March 23–25, 1988), 157–58.

Chapter 7
Elder-Care Solutions

1. R. Rieland, "When They're 64," *The Washingtonian* (January 1989), 108.
2. K. Bishop, "Studies Find Drugs Still Overused to Control Nursing Home Elderly," *New York Times* (March 13, 1989), 1.

3. J. Johnson, "Elderly Suffer Mental Ills Without Hope of Aid, Congressional Panel Told," *New York Times* (March 7, 1989), A-21.
4. "Study: Drug Misuse by Elderly Now a Major Problem," *Philadelphia Inquirer* (Febraury 16, 1989), 18A.
5. M. Burros, *New York Times* (February 1, 1989), C8.
6. *Fortune* and John Hancock report, 48.
7. Ibid.
8. "Eldercare in the Workplace: The What and the Why of Corporate Response," *International Personnel Management Association* (Alexandria, Va., August 1988), 14.
9. U.S. Senate, Special Committee on Aging, *Adult Day Health Care: A Vital Component of Long-term Care* (April 18, 1988), 105.
10. S. L. Zimmerman, "Adult Day Care: Correlates of Its Coping Effects for Families of an Elderly Disabled Member," *Family Relations* 35 (1986), 306.
11. Ibid.
12. U.S. Senate, *Adult Day Health Care*, 20.
13. C. Kopac and D. Price, "Bringing Together the Young and Old With Integrated Day Care," *Pediatric Nursing* 13 (July/August 1987), 228.
14. U.S. House, Select Committee on Aging, *Long-Term Care and Personal Impoverishment: Seven in Ten Elderly Living Alone at Risk* (October 1987), v.
15. American Association of Retired Persons, "Before You Buy: A Guide to Long-Term Care Insurance," (AARP, 1980), 6.
16. Ibid, 16.
17. *Fortune* and John Hancock report, 53–54.
18. J. E. Hanson, editorial, *Aging Network News* (August 1989), 2.

Chapter 8
Triple Responsibilities—The Sandwich Generation

1. U.S. House, Select Committee on Children, Youth, and Families hearings (May 3, 1988), 2.
2. *The Travelers' Employee Caregiver Survey* (Hartford, Conn.: The Travelers Corporation, 1985).
3. D. A. Miller, "The Sandwich Generation: Adult Children of the Aging," *Social Work* (September 1981), 419.
4. A. L. Otten, "Extended Families: As People Live Longer Houses Become Home to Several Generations," *Wall Street Journal* (January 27, 1989), A-1, A-4.
5. U.S. House, Select Committee on Children, Youth, and Families hearings, 32.
6. Ibid, 9–10.
7. A. C. Emlen, et al., *Child and Elder Care: Final Report of an Employee*

Survey at the Sisters of Providence (Portland, Ore.: Regional Research Institute for Human Services, Portland State University, 1988), 1–130.
8. U.S. House, Select Committee on Children, Youth, and Families hearings, 2.

Chapter 9
The Politics of Corporate Dependent Care

1. I. Heller, "An Employer Has Seen the Future, and Its Subsidized Day Care," *New York Times* (August 4, 1988), 34.
2. K. Hill-Scott, "No Room at the Inn: The Crisis in Child Care Supply" in *Caring for Children: Challenge to America*, ed. J. S. Lande et al. (Hillsdale, N.J.: Lawrence Erlbaum Associates, 1989), 211.
3. Bureau of National Affairs, *Employers and Child Care: Tax and Liability Considerations*, Special Report 7 (July 1988), 19–26.
4. J. Strickland, draft of *Status of Child Care and Human Service Liability*, report prepared for the Insurance Information Institute and National League of Cities (June 1, 1988).
5. A. J. Moore, "Child Care Makes Bottom Line Sense," *Child Care Action Campaign News* (September–October, 1988), 11.
6. *Corporate Child Care Initiations: The Potential for Employer Involvement in Child Care Programs* (The Massachusetts Industrial Finance Agency, March 1986).
7. Information in the author's possession.
8. Children's Defense Fund, *Child Care: The Time Is Now* (Children's Defense Fund, 1987), 1.
9. D. Tkac, "Day Care: Why It Makes Sense for Your Employer," *Children* (February 1988), 23.
10. Quoted in Auerbach, *In the Business of Child Care*, 21.
11. J. Auerbach, "The Privatization of Child Care: The Limits of Employer Support," presented at the conference of the American Sociological Association (August 28, 1988), 4.
12. M. Polatnik, "Why Men Don't Rear Children," (1974), 79.
13. Auerbach, "The Privatization of Child Care," 4.

Chapter 10
A Marshall Plan for Family Care

1. J. P. Fernandez, *Child Care and Corporate Productivity: Resolving Family and Work Conflicts* (Lexington, Mass.: Lexington Books, 1986), chapter 10; C. Wallis "The Child Care Dilemma," *Time* (June 22, 1989); B. Kitchen, "International Programs in the Work and Family," lecture in Toronto, Canada (December 1, 1988).
2. Information in the author's possession.

3. J. Templeman et al., "Grappling With Graying Europe," *Business Week* (March 13, 1989), 54.
4. P. Selby, M. Schechter et al., *Aging 2000: A Challenge for Society* (Boston: M.T.P. Press, 1982), 199.
5. J. Ostroff, *Successful Marketing to the 50+ Consumer* (Englewood Cliffs, N.J.: Prentice-Hall, 1989), 282.
6. Selby, Schechter, et al., *Aging 2000*, 199, 29–30, 54.
7. C. Nusberg, M. J. Gibson, and S. Peace, *Innovative Aging Programs Abroad: Implications for the United States* (Westport, Conn.: Greenwood Press, 1984), 170.
8. Ibid., 173.
9. B. V. Pifer, "Groups Get Emphasis in Japan's Dementia Programs," *Respite Report*, 2.
10. Ibid., 2.
11. Nusberg et al., *Innovative Aging Programs Abroad.*
12. Ostroff, *Successful Marketing to the 50+ Consumer*, 283.
13. Interview conducted by the author, November 24, 1989.
14. Cited in Klein, *Public Opinion Polls*, 1–24.
15. Ibid.
16. Information in the author's possession.
17. B. Reisman et al., *Child Care: The Bottom Line: An Economic and Child Care Policy Paper* (Child Care Action Campaign, 1988), 15–16.
18. Children's Defense Fund, *A Vision for America's Future: An Agenda for the 1990s: A Children's Defense Budget* (Children's Defense Fund, 1988), xx.
19. I. Garfinkle, *The Potential of Child Care to Reduce Poverty and Welfare Dependence* (Child Care Action Campaign (1988), 11.
20. Information in the author's possession.
21. D. DeVoss, "The Hero of Day Care, *Los Angeles Times Magazine* (September 1988), 10–20.
22. *Aging Network News* (April 1989), 10.
23. *Aging Network News* (December 1988), 8.
24. *Aging Network News* (March 1989), 10.
25. Information in the author's possession.
26. Hill-Scott, "No Room at the Inn," 212.
27. Reisman et al., *Child Care: The Bottom Line*, 50.
28. Ibid., 34.

Appendix

Various Solutions to Dependent-Care Needs

On- or Near-Site Day-Care Centers

An employer can develop a day-care center on or near company premises under a variety of financial and management arrangements. The program can be established as a wholly or partially owned subsidiary or as a new department of the company. The center might also be created as a separate, private, nonprofit entity, or as an employee-owned and -operated agency with credit backing by the company. Finally, the center can be contracted out to a nonprofit or profit-making agency to run for the company.

ADVANTAGES

- Employees miss fewer workdays because of the sudden loss of a child-care provider.
- The decrease in stress-related health problems translates directly into savings on health-insurance costs.
- High-quality standards are assured, which reduces parental stress. (High-quality care also enhances the social, physical, and educational development of children.)
- Employee turnover rates are reduced.
- Less productivity is lost due to child emergencies, since the employee can handle a problem without having to travel a long distance.

- The corporation can tailor the center's hours to corporate working hours.
- Labor recruitment and retention are enhanced.
- Parents have more time with their children during commuting, breaks, and lunch.
- The workplace is humanized for all employees, which may help morale.
- High visibility can improve public relations and community relations.

DISADVANTAGES

- Liability *may* be greater than other forms of child-care assistance.
- The initial investment may be costly.
- Utilization may fluctuate at the beginning.
- Cost of using the day-care center could become an issue, with some employees able to pay and others unable.
- Most day-care centers do not allow sick children to attend. This limits the benefit of reducing missed days at work.
- The limited number of slots and long waiting lists may engender bad feelings on the part of employees who see the child-care needs of others being met before their own.
- The needs of employees who work in the field, who do not normally come to the office every day, are not met.
- Day care may not be suitable for parents who commute on public transportation in rush hour or for parents who have difficult or long commutes.
- Most do not provide before-and-after-school care, which is a concern of many parents.

Child-Care Consortia

A child-care consortium is a group of employers who jointly share the costs, risks, and benefits of establishing and operating a day-care center. Each company is guaranteed a certain number of slots for its employees. Many of the advantages and disadvantages of the one-corporation-sponsored day-care center are also applicable here. In addition, the following advantages and disadvantages apply specifically to consortia.

ADVANTAGES

- The resources, liability, and cost for which any one company is responsible are limited.
- Employers with small workforces in specific geographic areas may participate.
- Larger employers that have small workforces in specific geographic areas can participate.
- The center is protected from underenrollment because of the large size of the combined labor pools.
- The humanization factor, in which corporations combine resources and cooperate, is emphasized; this means good publicity.
- The sense of community is strengthened.
- Consortia may prompt enthusiasm and cooperation from the city government, possibly in the form of zoning variances or waivers of development fees.

DISADVANTAGES

- They may involve complicated negotiations among participating companies.
- They may increase the complexity of policies and negotiations, especially if two or more unions are involved. (This was the case when the University of Southern California opened a center as a joint venture with the County Medical Center. Two separate waiting lists with different priorities were maintained to meet the different union packages.)
- The combined labor pools may be so large that the center can serve only a limited number of employees from each participating company.

- Location can be a problem. If consortium members are not clustered, the center is bound to be more convenient for some than for others.

Family Day Care

Family day care is an arrangement in which a neighborhood person—usually a woman—provides child care in her own home. Single providers may care for up to six children. In group-family-day care, approximately seven to twelve children are cared for by at least two adults. A family-day-care network is a group of family-day-care homes that operate under a central administration or that provide an informal coalition for support training.

ADVANTAGES

- Family-day-care homes may be located either close to home or near work, enabling a greater number of employees to be served.
- Family-day-care homes are much like the home environment.
- Many family-day-care homes provide before-and-after-school care.
- Employees with children of different ages can use the same provider.
- Programs can be tailored to the specific ages of the children.
- The flexible hours of some family-day-care providers are suitable to parents who work odd-hour shifts.
- Some family day-care homes provide overnight care for a limited number of days.
- Some family-day-care networks designate "sick bay" homes.
- Tuition is normally lower than that of day-care centers.
- Start-up and maintenance costs are low.
- The number of family-day-care homes can be expanded or reduced, depending on demand.

- The care may be more personalized in a family atmosphere.

DISADVANTAGES

- High provider turnover is a serious problem.
- The overall quality of the care in most family-day-care homes is far lower than that in day-care centers.
- Most family-day-care homes are neither licensed nor registered with state agencies.
- Unlicensed homes pose liability risks for the employer.
- Many states do not have well-defined licensing requirements for family-day-care homes.
- Private homes may have more safety hazards than formal day-care centers, increasing liability.
- Employees have less control over the quality of the care provided.
- Many of the caregivers are unskilled or poorly trained.
- Few family-day-care homes have education or developmental components.
- The services are low profile and offer little in the way of public relations or image-building for the company.
- The economics of family day care are limited. For example, if the fees per child are $60 per week (this estimate is probably high), a home serving five children takes in $300. Out of this amount comes the cost of meals, equipment, and janitorial services. What's left is the salary of the family-day-care providers—maybe as low as $200 per week. The provider could work fifty-five-hour weeks, with no coffee or lunch break and no benefits.

Before-and-After-School Programs

A before-and-after-school program (or latchkey program) provides care for school-age children before and after regular school hours. While a few companies provide this service for employees directly, most before-and-after-school care is found in the community: in public schools, in family day care, in YMCAs, in libraries, in senior centers, and in religious buildings.

ADVANTAGES

- Existing facilities that are in many cases underutilized are utilized.
- They provide an opportunity for public-private partnerships. Public relations benefit from such programs.
- Parents are less constrained to come in late or leave early.
- Parents make fewer phone calls "to check on the kids."
- The cost is usually relatively low, or there is none.
- Children receive constructive programs that keep them "off the street" and "out of trouble." This alleviates the stress on parents, allowing them to be more productive at work.

DISADVANTAGES

- Coordination of the programs may be complex and costly for companies whose employees commute from a wide radius of bedroom communities.
- The hours of before-and-after-school programs, if provided by anyone other than the employer, may not match the hours when care is needed; they may open too late or close too early. Employees for whom overtime is a consistent problem suffer most severely from the time constraints of community-based programs.
- Community-based programs vary in quality and scope.
- Many latchkey programs are not properly supervised. For instance, libraries don't have enough staff to watch all the children. Those children who are self-motivated read; others run rampant.

Vacation Care Programs

Working parents have a great deal of concern about their school-age children's care when schools are closed due to weather, holidays, or summer vacation. Employers can develop relationships with community organizations—such as drop-in day-care centers, family-day-care homes, or agencies that organize vacation-care programs for children during these periods.

ADVANTAGES

- Parents make fewer phone calls to check on the kids.
- Employee morale is improved because counterproductive worries about unsupervised children at home are reduced.
- Children are stimulated, and the incidence of delinquency is reduced through constructive educational programming.
- They provide an opportunity for public-private partnerships and the public receives benefits associated with such programs.
- They are an opportunity for corporations to improve community relations by directly subsidizing programs in the community or by donating in-kind services to accommodate programs. Significant subsidization of community programs increases a corporation's leverage over scheduling and programming.

DISADVANTAGES

- If the vacation program is not offered on- or near- the site, coordination becomes more complex and costly, especially in companies that are dealing with the different calendars of several school districts.
- Community programs vary a great deal in quality.
- Employees' personal vacation plans may produce fluctua-

tions in program attendance rates, making staffing difficult.

Care for Sick Children

Very few child-care programs can care for children when they are ill. Employers can create sick-child-care infirmaries, on-site or near-site; they can subsidize in-home nursing services; they can revise sick-leave policies to allow parents to stay home to care for sick children; and they can work with hospitals and private organizations that are setting up sick-child-care facilities.

Sick-child care is the principal cause of employee scheduling problems, and of all child-care concerns, it has probably the biggest influence on productivity. Research indicates that there is a high correlation not only between missed work and caring for a sick child, but also between caring for a sick child and leaving work early, coming in late, dealing with family issues during working hours, and on-and-off-the-job stress.

ADVANTAGES

- It reduces the incidence of employee absenteeism and stress.
- Employee morale is improved because the burden and inconvenience on coworkers, supervisors, and clients are reduced.
- Employee turnover is reduced.

DISADVANTAGES

- Childhood illnesses are generally unpredictable.
- The seasonal nature of children's illnesses (flu season) could cause staff shortages at particular times of the year.
- Sick-leave policies that allow parents to stay home with sick children could create problems with coordination.
- Children with chronic illnesses pose additional problems.

- The costs of providing sick-child care can be extremely high.

Adult Day-Health Care

Adult day-health care is a coordinated program of services in a nonresidential setting that cares for the frail elderly or for adults with physical or mental disabilities. The care may include social, medical, rehabilitative, recreational, and mental health services. Corporations can participate in adult day-health care directly or indirectly under a variety of financial arrangements on-site or near-site.

ADVANTAGES

- Families can continue working while caring for frail elderly or disabled adults in a noninstitutional setting. This can prevent inappropriate or premature placement in a nursing home.
- Employee productivity and attendance are increased.
- Absences and personal phone calls during work hours are reduced.
- It offers high visibility, which can improve community relations.
- It can be an effective labor-recruitment tool.
- It provides an equitable benefit for all employees since those without adult caregiving responsibilities benefit from the increased concentration and productivity of their coworkers.

DISADVANTAGES

- Liability may be a problem, depending on the arrangement.
- Cost may be a problem for the corporation.
- It may be costly to the employees.

- It is difficult to predict utilization. Demand may fluctuate due to the sudden and often temporary nature of crises.
- Coordination is complex and costly in companies whose employees commute from a wide radius of bedroom communities.
- The number of slots is limited. Long waiting lists can foster bad feelings among employees who see others' needs being met before their own.
- At this time, the number of adult day-health care facilities is limited. Therefore, some employees will not be able to use this option unless the company increases the supply.

Respite Care

Respite-care facilities and services provide for the short-term placement of individuals in response to family emergencies or to planned absences (such as vacation, business travel, or hospitalization). They can also simply allow family caregivers to shop or do errands. Respite care can be provided to employees under a variety of financial arrangements.

ADVANTAGES

- The stress experienced by employee caregivers and their families is relieved, thereby improving the productivity of employees.
- Employees can participate in corporate-sponsored events and after-hours meetings.
- Employee morale is improved.

DISADVANTAGES

- Utilization is difficult to predict. Caregiving responsibilities vary and demands are often subject to peaks and valleys. Corporate-sponsored events may strain the resources of qualified caregivers.

- There are potential difficulties in maintaining a pool of qualified caregivers.
- Multiple external providers limit the opportunity for quality control.

Intergenerational Programs

An intergenerational program provides programming for both child care and adult care. Employers can develop intergenerational programs under a variety of legal and financial arrangements, such as company owned and run, owned and operated by an independent contractor, cooperative ownership by employees, or owned and operated by a separate nonprofit entity.

ADVANTAGES

- Intergenerational programming wins broad employee support because it meets the needs of both young parents and adult caregivers.
- A corporation can tailor its program's hours to meet the specific needs of the employees.
- It benefits children and adults by allowing the two groups to reach across generational barriers and reap the mutual benefits of such stimulation.
- The standard of care is high, providing an important model of support for primary caregivers by demonstrating consistent and appropriate behavior.

DISADVANTAGES

- Programming for children and adults must remain separate. Carefully monitored, combined activities must be limited to two hours because the high energy level of young children can overwhelm frail elderly and impaired adults.
- The initial investments may be costly.

- Liability is unclear, depending on the ownership and management of the program.
- The limited number of slots (for which there are long waiting lists) can foster bad feelings on the part of employees who see others' child- and adult-dependent-care needs being met before their own.

Private Geriatric-Care Management

A private geriatric-care manager helps employees locate appropriate and qualified assistance to care for elderly or dependent adults within their own community. The service begins with an in-home needs assessment and is followed by a recommendation for services that best relieve the caregiver's burdens. This service may be limited to an information, consultation, and referral service, or it may continue as an ongoing service for the duration of required caregiving. Generally, these professionals are social workers or clinicians.

ADVANTAGES

- Employees are less stressed at work if they know that a qualified professional is on hand to manage crises as they arise.
- Care managers are on call twenty-four hours per day.
- Employee absenteeism, tardiness, and personal phone calls are reduced, so productivity is maximized.
- The distractions to other employees who do not have the problems are reduced.
- Employees can stabilize during a crisis and prepare their action plans for future crises.
- Employees can save money and strain in the long run through the professional consultation, since the care manager will educate them on the appropriateness of various options.

DISADVANTAGES

- The on-going service to employees can be expensive for the corporation, given the length of time that caregiving responsibilities can continue.
- Employees have disproportionate abilities to pay for services beyond what the corporation provides.
- Care-manager networks may vary in professional criteria for membership. Some may be limited to master's-degreed social workers, while others may open their membership to anyone with geriatric experience.

Resource and Referral

Resource and referral provides information about child care, elder care, and independent adult and family counseling for families attempting to select quality care. It refers individual families to local care providers that match the family's needs.

ADVANTAGES

- The amount of time parents take off from work to locate child care is often reduced.
- Employee needs can be identified, while planning data for future company initiatives is provided.
- It can stimulate the creation of new services.
- It works well for multisite employers.
- It is generally offered and available to all employees.
- An outside vendor limits the company's liability.
- Employees receive a wide array of solutions from which to choose.

DISADVANTAGES

- The needs of all parents may not be satisfied if the supply of services in the community is inadequate.

- It focuses primarily on family day care.
- A communications effort is required to publicize the availability of the service at the work site.
- The usage rate is quite low (2 to 4 percent).
- Some parents already have satisfactory child-care arrangements.
- Relative to usage, the costs are high and ongoing.
- There is no asset development or appreciation.
- It frustrates parents who use it and can't afford the care that is found.
- The reliability and the legitimacy of the recommendations are not guaranteed.
- The effectiveness initially depends on the supply of care in the community until provider recruitment programs take effect.

Employee Education Seminars

In employee education seminars, employees receive training in the resolution of caregiving problems and family/work conflicts. These seminars also highlight the advantages and disadvantages of various caregiving options.

ADVANTAGES

- The cost is relatively low.
- Corporations are assisted in reducing the productivity losses that result from caregiving problems.
- It provides a plausible first step toward dealing with caregiving problems and family/work conflicts for managers who approve of corporate involvement in family/work issues.
- It sends an inexpensive message to employees that the employer cares.
- All employees benefit from an increased level of under-

standing and sensitivity toward caregiving problems and family/work conflicts.
- Employees are assisted in reconciling work and family demands.

DISADVANTAGES

- It does not have any direct impact on the problems of the selection and supply of caregivers.
- The effectiveness of the seminars depends on corporate recognition of their value to *all* employees at *all* levels, regardless of whether they have caregiving responsibilities.
- Employees perceive this to be the least useful form of employer assistance.
- Education seminars, in which employees are encouraged to openly discuss their work/family conflicts, must provide some degree of anonymity in order to be effective.

Flex-time

Although employees continue to work a full-time schedule in flex-time, they have a choice in determining the start and end of that time. In flex-time, all employees generally work during the "core times," in midmorning and midafternoon, plus a variation. Employees who choose to use flex-time must establish a regular routine and cannot arbitrarily alter the hours they work from day to day.

ADVANTAGES

- The cost is low. This popular benefit is inexpensive to implement and easy to administer.
- The flexibility it provides can be useful to all employees in a variety of family situations.
- Employees' work performance and morale are improved

because of their increased control and flexibility in their work schedules.

- Employees receive latitude in matching their workdays with the schedules of their family-care providers.
- Commuting patterns are eased, and overall productivity is improved.

DISADVANTAGES

- Supervisors may resist.
- Problems in communication and staffing through the day may emerge.
- Not all types of work lend themselves to this solution.

Half-Day Vacations

Half-day vacations and individual vacation days are given to employees to deal with family problems without a loss of pay.

ADVANTAGES

- It incurs the least cost to the corporation.
- Employees who are permitted to take vacation time in half-days are much less likely to call in sick when there is a conflict between family/work schedules.
- The incidence of tardiness, leaving work early, and other related losses of productive time are reduced.

DISADVANTAGES

- The corporation is required to include a code for a half-day vacation in its management information and accounting systems.
- Union contracts must be revised to cover half-days for occupational employees, and company policy must be revised for management employees.

Compressed Work Weeks

In a compressed work week, the number of work days is fewer, but the hours per day are longer. Sometimes schedules are assigned on a fixed or a rotating basis, such as four days one week, three the next, or four ten-hour days.

ADVANTAGES

- The flexibility can be useful to employees in a variety of family situations.
- Work performance and morale improve because of employees' sense of increased control.
- The cost is low, but productivity is increased.
- Employees make the same money and retain the same benefits.

DISADVANTAGES

- Supervisors may resist.
- Problems in communication because of conflicting schedules may arise.
- Employees who feel that this schedule is thrust upon them may feel demoralized by a lack of control.

Flex-place

Flex-place is a work-at-home option for employees who do not need a traditional work-site base. This option is best suited for information-based jobs.

ADVANTAGES

- The recruitment and retention of those unable or unwilling to commute is improved.
- Productivity is improved because many at-home workers

can schedule their work at preferred times, and studies show that they work longer hours.

- The costs of office space are potentially reduced.
- Employees gain discretion in scheduling their work hours, which enables them to deal more effectively with work and family issues.
- Family-care costs, commuting costs, and stress are greatly reduced—even eliminated in some cases.

DISADVANTAGES

- Management is required to change the traditional supervisory methods.
- New ways of measuring performance are necessary.
- Some employees may feel that they must cover for at-home workers and resent them; or their jobs may not permit such arrangements.
- Special attention must be given to preserving the work rights of home-based employees, such as job security, pension, benefits, and job advancement.
- Employee problems related to isolation and loneliness may arise.
- Not all types of work lend themselves to this solution.

Job Sharing

In job sharing, two people share the work and responsibilities of one full-time position. Salary and benefits are usually pro-rated between the two.

ADVANTAGES

- It makes available part-time positions where they were previously not possible.
- A wider breadth of skills and experience can be provided in the job that is shared.

- It can help retain experienced employees.
- It can create a more effective job schedule.
- Continuity of coverage is allowed: if one person leaves, someone knowledgeable is still available.
- Frequently, the employer gains dedication, in the form of overtime worked in off hours.

DISADVANTAGES

- Benefit inequities may be perceived.
- A lack of information about how job sharing works can lead to middle-management resistance.
- It may be hard to evaluate performance if work assignments overlap.
- Peers may perceive that there is an inequitable distribution of the workload.
- Problems in communication with co-workers outside the job-sharing arrangement may arise.
- Employees' salaries are decreased.

Permanent Part-Time

In permanent part-time, employees are regularly scheduled and permanent, but they work fewer than the number of hours specified for full-time employment.

ADVANTAGES

- It opens a large labor pool that might not otherwise be available for recruitment because they cannot or do not want to work full-time.
- The employer can fit the size of the workforce to the size of the workload.
- Experienced employees who may want or need to cut back their working hours can be retained.

DISADVANTAGES

- It may involve extra costs because of fixed labor costs per employee.
- Management is required to change its perception that such workers are less committed.
- A careful reassessment of the organization's benefit program is essential before creating part-time positions.
- Treating employees fairly with regard to careers, promotions, and the like can become problematic.

Corporate Discount

In a corporate discount, the corporation negotiates an employee discount with a caregiving facility. Typically, a vendor lowers its fee by 10 percent, and the employer contributes 10 percent of the fees. Thus, the employees receive a 20 percent reduction in the costs of caregiving. In some cases the vendor offers the 20 percent discount directly to the employer in exchange for the purchase of a guaranteed number of slots.

ADVANTAGES

- Employees are assisted with the high cost of dependent care.
- The cost of implementation is relatively low.
- Little administration is required after the initial start-up phase.
- The program expands and contracts according to employees' needs.
- Liability is limited.
- It engenders favorable publicity for the employer as vendors promote their center to the media.

DISADVANTAGES

- Employees must use only the selected vendors.
- Employees can be turned away if the vendor is filled.

- Employees who have no immediate use for the service could see it as additional salary for employees who use the service.

Vouchers

Vouchers provide employees with full or partial reimbursement for the cost of employee-selected dependent-care arrangements.

ADVANTAGES

- Employees are assisted with the high cost of dependent care.
- Caregivers can choose from among care services.
- Family and community family-care services are supported without selecting from among deserving agencies.
- Administrative responsibility is limited if it is paid through payroll deductions.
- The supply of quality care services may be promoted.
- Capital expenditures are eliminated.

DISADVANTAGES

- The cost can be high, unless eligibility is limited.
- Limitations may cause equity problems (although every option has some element of an equity issue).
- If community care is not available or is not of high quality, employer subsidies do not significantly address the more serious problems that employees face.

Flexible Benefits

Recognizing that employees with dependent-care problems have different needs, the federal government has made a variety of tax benefits available to employers. The Economic Recovery Act of 1981 provided tax incentives for employer-sponsored dependent-care benefits. Many states are also implementing tax-incentive programs. At present, the federal government seems to be shifting its emphasis away from direct subsidies and direct support of day-care centers toward giving tax credits to parents and tax incentives to employers. This trend is expected to continue.

Flexible benefits allow employees to make individual choices from a menu of taxable and nontaxable benefits beyond the core benefit protection provided by employers. These benefits may be part of a comprehensive cafeteria plan, or they may be part of a flexible-spending-account or salary-reduction plan that allows employees to reduce a certain percentage of their income in order to receive pretax dollars to spend on dependent care.

The following is a list of provisions set forth by the IRS for the implementation of flexible benefits:

- *Dependent Care Assistance Programs (DCAPs).* DCAPs allow employers to provide dependent-care benefits—such as direct payments, services, or vouchers—that are sheltered from being taxed as part of the employee's gross income. The program must satisfy certain requirements regarding participants' eligibility, payment, and notification. Employers receive tax credits for implementing such a program. These programs may be funded through employer contributions, salary-reduction plans, or both.

- *The Comprehensive Cafeteria Plan.* This was created by Section 125 of the IRS Code (1978 Revenue Act), allowing employers to offer a choice of benefits. Employees receive a core set of benefits and the use of flexible credits to purchase more of the core benefits or optional benefits that are either taxable or nontaxable. A DCAP may be but is not required to be one of the benefits offered in a Comprehensive Cafeteria Plan.

- *Flexible-Spending Accounts and Salary-Reduction Plans.* These allow employees to make pre-tax contributions of up to $5,000 to the flexible-spending account, which reduces the amount of their salary subject to income and social security taxes. Pre-tax dollars can be used to pay for qualified care, insurance premiums, and health care and medical expenses. At the beginning of each year, employees must determine the amount of their salary that they wish to contribute to this spending option, and they must forfeit any spending dollars unused at year's end. These leftover funds become available to the employer for program management.

ADVANTAGES

- Equity in benefits is created, while a variety of dependent-care needs are met.
- Caregiving assistance is offered to employees in need without affecting those who do not have dependent-care problems.
- Greater control and reduction in the cost of benefits is allowed.
- More options in caregiving assistance are created, as needed by different employees in various locations.

DISADVANTAGES

- The implementation and administrative costs may be high.
- Increasing employee awareness of various options requires the employer to implement extensive marketing and education programs.
- Individual situations of caregiving require employees to assess the tax options that best meet their needs, since the various tax options may exclude other benefits.
- Financial assistance in the form of benefits may not be helpful in meeting employees' dependent-care needs if there is an inadequate supply of dependent care in the community.

Employee Tax Benefits

The Child and Dependent Care Tax Credit for Workers allows workers increased tax credits to pay for child- and adult-dependent care that is not covered by or paid by an employer-sponsored DCAP. Expenses for which the credit may be taken are limited to $2,400 for one dependent and $4,800 for two or more dependents. The expenses may be for services provided in or out of the home, for dependent children under the age thirteen, or for dependent adults over fourteen who are disabled and who live with the taxpayer.

ADVANTAGES

- Employee morale improves when companies educate employees on tax options that are offered directly to the employee at no cost to the corporation.
- Equity in benefits is created, while a variety of dependent-care needs are met.
- Caregiving assistance is provided to employees who need it, without affecting those who have no dependent-care issues.

DISADVANTAGES

- Employee awareness of various tax options is increased, requiring the employer to implement extensive marketing and education programs.
- Individual caregiving situations require employees to assess the tax options that best meet their needs since the various options may exclude other benefits.

Employee-Sponsored Long-Term-Care Insurance

Private health insurance provides coverage in the event of chronic illness or disability against catastrophic expenses. Long-term-care insurance is specifically designed to cover services not included by Medicare or medigap such as nursing-home care, adult day care, and home health-care services.

ADVANTAGES

- Reduced premiums purchased under a group-plan benefit employees.
- Increased service options covered by long-term-care insurance reduce the stress of caregiving.
- Employees are protected from the financial strain of supplementing long-term care and home care.
- Employee stress is reduced, which improves productivity.

DISADVANTAGES

- Availability is limited because of restrictions on the age of potential purchasers, health screening, and the absence of policies in many geographic areas.
- Eligibility for family members, such as spouse and parent, is sometimes limited by carriers.
- Policies vary considerably in cost and benefits and must be evaluated carefully.
- Lack of consistency among policies can make it difficult to compare policies and make an informed choice.
- Portability restrictions of the policy may limit the employee's perception of the benefit.

Medigap

Medigap, or Medicare supplemental insurance, is private health insurance that supplements or fills in many of the gaps in Medicare coverage, such as deductibles, copayments, and co-insurance amounts. This benefit may be offered through the employer with the employee assuming full or partial payment for premiums.

ADVANTAGES

- It protects employees from the financial strain of supplementing Medicare copayments and deductibles.

- It relieves employee stress, which improves employee productivity.

DISADVANTAGES

- Coverage generally has the same restrictions as Medicare—that is, length of stay and qualifications for coverage.
- The policies vary considerably in covered services and conditions of coverage.
- Implementation, marketing, and administration can be costly and time-consuming.

Bibliography

Accommodating Pregnancy in the Workplace. New York: National Council of Jewish Women, 1987.

Adolph, B., and K. Rose. *Employer's Guide to Child Care: Developing Programs for Working Parents.* New York: Praeger, 1985.

Adult Day Care in America; Summary of a National Survey. National Council on Aging, 1987.

Alpert, D., and A. Culbertson. "Daily Hassles and Coping Strategies of Dual Earner and Non-Dual Earner Women." *Psychology of Women Quarterly* (September 1987).

American Association of Retired Persons. *A Profile of Older Americans.* (AARP, 1988).

Aravanis, S. C., R. Levin, and T. T. Nixon, eds. *Private/Public Partnership in Aging: A Compendium.* Washington, D.C.: National Association of State Units on Aging and Washington Business Group on Health, November 1987.

Auerbach, J. *In the Business of Child Care: Employee Initiatives and Working Women.* New York: Praeger, 1988.

Bailey, J. E. "Personnel Scheduling With Flexshift: A Win Win Scenario." *Personnel* 63 (September 1986).

Barr, J. K., M. M. Duncan, T. Lucas, and L. J. Warshaw. *Assisting Employee Caregivers: Employers' "ElderCare" Programs.* New York: The New York Business Group on Health, Inc., February 1989.

Bass, D. M., and G. T. Diemling. "Family Caregivers and Their Support." *The Benjamin Rose Bulletin* (First Quarter 1988).

Beach, B. *Integrating Work and Family Life: The Home-Working Family.* Albany, N.Y.: State University of New York Free Press, 1989.

Becelia, M. "Reconcilable Differences: Business and Families Strike a Balance on the Issue of Parental Leave." *National Business Women* 68 (1987).

Beck, C. M., and D. Ferguson. "Aged Abuse." *The Journal of Gerontological Nursing* 7 (1981).

Bergstrom, J. M. *School's Out—Now What? Choices for Your Child's Time.* Berkeley, Calif.: Ten Speed Press, 1984.

Bloom, D. E., and T. P. Steen. "Why Child Care is Good For Business." *American Demographics* (August 1988).

Bohen, H. H. *Corporate Employment Policies Affecting Families and Children: The United States and Europe.* New York: Aspen Institute for Humanistic Studies, 1983.

———, and A. Viveros-Long. *Balancing Job and Family Life.* Philadelphia: Temple University Press, 1981.

Borrfield, P. K. "Working Solutions for Working Parents." *Management World* (February 1986).

Brody, E. M. "Women in the Middle and Family Help to Older People." *The Gerontologist* 21 (1986).

———, and E. B. Schoonover. "Patterns of Parent Care When Adult Daughters Work and When They Do Not." *The Gerontologist* 26 (1986).

———, M. H. Kleban, et al. "Work Status and Parent Care: A Comparison of Four Groups of Women." *The Gerontologist* 27 (1987).

Brooks, H., L. Liebman, and C. Schelling, eds. *Public-Private Partnerships; New Opportunities for Meeting Social Needs.* Cambridge, Mass.: Ballinger, 1984.

Brothers, J. *The Successful Woman: How You Can Have a Career, a Husband and a Family—and Not Feel Guilty About It.* New York: Simon and Schuster, 1988.

Burden, D. S., and B. K. Googins. *Balancing Job and Homelife Study.* Boston: Boston University School of Social Work.

Bureau of National Affairs. "Employers and Eldercare: A New Benefit Coming of Age." *The National Report on Work and Family.* Washington, D.C.: 1988.

Burud, S. L., et al. *Employer Supported Child Care: Investing in Human Resources.* Dover, Mass.: Auburn House, 1984.

———, P. R. Aschbacher, and J. McCroskey. *Employer-Supported Child Care: Investing in Human Resources.* Dover, Mass.: Auburn House, 1984.

Cadmus, R. R. *Caring for Your Aging Parents.* Englewood Cliffs, N.J.: Prentice-Hall, 1984.

Cain, C. "Stress-Related Claims Increasing." *Business Insurance* 20 (November 3, 1986).

Campbell, T. A., and D. E. Campbell. "71% of Employers Say They Could Be Part of the Child Care Solution." *Personnel Journal* (April 1988).

"Caregivers in the Workplace: Employer Support for Employees with Elderly and Chronically Disabled Dependents." *Medical Benefits* (July 30, 1987): Author.

Caregivers in the Workplace Survey. Washington, D.C.: American Association of Retired Persons, 1986.

Caro, F. G. "Relieving Informal Caregiver Burden Through Organizational Services." In *Elder Abuse: Conflict in the Family,* edited by K.S. Pillemer and R.S. Wolf. Boston: Auburn House, 1986.

Carter, John D., and Diane S. Piktialis. "What to Do about Mother in Milwaukee." *Business and Health* 5 (April 1988): 19–21.

Cherlin, A., and F. Furstenberg. *The New American Grandparent; A Place in the Family, a Life Apart.* New York: Basic Books, 1986.

Cherry, D., and M. Rafkin. "Adapting Day Care to the Needs of Adults With Dementia." *The Gerontologist* 28 (1988).

Child Care: A Work Force Issue. Secretary's Task Force on Child Care. Washington, D.C.: U.S. Department of Labor, April 1988.

Child Care Challenge; Report on Employer-Sponsored Child Care Services. Washington, D.C.: Congressional Caucus for Women's Issues, May 5, 1988.

Child Care: The Bottom Line; A Guidebook For Employers and Developers. State of California Commission for Economic Development, 1986.

A Children's Defense Budget; An Analysis of Our Nation's Investment in Children. Washington, D.C.: Children's Defense Fund, 1989.

Christenson, K. "Child Care as an Employee Benefit." *Compensation and Benefits Review* 3 (1987).

Cohen, D., and C. Eisdorfer. *The Loss of Self: A Family Resource for the Care of Alzheimer's Disease and Related Disorders.* New York and Scarborough, Ontario: New American Library, 1986.

Corporate Child Care Initiations: The Potential for Employer Involvement in Child Care Programs. The Massachusetts Industrial Finance Agency, March 1986.

Corporate and Employee Response to Caring for the Elderly: A National Survey of U.S. Companies and the Workforce. Sponsored by *Fortune* magazine and John Hancock Financial Services, 1989.

Creedon, M., ed. *Issues For an Aging America: Employees and Eldercare—A Briefing Book.* Bridgeport, Conn.: University of Bridgeport, Center for the Study of the Aging, 1987.

———. "The Corporate Response to the Working Caregiver." *Aging* 358 (1988).

———, and D. Wagnor. *Eldercare: A Resource Guide* (Produced for PepsiCo, Inc., by the Center for the Study of Aging, University of Bridgeport) Purchase, N.Y.: PepsiCo, 1987.

Creedon, M. A. *Issue for An Aging America: Employees and Eldercare.* Southport, Conn.: Creative Services, 1988.

Crichton, J. *The Age Care Sourcebook: A Resource Guide for the Aging and Their Families.* New York: Simon and Schuster, 1987.

Crossman, L. L., and C. Barry. "Older Women Caring for Disabled Spouses: A Model for Supportive Services." *The Gerontologist* 21 (1981).

Crouter, A. C. "Spillover from Family to Work: The Neglected Side of Work-Family Interface." *Human Relations* 37 (1984).

Cutler, L. "Counseling Caregivers." *Generations, Quarterly Journal of the American Society of Aging* 10 (1985).

Davidson, M., and C. Cooper. *Stress and the Woman Manager.* Oxford, England: Martin Robertson and Company, 1983.

Deimling, G. T., and D. M. Bass. "Symptoms of Mental Impairment Among Elderly Adults and Their Effects on Family Caregivers." *Journal of Gerontology* 41 (1986).

Demos, J. *Past Present and Personal: The Family and the Life Course in American History.* New York and Oxford: Oxford University Press, 1986.

DiBlase, D. "Easing Workplace Stress Cuts Costs: Experts." *Business Insurance* 20 (April 28, 1986).

Earl, J. H., and J. B. Wright. "Babysitting—Good for Business." *Management World* (February 1986).

Emlen, A. C. *Child and Elder Care: Final Report of an Employee Survey at the*

Sisters of Providence. Portland, Ore.: Regional Research Institute for Human Services, Portland State University, 1988.

———, P. E. Koren, and D. Louis. *1987 Dependent Care Survey: Sisters of Providence, Final Report.* Portland, Ore.: Regional Research Institute for Human Services, Portland State University, 1987.

———, and P. E. Koren. *Hard to Find and Difficult to Manage: The Effects of Child Care on the Work Place.* Portland, Ore.: Regional Institute for Human Services, Portland State University, 1984.

Employer Support for Child Care. New York: National Council of Jewish Women, August 1988.

Employer-Supported Child Care in Michigan. Lansing, Mich.: American Association of University Women, 1987.

Employers and Child Care: Tax and Liability Considerations. Bureau of National Affairs Special Report #7, July 1988.

Enright, R. B., and L. Friss. *Employed Caregivers of Brain-Impaired Adults: An Assessment of the Dual Role.* Family Survival Project, February 1987.

Etzion, D. "The Experience of Burnout and Work/Non Work Success in Male and Female Engineers; A Matched-Pairs Comparison." *Human Resource Management* 27 (Summer 1988).

Feder, J., and J. Holahan. *Financing Health Care for the Elderly: Medicare, Medicaid, and Private Health Insurance.* Washington, D.C.: The Urban Institute, 1979.

Fengler, A. P., and P. Rabins. "Men and Women: Do They Give Care Differently?" *Generations, Quarterly Journal of the American Society on Aging,* 10 (1985).

Fernandez, J. P. *Child Care and Corporate Productivity: Resolving Family and Work Conflicts.* Lexington, Mass.: Lexington Books, 1986.

Friedman, D. E. "Child Care for Employees' Kids." *Harvard Business Review* 64 (March/April 1986).

Friedman, E. "Elder Care: The Employee Benefit of the 1990s." *Across the Board.* New York: Conference Board, June 1986.

———. "Liberty, Equality, Maternity." *Across the Board* (March 1987).

Galinsky, E. *Child Care and Productivity.* Paper prepared for the Child Care Action Campaign Conference, New York, April 1988.

———. "Family Life and Corporate Policies." In *In Support of Families,* M. Yogman and T. B. Brazelton, eds. Boston: Harvard University Press, 1986.

———. "The Impact of Child Care Problems on Parents on the Job and at Home." (Unpublished paper). New York: Bank Street College of Education, 1987.

———. "The Impact of Supervisor's Attitudes and Company Culture on Work/Family Adjustment." Paper presented at the Annual Convention of the American Psychological Association, Atlanta, 1988.

———, and J. David. *The Preschool Years.* New York: Times Books/Random House, 1988.

———, and W. H. Hooks. *The New Extended Family: Day Care That Works.* Boston: Houghton Mifflin, 1977.

———, and D. Hughes. *The* Fortune *Magazine Child Care Study*. (Unpublished paper). New York: Bank Street College of Education, 1987.

———, D. Hughes, and M. Shinn. *The Corporate Work and Family Life Study*. (Unpublished paper). New York: Bank Street College of Education, 1986.

———, et al. *Work and Family: Research Findings and Models of Change*. Ithaca, N.Y.: New York State and Labor Relations, Cornell University, 1987.

Gibeau, J., J. Anastas, and P. Larson. *Breadwinners and Caregivers—Adult Health Services as an Employee Benefit: Supporting Workers Who Have Elderly Dependents*. Washington, D.C.: National Association of Areas on Aging, 1986–87.

Googins, B., and D. Burden. "Vulnerability of Working Parents: Balancing Work and Home Roles." *Social Roles* 32 (July/August 1987).

Gould, G., and M. Smith. *Social Work in the Work Place: Practice and Principles*. New York: Springer, 1988.

Grim, S. *Employers and Eldercare*. Washington, D.C.: Bureau of National Affairs, 1988.

Halcrow, A. "A New Twist on Child Care (Sick Child Care Program at Transamerica Life)." *Personnel Journal* (November 1986).

Harney, J. O., G. E. Groomes, N. Linsalata, and J. Luiz. "Aging in the Workplace." *John Hancock Newsletter* (Background Extra) 4. Boston: John Hancock Mutual Life Insurance Company, February 1987.

Hart, K. E. "Managing Stress in Occupational Settings: A Selective Review of Current Research and Theory." *Journal of Managerial Psychology* 2 (1987).

Hewitt Associates. *Eldercare: A Growing Concern*. Lincolnshire, Ill.: 1987.

Hill-Scott, K. "No Room at the Inn: The Crisis in Child Care Supply." In *Caring for Children: Challenge to America*, edited by J. S. Lande et al. Hillsdale, N.J.: Lawrence Erlbaum Associates, 1989.

Hofferth, S. L. "Child Care in the United States." In *American Families in Tomorrow's Economy*. Hearing before the Select Committee on Children, Youth, and Families, July 1, 1987. Washington, D.C.: U.S. Government Printing Office.

———. "What is the Demand for and Supply of Child Care in the U.S.?" Testimony presented before the House Committee on Education and Labor. Washington, D.C.: Urban Institute, 1989.

Holosko, M., and M. Feit. *Evaluation of Employee Assistance Programs*. New York: Haworth Press, 1988.

Hooyman, N. R., and W. Lustbader. *Taking Care: Supporting Older People and Their Families*. New York: Free Press, 1986.

Horne, J. *Caregiving: Helping an Aging Loved One*. Washington, D.C.: American Association of Retired Persons, 1986.

House, J. S. *Work Stress and Social Support*. Reading, Mass.: Addison-Wesley, 1981.

Hughes, D., and E. Galinsky. "Balancing Work and Family Life: Research and Corporate Application." In *Maternal Employment and Children's Development: Longitudinal Research*, edited by A. E. Gottfried and A. W. Gottfried. New York: Plenum Press, 1988.

————. *Relationships Between Job Characteristics, Work/Family Interference and Marital Outcomes.* (Unpublished paper.) New York: Bank Street College of Education, 1987.

Hunsaker, J. S. "Burnout, The Culmination of Long-Term Stress." *Industrial Management* 28 (Nov./Dec. 1986).

Johnston, W. B., and A. J. Packer. *Workforce 2000.* Indianapolis, Ind.: Hudson Institute, 1987.

Jump, T. L., and L. Hass. *Fathers in Transition: Dual Career Fathers Participating in Child Care. Changing Men: New Directions in Research on Men and Masculinity.* Newbury Park, Calif.: Sage Publications, 1987.

Kahn, A. J., and S. B. Kamerman. *Child Care: Facing the Hard Choices.* Dover, Mass.: Auburn House, 1987.

Kamerman, S. B. "Meeting Family Needs: The Corporate Response." Work in America Institute Studies in Productivity. New York: Pergamon Press, 1983.

Killian, M., and M. A. Brown. "Work and Family Roles of Women: Sources of Stress and Coping Strategies." *Health Care for Women International* 8 (1987).

Kopoc, A., and D. Price. "Bringing Together the Young and Old with Integrated Day Care." *Pediatric Nursing* 13 (July/August 1987).

Kraukopf, M. S., and S. H. Akabas. "Children With Disabilities: A Family Work Place Partnership Problem Resolution." 21, Los Angeles: University of Southern California, 1988.

Kurland, C. H. "The Constituency Speaks Out." *Perspective on Aging* (November/December 1985).

Labor Force Statistics Derived From Current Population Survey 1948–1987. Bulletin no. 2307, U.S. Department of Labor, Bureau of Statistics. Washington, D.C.: U.S. Government Printing Office.

Lamer, K. "The Constellation of Adult Day Care Services." *Perspective on Aging* (Nov./Dec. 1985).

Lang, A., and E. Brody. "Characteristics of Middle-Aged Daughters and Their Help to Their Elderly Mothers." *Journal of Marriage and the Family* 45 (1983).

Levi, L. *Stress Industry: Causes, Effects and Prevention.* Stockholm, Sweden: International Labour Organisation, 1984.

Levine, H. Z. "Alternative Work Schedules: Do They Meet Workforce Needs?" *Personnel* 64 (February 1987).

Lobosco, M. "Child Care Initiatives (Human Resources Managers' Attitudes)." *Personnel* 63 (August 1986).

Love, M., E. Galinsky, and D. Hughes. "Work and Family: Research Findings and Models for Change." *ILR Report* 25 (1987). Ithaca, N.Y.: Cornell University, New York State School of Industrial and Labor Relations.

McKay-Rispoli, K. "Small Children: No Small Problem." *Management World* (March/April 1988).

McLaughlin, M. "Stress Audit of Employees May Help Business Solve Costly Problem." *New England Business* 8 (April 21, 1986).

Miller, A. "The Sandwich Generation: Adult Children of the Aging." *Social Work* (September 1981).

Miller, D. B., N. Gulle, and F. McCue. "The Realities of Respite Care for Families, Clients and Sponsors." *The Gerontologist* 26 (1986).

Miller, T. I. "The Effects of Employer-Sponsored Child Care on Employee Absenteeism, Turnover, Productivity, Recruitment, or Job Satisfaction: What is Claimed and What is Known." *Personnel Psychology* 37 (1984).

Moen, P., and D. I. Demster McClain. "Employed Parents: Role Strain, Work Time, and Preferences for Working Less." *Journal of Marriage and the Family* (August 1987).

"Mothers in the Workplace (Selected Findings)." *NCJW Center for the Child Report.* New York: National Council of Jewish Women, 1987.

MuGurrin, L. "Should Corporate Benefits Include Helping With the Care of the Elderly Parents?" *New England Business* 8 (September 1, 1986).

Murphy, L. R. "Workplace Intervention for Stress Reduction and Prevention." *Causes, Coping and Consequences of Stress at Work,* edited by G. L. Cooper and R. Payne, (New York: John Wiley, 1988).

Myers, J. E. *Adult Children and Aging Parents.* Dubuque, Ia.: Kendall/Hunt Publishing Co., 1989.

The National Report on Work and Family; Special Report #2. Washington, D.C.: Buraff Publications, a subsidiary of the Bureau of National Affairs, 1988.

A National Survey of Caregivers, Final Report. Opinion Research Corporation. Washington, D.C.: American Association of Retired Persons, 1988.

Newgren, K. E., C. E. Kellogg, and W. Gardner. "Corporate Policies Affecting Dual Career Couples." *Advanced Management Journal* 52 (Autumn 1987).

Norfolk, D. "Putting A Price on Stress." *Chief Executive* (October 1987).

Nusberg, C., M. J. Gibson, and S. Peace. *Innovative Aging Programs Abroad; Implications for the United States.* Westport, Conn.: Greenwood Press, 1984.

O'Brien, P. *How to Select the Best Child Care Option for Your Employees.* Binghamton, N.Y.: Almar Press, 1987.

Odnoha, C. "Respite Program." *Caring* (December 1986).

Orians, V. "The Trainers Role in Stress Management and Prevention." *Journal of European Industrial Training* 10 (1986).

Ostroff, J. *Successful Marketing to the 50+ Consumer: How to Capture One of the Biggest and Fastest-Growing Markets in America.* Englewood Cliffs, N.J.: Prentice-Hall, 1989.

Perry, K. S. "Employers and Child Care: Establishing Services Through the Workplace." Washington, D.C.: U.S. Department of Labor, 1982.

Petty, D. and L. Friss. "A Balancing Act of Work and Caregiving." *Business and Health* 4 (October 1987).

Phillips, J. D. *Employee Turnover and the Bottom Line* (Working paper.) Rahway, N.J.: Merck and Co., 1989.

Pierce, Jon L. *Alternative Work Schedules.* Boston: Allyn and Bacon, 1988.

Pifer, A., and L. Bronte. *Our Aging Society: Paradox and Promise.* New York: W.W. Norton, 1986.

Pleck, J. H. "The Work-Family Role System." *Social Problems* 24 (1977).

Polniaszek, S. *Long-Term Care: A Dollar and Sense Guide*. Washington, D.C.: United Seniors Health Cooperative, 1988.

———, and K. J. Polniaszek. *Managing Your Health Care Finances: Getting the Most Out of the Medicare and Medigap Insurance*. Washington, D.C.: United Seniors Health Cooperative, 1989.

Quinn, S. J. "Elderly in Hospice: Older Parents Need Unique Kinds of Physical, Psychological, and Religious Support." *The American Journal of Hospice Care* 1 (1984).

Quinn, W. H., and G. H. Hutchinson, eds. *Independent Aging: Family and Social Systems Perspectives*. Rockville, Md.: Aspen System Corporation, 1984.

Ransom, C., P. Aschbacher, and S. Burud. *The Return on an Investment in Child Care Benefits—Is It Real? The Union Bank Story*. Unpublished manuscript, 1988.

Ransom, C., and S. Burud. *Productivity Impact Study Conducted for Union Bank Child Care Center*. Unpublished report, 1988.

Reisman, B., et al. *Child Care: The Bottom Line: An Economic and Child Care Policy Paper*. Child Care Action Campaign, 1988.

Ritzer, G. *Working: Conflict and Change*. Englewood Cliffs, N.J.: Prentice-Hall, 1977.

Rubin, S. S. *Family Caregivers: The Invisible Network of Long Term Care*. Boston: Unitarian Universalist Service Committee, 1986.

Schappi, J. *Improving Job Attendance*. Washington, D.C.: Bureau of National Affairs, 1988.

Schorr, B. "Professional Care for Victims of Alzheimer's Disease." *Health Policy Week* 17 (April 1988).

Schwab, T. *Caring for an Aging World: International Models for Long-Term Care, Financing and Delivery*. New York: McGraw-Hill Information Services, 1989.

Schwartz, L. *Parental and Maternity Leave Policies in Canada and Sweden*. Kingston, Ontario: Queen's University, Industrial Relations Centre, 1988.

Selby, P., M. Schechter, et al. *Aging 2000: A Challenge for Society*. Boston: M.T.P. Press, 1982.

Shamir, B., and I. Salomon. "Work-at-Home and the Quality of Life." *Academy of Management Review* 10 (1985).

Shinn, M., B. Oritz-Torres, A. Morris, P. Simko, and N. Wong. *Child Care Patterns, Stress and Job Behaviors Among Working Parents*. Paper presented at the Annual Convention of the American Psychological Association, New York, August 1987.

Silverstone, B., and H. Hyman. *You and Your Aging Parent*. New York: Pantheon, 1982.

Skinner, D. A. *Managing in Dual-Employed Families: Policies and Perspectives That Would Help*. Paper presented at the National Council on Family Relations, San Francisco, October 16–20, 1984.

———. "Dual Career Family, Stress and Coping: A Literature Review." In

Work and Family, edited by P. Voyandoff. Palo Alto, Calif.: Mayfield Publishing Co., 1984.

Stackel, L. "Eldercare: An Emerging Phenomen." *Employment Relations Today* 13 (Winter 1986/1987).

Staines, G. L., and J. H. Pleck. *The Impact of Work Schedules on the Family.* Ann Arbor, Mich.: The Institute for Social Research, 1983.

Stone, R. I., and P. Kemper. *Spouses and Children of Disabled Elders: Potential and Active Caregivers.* Washington, D.C.: U.S. Department of Health and Human Services, January 1989.

Stone, R. I., and P. F. Short. *The Competing Demands of Employment and Informal Caregivers to Disabled Elders.*

Susser, P. A. "Balancing Work Place and Family Concerns." *Employment Relations Today* 13 (Autumn 1986).

Symposium on Workforce Research on the Family. Sponsored by the Conference Board, Arden House. Harriman, N.Y., March 23–25, 1988.

"There's No Place Like Home." *U.S. News and World Report* (January 25, 1987).

Thirty-three Ways to Ease Work/Family Tensions: An Employee's Checklist. Bureau of National Affairs, 1980.

Thwaites, L. "We All Benefit When Society Shares the Burden of Alzheimer's." *Continuing Care* (December 7, 1987).

Towler, J. "Mental Health is a Corporate Concern." *Industrial Management* 10 (February 1986).

The Travelers' Employee Caregiver Survey. Hartford, Conn.: The Travelers Corporation, 1985.

U.S. Department of Health and Human Services. *Aging America: Trends and Projections.* Washington, D.C.: U.S. Government Printing Office, 1987–88.

U.S. Department of Labor, Report of the Secretary's Task Force on Child Care. *Child Care: A Workforce Issue.* Washington, D.C.: U.S. Government Printing Office, April 1988.

U.S. House, Select Committee on Aging. *Long-Term Care and Personal Impoverishment: Seven in Ten Elderly Living Alone at Risk.* Washington, D.C.: U.S. Government Printing Office, October 1987.

U.S. House, Select Committee on Aging, Subcommittee on Human Services. *Exploring the Myths: Caregiving in America.* Washington, D.C.: U.S. Government Printing Office, January 1987.

U.S. House, Select Committee on Children, Youth and Families Hearings, May 3, 1988.

U.S. Senate, Special Committee on Aging, in conjunction with the American Association of Retired Persons, the Federal Council on the Aging, and the U.S. Administration on Aging. *Aging America.* Washington, D.C.: U.S. Government Printing Office, 1988.

A Vision for America's Future: An Agenda for the 1990s: A Children's Defense Budget. Children's Defense Fund, 1988.

Voluck, P. R., and H. Abramson, "How to Avoid Stress-Related Disability Claims." *Personnel Journal* 66 (May 1987).

Von Behern, R. "Adult Day Care: Progress, Problems, and Promise." *Perspectives on Aging* (Nov./Dec. 1985).

Wagel, W. H. "Eldercare Assistance for Employees at the Travelers." *Personnel* 64 (October 1987).

Warshaw, L. J., J. K. Barr, and M. Schachter. "Caregivers in the Workplace: Employer Support for Employees with Elderly and Chronically Disabled Dependents." *Journal of Occupational Medicine* 29 (June 1987).

Warshaw, L. J., Barr, J. K., Rayman, I. *Employer Support for Employee Caregivers.* The New York Business Group on Health, 1986.

Winfield, E. "Workplace Solutions for Women under Eldercare Pressure." *Personnel* 64 (July 1987).

Workforce 2000: Work and Workers for the 21st Century. Washington, D.C.: Hudson Institute, for the U.S. Department Labor, 1987.

Zigler, E. F., S. L. Kagan, and E. Klugman, eds. *Children, Families and Government: Perspectives on American Social Policy.* Cambridge, Mass.: Harvard University Press, 1983.

Zigler, E. F., and E. W. Gordon, eds. *Day Care: Scientific and Social Policy Issues.* Dover, Mass.: Auburn House, 1982.

Zimmerman, S. L. "Adult Day Care: Correlates of its Coping Effects for Families of an Elderly Disabled Member." *Family Relations* 35 (1986).

Index

About the Author

JOHN P. FERNANDEZ graduated magna cum laude from Harvard in 1969 and received his Ph.D. in sociology from the University of California at Berkeley in 1973. He has extensive experience both as a researcher and teacher and as a manager with AT&T for fifteen years. While with AT&T, he served as a division-level manager in the areas of operations, labor relations, personnel, and human resources forecasting and planning. In addition to his many publications and speaking engagements, he has published four previous books: *Survival in the Corporate Fishbowl: Making it into Upper and Middle Management; Child Care and Corporate Productivity: Resolving Family and Work Conflicts; Racism and Sexism in Corporate Life: Changing Values in American Business;* and *Black Managers in White Corporations.* He is currently the president of Advanced Research Management Consultants, a Philadelphia-based consulting firm that specializes in human-resource issues such as survey research, managing a culturally diverse workforce, dependent care, human resources, forecasting and planning, and developing a proactive workforce.